The Destructive Power of Religion

**Recent Titles in
Contemporary Psychology**

Resilience for Today: Gaining Strength from Adversity
Edith Henderson Grotberg, editor

THE DESTRUCTIVE POWER OF RELIGION

Violence in Judaism, Christianity, and Islam

Volume 1
Sacred Scriptures, Ideology, and Violence

J. Harold Ellens, Editor

Foreword by Martin E. Marty
Ad Testimonium by Archbishop Desmond Tutu

Contemporary Psychology
Chris E. Stout, Series Editor

Westport, Connecticut
London

Library of Congress Cataloging-in-Publication Data

The destructive power of religion : violence in Judaism, Christianity, and Islam /
edited by J. Harold Ellens; foreword by Martin E. Marty.

    p. cm.—(Contemporary psychology, ISSN 1546–668X)
  Includes bibliographical references and index.
  ISBN 0–275–97958–X (alk. paper)
  1. Violence—Religious aspects. I. Ellens, J. Harold, 1932– II. Contemporary
psychology (Praeger Publishers)
BL65.V55D47 2004
291.1'78—dc21   2003051061

British Library Cataloguing in Publication Data is available.

Library of Congress Catalog Card Number: 2003051061
ISBN: 0–275–97958-X (set)
        0–275–97972–5 (vol. I)
        0–275–97973–3 (vol. II)
        0–275–97974–1 (vol. III)
        0–275–98146–0 (vol. IV)
ISSN: 1546–668X

First published in 2004

Praeger Publishers, 88 Post Road West, Westport, CT 06881
An imprint of Greenwood Publishing Group, Inc.
www.praeger.com

Printed in the United States of America

The paper used in this book complies with the
Permanent Paper Standard issued by the National
Information Standards Organization (Z39.48–1984).

10 9 8 7 6 5 4 3 2 1

For my father, John S. Ellens, who was without exception and by a wide margin the very best man I ever knew; because of his character God can never be for me less than healing and redemptive, though religions may prove destructive. In the face of everything he was faithful.

For my mother, Grace Kortmann Ellens, whose quality of spirit more fully defined her name than most sacred scriptures and than those who named her could ever have known; because of her I am persuaded that finally, in life and death, only grace works. Grace did not define her, she defined it. Always lively and often in the valley of the shadow, she was full of faith.

So divine incarnation is easy for me to perceive; I keep expecting it everywhere. Though regularly disappointed, it is surprising where I see it; John and Grace gave me "eyes to see and ears to hear."

CONTENTS

FOREWORD

"Too bad this set of books is so relevant." That phrase is not a dismissal of, but an advertisement for, this work that will inform and provide perspective for people anywhere who are trying to make sense of the outburst of religiously based violence around the world.

That phrase also echoes the title and theme of the talk, "Too bad we're still relevant!" that I gave at the annual meeting of the American Academy of Arts and Sciences (AARS) in 1996, while closing the books on a six-year, twelve-conference, hundred(s)-scholar, five-volume work, *The Fundamentalism Project*, that the AARS had sponsored between 1988 and 1994.

For more than six years, my associate R. Scott Appleby and I labored with that anxiety, "What if we are irrelevant by the time this is finished?" while we directed the project. My talk included a reminder to the academy that in 1988 they could have chartered all kinds of relevant studies (e.g., U.S.-Soviet Relations in the Twenty-First Century, or Exporting Apartheid from South Africa) that would have been irrelevant by 1996. Since he and I had not asked for the work but had been chosen by the academy, we armed ourselves with yellow highlighters and daily marked the newspaper references that dealt with our subject. We went through many yellow markers, and found the number of references to such hard-line religion increasing.

That report foresaw frustrations and rages of religion-rooted conflict in the new millennium and mentioned that even terrorism would be an instrument of the religiously violent. Still, there were some reasons to hope for a measure of decreased religious conflict, even if it was only to be replaced by other kinds, such as territorial or ethnic conflict, as in Kurdish areas of Turkey or in Rwanda or the former Yugoslavia. Yet all of these conflicts are eclipsed by religious furies and violence.

It is in that context that I help J. Harold Ellens turn this subject over to you who, in libraries, at desks, in classrooms, or at home, are working your way through bafflement over the explosion of violence that grows out of the dark side of religion. "Too bad it's relevant."

Twenty years ago I was blithely teaching American religious history, remarking on the relative tolerance to which we citizens had worn each other down in values and practice. On days off from history, as a former pastor and a theologian-at-the-margins I also found many ways to affirm the healing side of religion. As peers in my generation face the debilitation and death that come with our advanced years, we find ourselves consoling each other with stories about the promises of God the healer. At the same time, many of us have joined forces, professionally, to measure and encourage efforts at employing spiritual means to address issues of health and healing.

We see religion represented through churches, synagogues, and mosques, located cozily next to each other in the alphabets of the Yellow Pages. There are few dead bodies in America as a result of religious conflict. Of course, there were always tensions, bloodless schisms, arguments, and contentions, but the violence related to each has been reasonably held in check.

Then *The Fundamentalism Project* forced me and people with whom I worked to "go global," where we got a very different perspective. Domestically, as we listened to the voice of people who had been victimized or oppressed in the name of religion, we noted how many other words ending in *–press* matched "oppress": repressed, suppressed, and so on, suggesting the negative and destructive roles of religion. We had begun to explore an underside of the presence and power of this force in life and history.

Two days after 9/11 I was scheduled to lecture at the University of Illinois on a theme chosen a year before: "Religion: The Healer that Kills; the Killer that Heals." When the terrorists struck in the name of God in New York, they ensured good crowds for talks like that and gave new impetus for scholars to explore the themes gathered so conveniently in these four books on *The Destructive Power of Religion, Violence in Judaism, Christianity, and Islam.*

I am no newcomer to this field, and I know that most of the authors in these volumes, from biblical scholars to psychoanalysts, have long been at their inquiries. Many of them include just enough autobiography for us to learn that they themselves were often among those who experienced the destructive side of religion. They tell us how they countered it, and some testify to its lasting effects. As I read those chapters, however, I noticed also how often they "kept the faith," pursued the spirit, or stayed with religion, however one wishes to put it, even as they wanted to rein in the destructive forces that issue from it. Professor Ellens himself slips in a word that he thinks characterizes the dimensions of religion that one can affirm: *grace.*

How does one square the study of destruction and the affirmation of construction in this one area of life, religion, as many of the authors undertake to do on these pages? Rousseau once said that readers could expect his thoughts to be consistent with each other, but they could not expect him to express them all at the same time. So here, too, one pictures that when assigned another topic, when placed in the role of the therapist, healer, or pastor, these authors could write essays of note about the constructive side.

But if there is anything consistent in these essays, or, rather, because there is much that is consistent in these essays, it is this coherence that the authors bring to their theme, namely, "it is futile to experience grace or healing so long as":

- People think that all would be peaceful if the whole world turned godless, secular, free of religion.
- Humans live with delusion or illusion about the really destructive aspects of faith and faiths.
- We believe that the dark side of religion is all in the mind, heart, and company of "the other," those people who have the wrong God, the wrong books, the wrong nation in which to live.
- People fail to explore their own scriptures, traditions, and experiences, as they have inherited them from ancestors (e.g., when Christians see *jihad* as the main mark of Islam or when Muslims think *crusades* against infidels are what Christians are all about).
- Humans do not engage in psychological probing of themselves and others, to unearth the tangle of themes and motifs that are destructive when faith or God enters the scene.

The authors of these books are helpful to all who want to effect change in the destructive power of religion. For example, the biblical scholars among them bring to light many destructive stories in scrip-

tures that adherents want to overlook. More and more we learn from
these volumes the complex, nether-side of the animating stories of
the strangers' faiths. We are compelled here to look at their traditions
and sacred scriptures: Qur'an, Torah, New Testament, and more. Too
often we read them only in ways that portray an ugliness associated
with the other person or company.

Since most writers of these volumes stand in biblical traditions,
they take on the stories most would like to overlook: Abraham and
Isaac, Jephthah and his daughter, some aspects of God the Father and
Jesus the Son relations. They see no way around such texts, and do
not offer trivializing pap to give them easy interpretations; but they
give us instead tools for interpreting those narratives. These can
make us aware and can be liberating.

Psychology plays a very big role in these volumes, in keeping with
their auspices and intentions. During the six years of *The Fundamentalism Project*, Dr. Appleby and I, with our board of advisers,
jokingly said that we would not let the psychologists in until the
third or fourth year. Then we did, and they were very helpful. What
we were trying to show the academy and readers around the globe
was the fact that there were some irreducibly religious elements in
Fundamentalisms.

Of course, religious Fundamentalists think they are *purely* religious; but many scholars in the social sciences "reduced" them: their
hard-line views were considered by such scholars to be "nothing but"
a reflection of their social class (Marx), or of their relations to their
fathers (Freud), or a reflection of their descent from particularly
vicious simian strands (Darwin).

In our project we were not able to disprove all that the reducers
claimed, and had no motive to do so. *The Fundamentalism Project*, like
this one, was to issue new understanding, not new evasion or new
apologetic sleights of hand. We simply wanted readers of those books
to see, as readers of *The Destructive Power of Religion* should see, the
psychological dynamics that are present at the center of all human
faith commitments and explanations. One sees much of such connection and illumination in these essays. The introduction of insights
from the humanities balances those of social scientists. The religiously committed authors, and those who, at least in their essays, are
noncommittal, together with numerous other aspects of these important volumes, help produce a balanced depiction.

What I took away from the chapters, especially, is a sense of the
pervasiveness of violence across the spectrum of religions. Not

many years ago, celebrated students of myth, or romantic advocates of anything-but-our historic religious traditions, won large enthusiastic audiences for their romantic pictures. *If only* we could get away from Abraham's God, Jesus' Father, and Mother Church's Mary; if only we could move far from Puritan Protestantism with its angry God; if only we left behind Judaism with its Warrior God; if only. . . .

There was great confidence in and propaganda for the notion that we could find refuge in any number of alternatives: gentle, syncretic Hinduism; goddess-rule; mysticism; transcendentalism; animism; Native American thought. However, closer scrutiny showed that only relative distance and the intriguing exoticism of nonconformist alternatives made these other models seem tolerant and gentle. The closer and informed view found violent stories of Hindu-Muslim warfare, tyrannies by what were proposed as the "gentle" human sacrifice, and tribal warfare everywhere. All this is not designed to violate what we are not supposed to violate after reading *The Destructive Power of Religion*, namely, the principle that we are to be self-critical and not irrationally attacking the "other" with finger-pointing. Of course, the "others" *are* in some degree also victims and often perpetrators of the violent and destructive sides of faith.

What goes on, however, as these chapters show, is that there is a dark underside, a nether, shadowed side to every enduring and profound system of symbols and myths, hence to every religion. That may result from deep psychic forces discerned by many of the scholars authoring these volumes. It may result from the realization that the grand myths and stories deal with the wildest and deepest ranges of human aspiration and degradation.

Most of these authors are anything but fatalistic. While there are no utopians here, no idealists who think all will always be well, most of them have a constructive purpose that becomes manifest along the way.

We historians learned from some nineteenth-century giants that we overcome history with history. That is, there is no escape from the world of events and stories and constructions; but we are not doomed to be confined among only violent actions. So with these essays, they make it plain that we are to overcome analysis with analysis, analysis of destruction, which gives insight that can lead to construction. These essays are not preachy: the authors set forth their cases and let readers determine what to do with whatever emerges. I picture a good deal of self-discovery following the discovery of this important work. One hopes that here will be found some glint of discernment that is an expression of—yes, grace!

Martin E. Marty

**Fairfax M. Cone Distinguished Service Professor Emeritus
University of Chicago Divinity School**

Lent 2003

AD TESTIMONIUM

The Destructive Power of Religion is a work of profound research and engaging writing. It is a groundbreaking work with tremendous insight, a set of books that will inform and give perspective to people anywhere trying to make sense of religiously based violence. Professor Ellens has assembled a brilliant stable of insightful and concerned authors to produce four volumes of readable, thoughtful analysis of our present world situation. This contribution will have permanent value for all future research on the crucial matter of religion's destructive power, which has been exercised throughout history, and continues today to give rise to violence in shocking and potentially genocidal dimensions. Future work on this matter will need to begin with this publication. This will become a classic.

Professor Ellens and his team have not produced this important work merely out of theoretical reflection or as viewed from a distant ivory tower. I first met Professor Ellens while he was heavily engaged in psycho-social research in the Republic of South Africa in the 1970s and 1980s, when my country was struggling with some of the worst oppression wreaked upon much of its citizenry by the religiously driven, destructive policies of Apartheid. His comparative studies of educational, health care, and psycho-spiritual resources provided for the black South Africans and the black citizens of the United States were important contributions at a critical time. His orientation is always from the operational perspective, down on the ground where real people live and move and have their being.

In consequence, this massive work is a challenge to those in the professional worlds of psychology, sociology, religion, anthropology, pastoral care, philosophy, biblical studies, and theology. At the same time, it is so highly readable that it will be accessible and downright informative to the layperson or general reader who finds these volumes at the local library. These books are helpful to all who want to effect change in the destructive process in our world, a process too often created or fostered by religious fervor.

It must be noted with equal enthusiasm that the four volumes of *The Destructive Power of Religion* are as urgent in their emphasis upon the positive power—religion's power for healing and redemption of personal and worldwide suffering and perplexity—as they are in boldly setting forth the destructive side. Particularly, the numerous chapters by Professor Ellens, as well as those by Professors Capps, Aden, Wink, Sloat, and others, constantly move us toward the healing perceptions of grace and forgiveness.

Professor Ellens has repeatedly, here and in other works on his long list of publications, called attention to the role redemptive religious power played in the formulation and operation of the Truth and Reconciliation Commission in my country at a time of extreme crisis, thus making possible a thoroughgoing sociopolitical revolution with virtually no bloodshed. He claims, quite correctly, I think, that if it had not been for the pervasive presence of biblical concern and religious fervor in the black, white, and colored populations of our republic at that time, there would have been no way through that sociopolitical thicket without a much greater denigration of the quality of life in our society, and an enormous loss of life itself. I am grateful to him for his insight and his articulation of it for the larger world community. That is typical of the practical approach evident in his work and that of his entire team, which has provided us with this very wise work, *The Destructive Power of Religion.* I commend them unreservedly. I am honored that I have been asked to provide this testimony to the profound importance of these volumes for the worldwide community of those who care.

Archbishop Desmond Tutu
Pentecost 2003

PREFACE

While deeply occupied with the preparation of these volumes, during the Christmas season of 2002, I fell rather inadvertently into a conversation with a young and thoughtful woman, Mollie, who has, consequently, become a genuine friend. Pain prompted our connection; hers, which was more than anyone so young and vital should have to bear, reawakening mine, long, old, deep, soaked in my earliest memories from when I was less than five. Mollie was injured at a tender age and in a manner that made her feel betrayed by God and humankind. My particular personal perplexity started with my mother's frequent illness and absence in my infancy, and was fixed forever in my character and consciousness by the death of my dearest friend on August 3, 1937. Her name was Esther Van Houten, we were both five years old, and we were madly in love. We talked all that summer of starting school together in the fall. We were infinitely joyful. We were gracefully oblivious of the Great Depression in which both our families were caught, and of the lowering clouds of war which would soon take away my older brother and five of hers.

August 3 of that year was a brilliantly sunny day on our remote farmstead southwest of McBain, Michigan. I was standing by the well outside the kitchen window of our farmhouse, vaguely conscious of my mother's image in the window as she prepared my father's mid-morning "lunch." I was thinking of Esther and expected any moment to run across the country road and up the driveway to her yard to while away the morning with her. I heard the screen door of her home slam shut.

My heart leaped, and I looked up anticipating seeing her with her long blond hair and bright blue eyes—like my mother's eyes. There she stood, at the top of the driveway, completely on fire, and she burned to death right there. I helplessly called for my mother, but there was nothing one could do out in that remote place on August 3, in 1937. A sheet of darkness came down on me and did not begin to rise again until I was seven. During those two years, my brother Gordon died, my sister, my dear grandfather, and two neighbor children. Death seemed everywhere. The darkness has never completely gone away.

What connected me with Mollie is our common "case regarding God." It is our common case in that we discovered that we hold it in common and that is how we found each other; but it is also a common case because the longer I live and the more I learn the clearer it is that this is the case every thinking and feeling person has regarding God. It is common among humans to live with this perplexity. The ancient Israelites who gave us their Bible, and with it the heritage Jews, Christians, and Muslims hold in common, formulated the perplexity in the question, "How is God in history, particularly our usually troubled and often wretched history of wickedness, destruction, and death?" How can God promise so much prosperity and security through the prophets and deliver so little safety for faithful, vulnerable, hopeful humans? How can God entice a fourteen-year-old girl into the quest for faith and in that very context fail to protect her from injury and betrayal? God seems perfectly capable of engineering a majestic creation and strategizing its evolution through eons of productive time, but he cannot keep a five-year-old girl from death by fire? I spent my entire life, from age seven on, devoted to a single course toward, into, and in the ministry of theology and psychology, confidently trying to recover the trust that God, in a prosperous providence, would embrace my children and carefully shepherd them into health, wisdom, safety, and success; in the faith, in fruitful marriages, in joyful parenting, and in the fulfillments of love. I entrusted my children to God's care while I was busy "doing the work of God's Kingdom." I did my side of the "bargain" very well. God did not do as well on his side of the equation.

All this has caused me to work very hard to rethink my entire notion of God, and especially my theology of sacred scriptures. I do not see how any honest and honorable person can get through an entire lifetime without being forced to do this very same thing, forced by what has always been the ordinary horror and daily trauma of life, personal and universal. Unless one is able to see the unsacred in sacred scriptures, what can the sacred mean? Unless one has a comprehensive way to come to terms with the horror of life, how can celebration of the gracious be anything but psycho-spiritual denial? There can be no question that the God of the Hebrew Bible, and the God who is reported to have killed Jesus because, after getting ticked off at the human race, he could not get his head screwed on right again unless he killed us or somebody else, is abusive in the extreme. To salvage a God of grace out of that requires some reworking of the traditional Judaic, Christian, and Muslim theologies of sacred scripture. The difficulty that prevents us from writing God off completely and permanently is the fact that both the Old Testament and the New Testament, as well as the Qur'an, have woven through the center of their literary stream a more central message as well. The notion, unique in all human religions, that Abraham seems to have discovered, which is so redemptive in these sacred scriptures, is the claim that the real God is a God of unconditional grace—the only thing that works in life, for God or for humans. The human heartache is universal. The perplexity pervades everything in life. The question is, "Is there any warrant that the claims for grace do too?"

I do not feel like the Lone Ranger in this matter. Of course, there is Mollie's case, but everyone who has been around for a while knows a long list of the Mollies in this world. I have sat in my psychotherapist and pastoral counselor chairs for 40 years and have noticed that this is the "case regarding God" that perplexes most thoughtful and informed people; and most have been afraid to say it aloud, or have had no good opportunity to do so. Mollie said it aloud to me and immediately I recognized the sound of it. It is our common human story. It has ever been so, since reflective humans first opened wondering eyes upon this planet. Many years ago Barbara Mertz wrote a telling book about ancient Egypt. She called it, *Red Land, Black Land*.[1] She noted that we cannot speak of those mysterious days and people of so long ago without being awed by their way of dying and their funerals. They recorded them grandly in their even grander tombs. It is a simple story, the same as ours; a story in Mertz's sensitive words, "of our common human terror and our common hope."

The Destructive Power of Religion, Violence in Judaism, Christianity, and Islam, is a work in four volumes about our common human terror and our common hope. I hope you will find it stirring, disturbing, and hopeful.

J. Harold Ellens
Epiphany 2003

Note

1. New York: Dell Publishing, 1966, 367.

ACKNOWLEDGMENTS

Dr. Chris Stout invited me to write a chapter in his earlier, remarkably important four-volume set, *The Psychology of Terrorism*. I was pleased to do so, and we published my chapter there under the title "Psychological Legitimization of Violence by Religious Archetypes." Debbie Carvalko, acquisitions editor at Greenwood Press, found the chapter valuable and asked me to expand it by editing a work, which I have titled *The Destructive Power of Religion*. Thus, these four volumes were thoughtfully conceived and wisely midwifed. The birth is timely, since it seems everywhere evident that the world needs these reflections just now, more than ever. I wish, therefore, to acknowledge with honor and gratitude, Debbie's kind proficiency and Chris' professional esteem. I wish, as well, to thank the 30 authors who joined me in creating this work. I wish to express my gratitude to Beverley Adams for her meticulous work in reading the proofs of these volumes, while I was too ill to do so.

CHAPTER 1

INTRODUCTION: THE DESTRUCTIVE POWER OF RELIGION

J. Harold Ellens

Religion is a source of remarkable consolation and hope. It accounts for human endurance through the long reach of our species' precarious history. It is stimulated by and at the same time drives our spirituality, that is, our hunger and quest for meaning in life. Religion responds to our innate sense that the ultimate meaning of our lives is transcendental, and it offers the worldviews and rituals, the ideas and programs, that help us formulate and express our sense of linkage with transcendental reality—with God.

Religion has taken many forms in human history. Those numerous forms have focused on a great variety of points, claiming each of them in various times and settings as the central meaning or truth for humankind. Some religion is formalistic and full of programs and projects. Other kinds are meditative, touching a very fiery personal inner thirst for meaning. Programmatic and project-oriented religions may be called extrinsic in their spirituality, while interior and reflective religions seem more intrinsic. Which suits each human best is a matter of style rather than one's degree of spiritual authenticity or genuineness.

Some religious practice is most focused on dogma or liturgy, some depends nearly completely upon intuitive illumination and psychospiritual interiority. As Toynbee is said to have remarked on history in general, it is certainly true of the history of religions. The formalistic aspects of religious institutions, creeds, dogmas, canon law; the notable records of bishops, archbishops, curias, and popes; and the decrees of councils, consistories, or confraternities, while of temporary usefulness, constitute the flotsam and jetsam that wash down the stream of history into the ocean of relative irrelevance. The real history of religions is rather the variegated life that is at play deep in the stream of history, where all the unnoticed schools of colorful life forms gambol, and on the banks of the river where both simple and sophisticated folk from the hamlets, villages, and glass skyscrapers everywhere, live and move, sing and dance, fear and hope, touch each other with hands and hearts, love and make love, bear children and catechize them, comfort them in their losses, and bury their dead with faith, hope, and dignity.

It has long seemed to me quite clear that the authenticity of any form of religion or personal spirituality depends upon whether it will bury a child. Can the spirituality that shapes my sense of meaning, the religious ritual that comforts and consoles me, empower me to endure the terror of standing at the edge of the empty tomb into which I must finally lower my own little one? Humans have crafted this question in a variety of ways. Usually our way of saying that unspeakable sentence is designed to mask the horror of it, but neither the most intensely devout form of spirituality, nor the most prayerfully confident hope, protects us from this terror. If we can get through a lifetime without that broken child being our own personal progeny, it is some inexpressible grace, but, nonetheless, we do not get clean away. For me, and every sensitive person, every broken child is mine. That death is a form of terror. Can a religion speak spiritually to such a time of terror and save one's sense of meaning? What does that take?

Exposition

Too often religion has spoken with an opposite voice. We look to our sacred scriptures for the words of consolation and hope and we find them there pervasive, but many of the words in sacred scriptures express threat and violence. Western cultures have been shaped by religions that, at best, have sounded uncertain trumpets. Judaism, Christianity, and Islam are all forms of spirituality and religious practice that derive directly from ancient Israelite religion, and that religious tradition speaks with remarkable and disappointing ambiguity. It is my conviction that the main psychosocial and political problem in modern and postmodern culture arises from the apocalyptic worldview willed to us by that ancient ambiguous religion. From the

Hebrew Bible's earliest cadences come the sounds of a world split apart. Good and evil are ranged against each other, and from the outset they are given cosmic dimensions. Good and evil quickly become God and devil, and the real arena of the problem becomes transcendent and hence all-encompassing. This ultimate dualism then becomes the model for explaining the meaning of everything, and this schizophrenia is internalized to the unconscious level in every aspect of Western culture and every Western person. It becomes the primal archetype of our understanding, reflecting a schizoid misunderstanding of the real way things are.

The notion that evil is cosmic and that reality is split, from the transcendental level down to our empirical experience, is profoundly untrue. There is no evidence on the basis of which to conclude that there is such a thing as cosmic evil or that some grand warfare between good and evil, God and devil, rages in the universe or in our personal worlds. We have no data in terms of which to conclude that any evil exists in this world except that which humans do to each other from illness, ignorance, or ill will. Tragedies happen, of course. Mud slides kill Columbians. Vesuvius killed Romans in 79 C.E. On January 21, 2003, an earthquake of 7.8 on the Richter scale killed at least 22 citizens of Mexico. Children die daily somewhere. These are tragedies, but not cosmic evil. They are evil in that they terrorize and torture humans, sometimes beyond what is supportable. They are inconveniences of the body, mind, or spirit. However, the suffering of this world arises from our actions or our failure to act, either from inadequate or bad will, or from inadequate or bad information, or from inadequate or inefficient effort, or from lack of power or ability to do better or differently.

Humankind is caught in a world that challenges us beyond our incompletely evolved human capacities, a world in which our incapacity to meet the challenge turns naturally back upon us with cruel pain. If you do not have enough men to lift the barn beam, it will fall upon you and crush you, not because the beam or the world in which it functions is evil, or because barn raising is evil, but because the challenge was still beyond you. A microbe infects a blade of grass munched by a cow whose dangerous milk is offered an infant and kills him. Great achievement for the parasite. Great tragedy for the child and his loved ones—not because the world is evil but because we have not yet imagined an adequate medical management of microbes.

So we live out our quest for meaning, spirituality, and authentic religion in a world of human pathos, vulnerability, and pain. There is no way around that. It is surely the best of all possible worlds, nonetheless, in which microbes, cows, babies, and their parents are free, although immature, inadequate, incomplete, and endangered species. The challenges are God-sized and our resources are only human, so the task could easily become overwhelming. For many it does. For all of us it would if we could find no comfort and consolation. The tragic side of human experience, therefore, is greatly and unnecessarily exaggerated when the main sources to which we look for consolation and empowerment, our religious traditions, are infested with ambiguity. The greatest tragedy is religion that sounds the trumpet of violence and champions the metaphors of abuse, exploitation, legalisms, and merely a conditional grace.

As I mentioned above, the Western religious traditions, which go back to the ancient Israelite religion of the Hebrew Bible, have internalized this violent metaphor of the cosmic contest between transcendental good and evil. It is an old pagan idea that derives from ancient Mesopotamian, Egyptian, and Canaanite legend, reinforced by the apocalypticism of Zoroastrian influences from the sixth century B.C.E. This violent metaphor of divine warfare and of a God who kills his son has become the central metaphor of the Master Story of Western culture. It has settled into the center of the psyche of the communities of faith we know as Judaism, Christianity, and Islam. Through them it has shaped the unconscious psychosocial assumptions of our cultures. This set of unconscious apocalyptic assumptions forms the sources and stage set for what we find meaningful in our cultures, from the violent game machines in the arcades our teenagers frequent to the actions of the Islamic Fundamentalists who flew airplanes into the World Trade Center. It is a short psychospiritual step from the vicarious forms of wishful mythic violence in the arcade machine to the mythic wishes that hurled gasoline-laden flying machines into the workplace of twenty thousand New Yorkers.

The hero-touting movies, popular literature, money-making music, and crowd-gathering Fundamentalist TV evangelists are all pushing the same apocalyptic model. Cosmic good and transcendental evil are depicted as being in mortal combat on the battlefields of our political policy, our international relations, our social values, and our spiritual quests in the arena of the human heart. Meanwhile, the truth is that none of this is so. But how many of the movies produced in the last 10 years would have gained any audience or financial success, if they had not exploited this false apocalyptic vision? What would happen to a movie that simply told the truth that humans are up against some

The Statue of Liberty stands in the foreground as New York City is shrouded in smoke after two hijacked planes crashed into the World Trade Center, Tuesday, September 11, 2001. AP/Wide World Photos.

massive challenges to form a congenial world, safe for children and those who love them? Who would make money on a film that refused the apocalyptic vision and instead set before us the hardheaded enigmas of the creation of a more blessed world?

Apocalyptic evangelists, film producers, arcade machine purveyors, designers of the violent Disney videos, and those Fundamentalist Islamic terrorists are all in the same category in terms of the unconscious metaphors by which they are shaped, to which they appeal, and that they constantly reinforce in our cultures. Moreover, the Master Story from which they derive their unconscious metaphors is the tradition of Western religions: Judaism, Christianity, and Islam. The Western world will need to decide whether it wishes to change this destructive story and its vicious core metaphors, or continue to wreak increasing psychospiritual havoc upon itself until the metaphor becomes so pervasive that we will all feel relieved with the impending prospect of a final cataclysmic Armageddon, closing out history. Does this seem far-fetched? It is the palpable vision of the Zionist Christian

Fundamentalists and Evangelicals, of the Islamic terrorists, and can it not be of the Israeli Zionists who would rather fight than switch. Such folk are serious and sincere about their vision and are quite sure they are closer to God's truth than any of the rest of us who seek spiritual authenticity and religious integrity and peace. The metaphor of cosmic evil and violence has taken over their center.

It is of great interest that Western religions are the action-oriented religions. In this regard they differ greatly from the spirit and style of the historic Eastern religions, Hinduism, Buddhism, and Confucianism. Eastern religions are characterized by a movement inward, while Western religions tend to externalize their values in sociocultural influences. The inward-oriented religions of Asia and India emphasize the importance of individual and intrinsic spirituality that moves toward transcendence of self, society, and world. The outward-acting religions of the West emphasize human responsibility for the shape and function of society, and tend to make ethical claims in the name of religion and religions' God. This extrinsic spirituality is advantageous in many ways, especially in terms of attempts at managing material resources for the enhancement of the material comfort, safety, health, and quality of human life. One needs only compare the sewer systems of India and the United States to discern the difference a socially responsible extrinsic spirituality makes compared with an individualistic, interiorizing transcendental religion.

However, the underside of this very same extrinsic and action-oriented nature of the Western religions carries with it the monstrous danger that externalizing the metaphors and models of apocalyptic religion into culture building and social function produces enormous potential for violence at both the individual and societal levels. If the world is a stage for the cosmic battle between good and evil, God and devil, mediated through human agency, humans who want to undertake what they consider responsible courses of action are likely to resort to violence to win the war for God and the good. Each highly motivated religionist conceives of his or her religio-cultural stance to be the one that is on God's side. Thus those who have the posture of one of the other action religions tend to be placed in the religio-cultural category of the evil one—the other side of the cosmic conflict. Thus Fundamentalist Muslims resort to terror to oppose the influences of American culture and political presence in their world, the generally secular character of which is identified with Christian or Judeo-Christian traditions. It was these people who assassinated Anwar Sadat for his inclination toward American policy and toward peace.

So also Fundamentalist Jews tend to side with the aggressive right-wing politics in Israel today and demonize the Palestinian activists as belonging to the enemies of God and God's people. It was such Jews who assassinated Rabin because of his quest for peace and reconciliation. In like manner, American Fundamentalist Christians support Zionist causes, not because they hold to the original Zionist principles, but because they believe that doing so hurries the onset of the ultimate conflict between the cause of God, identified with their form of Christianity, and the cause of the devil, identified with Muslim religion and politics. Their ambition is to precipitate the ultimate conflict, bringing the world into a cataclysmic Battle of Armageddon. This prospect is of high value to these Christian Fundamentalists because they are sure that the final battle will end the travail of history as we know it with its cosmic conflict, it will defeat the powers of the devil, and it will bring Jesus, as "the Son of Man, on the clouds of heaven, with all the Holy Angels, in the glory of his Father." It will give us a new heaven and a new earth, devoid of the tiring cosmic conflict.

All three of these action-oriented Western religions have a common psychological need and archetype. It is that of the quest for a final solution. This is not just the final solution to present practical political or social problems, not simply the final solution to misunderstandings between Jews and Arabs, not even the final solution to high threat levels in the oily Middle East, nor the definitive final solution to disagreements between Europe, Asia, and America on how to shepherd the world to peace and prosperity. This is not a conscious level quest for a strategy of political and social well-being. It is an unconscious urge, a psychological desperation, a sociopolitical lust for the final solution to the underlying cosmic conflict between God and devil, between all things good and all things evil.

If you asked human beings on the streets of our cities if this is their need and hunger, most would not be conscious of this as the driver behind their enthusiasm for the causes they espouse. Nonetheless, it is true for religionists and secularists alike. The deep-structure drivers behind the institutional and societal violence in our Western culture—political and economic manipulation and military action—are the psychological archetypes that compel us to lunge for those final solutions. Each war is the war to end all wars—although it never does and never will. These deep-structure psychological archetypes are shaped by the religious models of violent cosmic conflict that derive from ancient Israelite religious narratives in the Bible and lie at the core of all Western religions. This lust and lunge for final solutions express the weariness of Western humanity under the burden of the cosmic-conflict model of reality. It is a failure of verve and a failure of nerve in the West. It expresses a universal unconscious longing to get out from under this religio-cultural burden. It is a longing for the end—and for the relief of death.

Conclusion

The central problem with which we are perpetually faced throughout the world today, given the prominent influence of Western culture nearly everywhere on this planet, is complex but relatively easy to outline. As we noted, it is rooted in the core metaphor of a violent cosmic contest between good and evil in terms of which all of reality is consciously viewed and that is derived from the ancient Israelite root of all of our religions. This metaphor appeals to our primal communal survival instincts and feeds those aggressive drives, giving form to unconscious psychological archetypes regarding us versus them, those on the side of God and the good versus those on the side of evil and the demonic. This set of archetypes prompts the lust for comfort and safety gained by force: political, economic, or military; and the lunge for an ultimate resolution by cataclysm—an apocalyptic death wish. This is a particularly obscene state of affairs, since the root hypothesis is erroneous. There is no reason to claim that there is such a thing as ontological evil in this world, and there is no evidence for a transcendental cosmic conflict. There are just communities of inadequate, ignorant, and sick humans trying to find their way to meaning in a world of radical freedom, constant growth, the perpetual change attendant upon growth, and the pervasive pain that accommodating change always brings.

Some years ago, I am told, the cartoon editor of the Kansas City *Star* retired. He had served a long lifetime career for that paper, and they honored him with a congratulatory dinner. He had wielded a particularly cynical and acerbic pen all his long years as a cartoonist, severely lacerating the pomposity, presumptuousness, narcissism, acquisitiveness, and general bad manners of humanity. Now, at his dinner he was expected to make some memorable remarks. They asked him to comment upon what he really thought of the human race. He simply said, "I think we ought to be kind to it. It is the only one we've got!" I think it is time for us to begin to treat and nurture the human race and its pilgrimage with gentle kindness and enticing nurture, by providing it a vision of life as an intriguing, though painful, growth quest, in the congenial environment of simple pleasures, consoling love, and amazing grace. To do this we must rid ourselves once and for all of the great lie. We must transcend the awful betrayal in our earliest religious metaphors that make us feel unconsciously that we are up against cosmic evil, divine threat, inherent failure, insurmountable guilt, final resolution by calamity and cataclysm, and ultimate self-inflicted disaster. That is not the meaning of things. The meaning is in growth and grace.

In this first of four volumes of *The Destructive Power of Religion: Violence in Judaism, Christianity, and Islam*, 10 senior scholars from the United States and Canada address that appalling enigma. Volume I investigates its root and source under the title *Sacred Scriptures, Ideology, and Violence*. Volume II, with seasoned scholars from Latin America and the United States, deals with the theme *Religion, Psychology, and Violence*. Volume III, entitled *Religion and Violence: Models and Cases*, features 10 professional psychotherapists, university professors, and research scholars from the United States and the Republic of South Africa. Volume IV, *Contemporary Views of the Relationship of Spirituality and Violence*, offers essays by renowned professionals in the fields of psychology, religion, history, and jurisprudence. Perhaps the weighty but stimulating argumentation of these volumes will contribute to freeing the Western world from its addiction to its inherently self-destructive core metaphor.

CHAPTER 2

THE ZEAL OF PHINEHAS, THE BIBLE, AND THE LEGITIMATION OF VIOLENCE

John J. Collins

"The Bible, of all books, is the most dangerous one, the one that has been endowed with the power to kill," writes Mieke Bal.[1] Like many striking aphorisms, this statement is not quite true. Some other books, notably the Qur'an, are surely as lethal, and in any case, to coin a phrase, books don't kill people. But Professor Bal has a point nonetheless. When it became clear that the terrorists of September 11, 2001, saw or imagined their grievances in religious terms, any reader of the Bible should have had a flash of recognition. The Muslim extremists drew their inspiration from the Qur'an rather than the Bible, but both scriptures draw from the same wellsprings of ancient Near Eastern religion. While it is true that both Bible and Qur'an admit of various readings and emphases, and that terrorist hermeneutics can be seen as a case of the devil citing scripture for his purpose, it is also true that the devil does not have to work very hard to find biblical precedents for the legitimation of violence. Many people in the modern world suspect that there is an intrinsic link between violence and what Jan Assmann has called "the Mosaic distinction" between true and false religion,[2] or even between violence and monotheism or monolatry.[3] Such claims are, no doubt, too simple. Violence and the sacred went hand in hand long before the rise of Akhenaten or Moses, and polytheism can be used to legitimate violence just as easily as monotheism.[4] But it is biblical monotheism that has dominated the Western world for the last two thousand years,

Moses with the Tablets of the Law, by Claude the Elder Vignon. Erich Lessing/Art Resource, New York.

and it is the Bible that concerns us here. At a time when the Western world is supposedly engaged in a war on terrorism, it may be opportune to reflect on the ways in which the Bible appears to endorse and bless the recourse to violence, and to ask what the implications may be for the task of biblical interpretation.

Violence, of course, has many forms. On a broad level, it has been defined as "the attempt of an individual or group to impose its will on others through any nonverbal, verbal, or physical means that inflict psychological or physical injury."[5] Often the term is reserved for coercion or force that is illegitimate, and associated with social disorder, although states and governments routinely use forceful and coercive methods to impose order.[6] For the present, I will restrict myself to the most obvious, even crude, forms of violence—the killing of others without benefit of judicial procedure. It is important to bear in mind, however, that the line between actual killing and verbal, symbolic, or imaginary violence is thin and permeable. The threat of violence is a method of forceful coercion, even if no blood is actually shed.

The ḥerem, or Ban

"The Lord is a warrior," says the song of Moses (Exod. 15:3), in one of the earliest attempts to characterize the God of Israel.[7] Many of the oldest hymns in praise of this god celebrate "the triumphs of the Lord" (Judg. 5:11). "It is as good as certain," wrote Gerhard von Rad, "that the concept of faith—in other words, that confident trusting in the action of Yahweh—had its actual origin in the holy war, and that from there it took on its own peculiar dynamic."[8] Even if we regard von Rad's statement as exaggerated, it is certainly true that YHWH's putative power in battle was a major consideration in early Israelite worship.[9] Moreover, the Israelites were expected to "come to the help of the Lord" in battle, and were subject to sanctions if they did not, as can be seen from the cursing of Meroz in the Song of Deborah (Judg. 5:23). Only in much later times would the power of the deity be taken as a reason for quietism on the part of human worshipers.[10]

The violence associated with the worship of YHWH in antiquity is most vividly illustrated by the practice of the ḥerem, or ban, the practice whereby the defeated enemy was devoted to destruction.[11] The practice was not peculiar to Israel. A famous parallel is provided by the Moabite stone, erected by the ninth-century king Mesha:

> And Chemosh said to me, "Go, take Nebo from Israel. So I went by night and fought against it from the break of dawn until noon, taking it and slaying all, seven thousand men, boys, women, girls, and maid—servants, for I had devoted them to destruction for (the god) Ashtar-Chemosh."[12]

The practice was evidently known in Israel and its environs, although it is not widely attested in the ancient Near East.[13] It was not just a figment of the imagination of later writers.

The Moabite example shows that the slaughter has a sacrificial character; the victims are offered to the god.[14] In the Bible, this is sometimes done at the deity's command. 1 Samuel 15:3 may serve as a representative example: "Thus says the Lord of hosts, 'I will punish the Amalekites for what they did in opposing the Israelites when they came up out of Egypt. Now go and attack Amalek, and utterly destroy [herem] all that they have; do not spare them, but kill both man and woman, child and infant, ox and sheep, camel and donkey." The herem can also be undertaken on human initiative. In Numbers 21:1–3, the Israelites respond to a setback at Arad by making a vow to the Lord that "if you will indeed give this people into our hands, then we will utterly destroy their towns." When the Lord duly hands over the Canaanites, the Israelites "utterly destroy them and their towns." The fulfillment of the promise shows that more than the destruction of property was involved. We are reminded of the vow of Jephthah in Judges 11:31: "If you will give the Ammonites into my hand, then whoever comes out of the doors of my house to meet me . . . shall be the Lord's, to be offered up by me as a burnt offering." Jephthah clearly intended human sacrifice, although not the sacrifice of his daughter, as transpired.[15] The parallel underlines the fact that the ban, too, involves human sacrifice. The *do ut des* mentality may also be implied in other cases where no rationale is given for the ban: the assumption is that the offering wins the support of the deity. In any case, there is assumed to be a connection between the fulfillment of the ban and success in battle, as is clear in the story of Achan and the conquest of Ai in Joshua 7–8, where defeat is attributed to Achan's violation of the ban.

The ritualistic character of the herem, which leaves no room for individual decision, has sometimes been viewed as a mitigating factor in its morality. It eliminated plunder and exploitation. "Paradoxically," writes Susan Niditch, "the ban as sacrifice may be viewed as admitting of more respect for the value of human life than other war ideologies that allow for the arbitrary killing of soldiers and civilians."[16] The enemy is deemed worthy of being offered to God. One hopes that the Canaanites appreciated the honor. Rather than respect for human life, the practice bespeaks a totalistic attitude, which is common in armies and warfare, wherein the individual is completely subordinated to the interests of the group.[17] Niditch is quite right, however, that the ban as sacrifice requires "a God who appreciates human sacrifice," and that those who practiced the ban "would presumably have something in common with those who believed in the efficacy of child sacrifice."[18] All of this helps put the practice in context in the ancient world, but increases rather than lessens its problematic nature from an ethical point of view.

It is now widely recognized that human sacrifice was practiced in ancient Israel much later than scholars of an earlier generation had assumed.[19] Abraham is not condemned but praised for his willingness to offer up his son, even though he is not required to go through with it.[20] Exodus 22:28–29 appears to require the sacrifice of the first-born, and does not provide for substitution in the manner of the parallel text in Exodus 34:19–20.[21] Kings of Judah, Ahaz and Manasseh, are accused of child sacrifice.[22] Their practice cannot be dismissed as due to foreign influence, but had venerable precedents in the cult of YHWH. Nonetheless, by the time of the Deuteronomists this practice had been denounced by prophets,[23] and Deuteronomy explicitly condemns it as an abhorrent Canaanite custom.[24] Yet the same Deuteronomy has no qualms about the practice of the ban, and in fact most of the passages dealing with ḥerem are found in the Deuteronomistic corpus.

Deuteronomy does not eradicate the sacrificial aspect of the ban but it seeks to rationalize the practice by justifying it.[25] Deuteronomy 20 distinguishes between "towns that are very far from you" and "the towns of these peoples that the Lord your God is giving you as an inheritance." In the latter, "you must not let anything that breathes remain alive . . . so that they may not teach you to do all the abhorrent things that they do for their gods, and you thus sin against the Lord your God." Ethnic cleansing is the way to ensure cultic purity. In the case of faraway towns, only the males need be put to the sword. In this case, no justification is deemed necessary; the slaughter is normal procedure in warfare; it is the restraint that is remarkable. Reasons other than the danger of false worship are occasionally offered. Sihon, king of Heshbon, is condemned for his lack of hospitality to the Israelites in Deuteronomy 2:26–35, and not a single survivor is left. Perhaps the most practical justification is given in Numbers 33:55: "but if you do not drive out the inhabitants of the land from before you, then those whom you let remain shall be as barbs in your eyes and thorns in your sides; they shall trouble you in the land where you are settling." The predominant justification for the slaughter, however, is as a precautionary measure against false worship.[26]

Insofar as the ḥerem applies primarily to the promised land, it also rests on the premise that this land is legitimately given to Israel by its God. The command in Deuteronomy 7 is typical and foundational:

When the Lord your God brings you into the land that you are about to enter and occupy, and he clears away many nations before you—the Hittites, the Girgashites, the Amorites, the Canaanites, the Perizzites, the Hivites, and the Jebusites, seven nations mightier and more numerous than you—and when the Lord gives them over to you and you defeat them, then you must utterly destroy them. Make no covenant with them and show them no mercy. Do not intermarry with them, giving your daughters to their sons or taking their daughters for your sons, for that would turn away your children from following me, to serve other gods. Then the anger of the Lord would be kindled against you, and he would destroy you quickly. But this is how you must deal with them: break down their altars, smash their pillars, hew down their sacred poles and burn their idols with fire. For you are a people holy to the Lord your God; the Lord your God has chosen you out of all the peoples on earth to be his people, his treasured possession.[27] (Deut. 7:1–6)

There are two primary factors in these passages that are taken as warrants for violence on the part of Israel. One is the demand that Israel worship only one god, YHWH. Other peoples who might interfere with that demand, and Israelites who fail to comply with it, may legitimately be killed. The second is the claim that a land is given to Israel by divine grant and that consequently the previous inhabitants not only may be driven out or killed, but should be. The legitimation for violence is not simply monotheism as such. There is no demand that all people must worship YHWH, although that is envisioned as a desirable goal in some prophetic texts.[28] The issues concern the status of Israel as YHWH's chosen people and covenant partner, and the claim of a land as its inheritance. In short, the issue is not monotheism, as such, but the advancement of a particular people and the imposition of its cult within the territory it controls.

The command to slaughter the Canaanites is not without a certain irony in the context of Deuteronomy. As Moshe Weinfeld has shown, Deuteronomy is one of the great repositories of humanistic values in the biblical corpus.[29] This is the book that repeatedly tells the Israelites to be compassionate to slaves and aliens, remembering that they themselves were slaves and exiles in the land of Egypt.[30] The ethical principle, to do unto others as you would have them do unto you, was not an innovation of the New Testament.[31] The laws on slaves and aliens in Deuteronomy show an appreciation of what Emmanuel Levinas calls "the face of the other"[32] as human, and they call for empathy with our fellow human beings. But this empathy does not extend to the Canaanites or the peoples of the land. At least by the time Deuteronomy was written, the people of Israel and Judah should have known the heart of the conquered and known what it was like to have their land overrun and their shrines burned down. Yet there is no appreciation here of the face of the Canaanite and no misgiving about doing to others what they themselves had suffered.

There is also some irony in the way in which these commands of destruction are embedded in the story of the Exodus, which has served as the great paradigm of liberation in Western history.[33] But the liberation of the Israelites and the subjugation of the Canaanites are two sides of the same coin. Without a land of their own, the liberated Israelites would have nowhere to go, but the land promised to them was not empty and had its own inhabitants. Read from the Canaanite perspective, this is not a liberating story at all.[34]

Of course, those who have read and recited the story of the Exodus over the centuries have been Jews and Christians who identify with Israel in the story. In the not too distant past, biblical scholars gave the Canaanites short shrift. "From the impartial standpoint of a philosopher of history," wrote Albright, "it often seems necessary that a people of markedly inferior type should vanish before a people of superior potentialities."[35] In a more explicitly theological vein, G. E. Wright could claim that "the Canaanite civilization and religion was one of the weakest, most decadent, and most immoral cultures of the civilized world at that time," and that God had a purpose in choosing Israel and giving her the land.[36] Most scholars, we should hope, have learned by now that biblical denunciations of the Canaanites cannot be taken at face value and that these texts may tell us more about the purposes of their human authors than about the purposes of God.[37]

History and Ideology

The context of the discussion has changed significantly in recent years with the recognition that the biblical texts are not historically reliable accounts of early Israelite history, but ideological fictions from a much later time. The archaeological evidence does not support the view that marauding Israelites actually engaged in the massive slaughter of Canaanites, either in the thirteenth century or at any later time.[38] Recent scholarly hypotheses about the origins of Israel tend to be more compatible with modern moral sensibilities, whether the early Israelites are imagined as peasants in revolt,[39] or as quiet, hardworking settlers in the hill country.[40] But this scarcely relieves the moral problem posed by the biblical texts, which portray Israel as an aggressive, invading force, impelled by divine commands.[41] In the words of James Barr: "the problem is not whether the narratives are fact or fiction, the problem is that, whether fact or fiction, the ritual destruction is *commended*."[42] The texts are not naive reflections of primitive practice, but programmatic ideological statements from the late seventh century B.C.E. or later. We can no longer accept them as simply presenting what happened. Whether we see these texts as reflecting expansionistic policies of King Josiah or as mere fantasies of powerless Judeans after the Exile, they project a model of the ways in which Israel should relate to its neighbors. In this perspective, ownership of the land of Israel is conferred by divine grant, not by ancestral occupancy or by negotiation, and violence against rival claimants of that land is not only legitimate, but mandatory, especially if these people worship gods other than YHWH, the God of Israel.

It is a commonplace of modern scholarship to say that the books of the Torah and the Deuteronomistic history are engaged in the construction of the identity of "Israel." What they reflect is not Israel as it was, but Israel as the authors thought it should be. Identity is defined negatively by a sharp differentiation of Israel from the other peoples of the land and positively by the prescriptions of a covenant with a jealous sovereign god. In Deuteronomy 7, the peoples of the land are identified chiefly by their worship, which involves sacred poles and pillars and idols. At least some of these cultic accoutrements are associated with the worship of YHWH in Genesis.[43] In Deuteronomy 12 we find that any cultic worship outside of "the place that the Lord your God will choose" is illegitimate. The reform of King Josiah, described in 2 Kings 22–23, is evidently an attempt to implement the cultic demands of Deuteronomy, or, to put it differently, Deuteronomy, in some form, was promulgated to authorize the actions of Josiah. Josiah's actions were not directed against actual Canaanites, but against Israelites whose cultic practices did not conform to Deuteronomic orthopraxy. There is much to be said then for the view that neither Deuteronomy nor Joshua, in the historical context of their composition, was intended "to incite literal violence against ethnic outsiders" but was rather directed at "insiders who pose a threat to the hierarchy that is being asserted."[44] Whether this really relieves the moral problem might be debated.[45] In fairness to Josiah, we are not told that he practiced ḥerem against anyone, although he certainly used violence to suppress the high places. But texts have a life of their own, and the effective history of the conquest stories is based not on critical reconstructions of the underlying history but on the prima facie meaning of the texts.

Story and Example

Two examples may suffice here to illustrate the ways in which these biblical texts have served to legitimize violent action.

The first is drawn from ancient Judaism, from the book of 1 Maccabees, which, ironically, has the status of scripture in Catholic Christianity but not in Judaism. It is easy enough to sympathize with the story of the Maccabean revolt.[46] In view of the alleged persecution of observant Jews by Antiochus Epiphanes, the actions of Mattathias and his sons can be viewed as self-defense, and therefore legitimate by the standards of any culture. But this is not the only, nor even the primary, aspect of the situation emphasized in 1 Maccabees. Mattathias, we are told, "burned with zeal for the law, just as Phinehas did against Zimri the son of Salu."[47] The reference is to the incident at Baal-Peor in Numbers 25, when the Israelites incurred the wrath of the Lord by having sexual relations with Moabite women and participating in the sacrifices of pagan gods.[48] The unfortunate Zimri brought a Midianite woman into his family in the sight of Moses and the congregation. Phinehas took his spear and followed them into the tent and pierced the two of them. His action was approved in an oracle spoken by Moses:

> Phinehas, son of Eleazar, son of Aaron the priest, has turned back my wrath from the Israelites by manifesting such zeal among them on my behalf that in my jealousy I did not consume the Israelites. Therefore say, "I hereby grant him my covenant of peace." It shall be for him and for his descendants after him a covenant of perpetual priesthood, because he was zealous for his God, and made atonement for the Israelites.[49]

A recent monograph on Old Testament ethics assures us that "the exemplary dimension of his act was not its violence ... but Phinehas's zeal for the Lord and his atoning for the people. These were hallmarks of true priesthood."[50] Mattathias, however, was in no doubt as to what the exemplary dimension of the act required. Like

Phinehas, he first kills a compatriot, thereby lending credence to the view that a primary purpose of violence in the biblical texts is to enforce conformity within the people of Israel. But Phinehas also participates, as priest, in the massacre of the Midianites, which follows the practice of the ḥerem, or ban, although that word is not used.[51] Mattathias also proceeds to wage war against the Gentiles. Moreover, the example both of Mattathias and of Phinehas became the model for the Zealots who fought against the Romans in the first century C.E.,[52] and whose methods would surely qualify for the label *terrorist* in modern political rhetoric.[53]

The second example is drawn from Christian history. The English Puritan revolution was justified repeatedly by biblical analogies drawn from the Old Testament. Using a rather dubious interpretation of the Book of Daniel, the revolutionaries saw themselves as "the Saints of the Most High," commissioned to execute judgment on kings and nobles.[54] Oliver Cromwell drew a parallel between his revolution and the Exodus[55] and proceeded to treat the Catholics of Ireland as the Canaanites. He even declared that "there are great occasions in which some men are called to great services in the doing of which they are excused from the common rule of morality," as were the heroes of the Old Testament.[56] A generation later, the Puritans of New England applied the biblical texts about the conquest to their own situation, casting the Native American Indians in the role of the Canaanites and Amalekites. In 1689, Cotton Mather urged the colonists to go forth against "Amalek annoying this Israel in the wilderness."[57] A few years later, one Herbert Gibbs gave thanks for "the mercies of God in extirpating the enemies of Israel in Canaan."[58] He was not referring to biblical times. Similar rhetoric persisted in American Puritanism through the eighteenth century, and indeed biblical analogies have continued to play a part in American political rhetoric down to the present.[59]

Of course Americans are not alone in looking to the Hebrew Bible or Old Testament for an exemplary paradigm. The Boers of South Africa applied the story of the Exodus to their situation under British rule, and black African liberationists later applied it to their situation under the Boers.[60] Most obviously, biblical narratives have been a factor in the Zionist movement in Israel, shaping the imagination even of secular, socialist Zionists and providing powerful precedents for right-wing militants.[61] Biblical analogies also provide the underpinnings for support of Israel among conservative Christians.[62]

Eschatological Vengeance

The examples of the Zealots and the Puritans may help to dispel any notion that religion evolves in a linear way and that the violence of Joshua or of Phinehas was a vestige of primitive religion, transcended in later Judaism and Christianity. It is true, however, that most of the biblical endorsements of violent human action are set in the context of early Israel, even if they were written later. The highly ritualized accounts of warfare in the books of Chronicles are also set in an earlier time and are unlikely to stir the blood in any case. In the literature of the Second Temple period, however, the focus is often on the future rather than on the past.[63] The late prophetic and apocalyptic literature is not necessarily less violent in its rhetoric than Deuteronomy or Joshua, but it has less emphasis on human action and more on the expectation of the eschatological judgment of God.

Again, a few examples may suffice. The prophet of the latter chapters of the book of Isaiah imagines God as a warrior spattered in blood, like a person who has been treading the wine press (Isa. 63).[64] The day of redemption must also be a day of vengeance on God's enemies. Here, no one is asked to "come to the help of the Lord":

> I looked, but there was no helper;
> I stared, but there was no one to sustain me;
> So my own arm brought me victory and my wrath sustained me.

In the apocalyptic literature of the Hellenistic and Roman periods, the faithful people are to wait for this divine intervention. The Book of Daniel tells how in a time of persecution the wise among the people will instruct the many, even though some of them will fall, "so that they may be refined, purified, and cleansed, until the time of the end." The archangel Michael does the fighting on their behalf. At the end, when Michael prevails, they are elevated to shine like the stars forever (Dan. 12:1–3). In this literature there is a new factor to be considered: the hope of resurrection. Martyrdom becomes an option, because the reward of the righteous is not in this world but in heaven.[65] The apocalyptic literature is not necessarily quietistic. One apocalypse in the book of Enoch, known as the Animal Apocalypse, apparently endorses the militancy of the Maccabees.[66] The War Scroll from Qumran is written in anticipation of human participation in the final conflict, but this is compatible with the pledge to avoid conflict with "the men of the pit" until the Day of Vengeance (1QS 10:19).[67] But the dominant tendency of this literature is quietistic, in the sense that it encourages endurance and even martyrdom in the present era. This is also true of the Book of Revelation in the New Testament, which holds up the crucified messiah, the lamb that was slain, as the model for Christians to emulate.[68] We find a similar combination of present restraint, in the hope of future vengeance, in the rabbinic tradition.[69] The Mekhilta cites Exodus 15:6: "Your right hand shatters the foe," and comments: "it does not say 'has shattered the foe' but 'will shatter the foe'—in the Age to Come."[70] And again, quoting Deuteronomy 32:35: "Vengeance is mine and recompense— I will punish them myself. Not through an angel and not through a sent one."[71]

There is, in fact, an intrinsic connection between present forbearance and eschatological vengeance in this literature.[72] In the Epistle to the Romans, Paul cites the same verse from Deuteronomy 32, to illustrate the point that his readers should "never avenge yourselves, but leave room for the wrath of God. . . . No, 'if your enemies are hungry, feed them; if they are thirsty, give them something to drink; for by doing this you will heap burning coals on their heads.'"[73] As Krister Stendahl showed in a famous article, this attitude has more to do with the perfection of hatred than with disinterested love: "With the Day of Vengeance at hand, the proper and reasonable attitude is to forgo one's own vengeance and to leave vengeance to God. Why walk around with a little shotgun if the atomic blast is imminent?"[74] The expectation of vengeance is also pivotal in the Book of Revelation.[75] The coming fall of Rome is heralded in gloating terms in chapter 18. In chapter 19, Christ appears from heaven as a warrior on a white horse, from whose mouth comes a sharp sword with which to strike down the nations and who will tread the wine press of the fury of the wrath of God. Even in the Synoptic Gospels, Jesus' teaching about loving one's enemies is framed by the prospect of a final judgment when the wheat will be definitively separated from the tares.[76]

The effective history of apocalyptic literature has varied with the patience of believers. As we have seen, books like Daniel and Revelation were originally intended to encourage patient endurance, and they have often inspired quietistic movements through the centuries.[77] But there also have been numerous examples of people who took it upon themselves to "force the end."[78] In Christian tradition, there are several striking examples of this in the late Middle Ages and the period of the reformation: the Taborites in Bohemia, Thomas Müntzer and the Peasants' Revolt, John of Leyden, the messiah of

Münster.[79] Apocalyptic expectations played a part in the Puritan revolution in England.[80] In most of these cases, however, the revolutionaries drew their inspiration not just from Daniel or Revelation but from an apocalyptic reading of the entire Bible. The examples of Joshua and Phinehas were all the more relevant in the throes of eschatological crisis. Even when the millenarian movements did not initiate violence themselves, they often provoked it by their uncompromising criticism of the authorities and their refusal to compromise. The Branch Davidians in Waco, Texas, provide a modern example.[81] In some cases, the violence was self-inflicted, as in the latter-day instances of Jonestown and Heaven's Gate.[82]

The expectation of a final Armageddon may not be as directly conducive to violence as a command to kill the idolaters next door, but in fact the impact of eschatological texts may not be very different from that of history-like narrative precedents. Few people in any age have taken the ḥerem texts of the Hebrew Bible as commandments for their own time. Strictly interpreted, they apply only to specific peoples who no longer exist.[83] Equally, eschatological violence is properly the prerogative of God. But in both cases, the approval of violence in the texts offers dangerous encouragement for militants, which has, on occasion, contributed to disaster.

Like the commands to slaughter the Canaanites in the Deuteronomic literature, the predictions of eschatological judgment also shape group identities. In the Jewish apocalyptic literature, the national identity is already qualified. The elect, or the sons of light, are not simply identical with Israel. The land remains important in the Jewish works, but even there it is relativized. In many cases, the ultimate hope of the elect is for life with the angels in heaven. In the New Testament, identity is no longer tied to ethnicity or to possession of a particular land. What this literature shares with Deuteronomy, however, is the sharp antithesis with the Other, whether the Other is defined in moral terms, as sinners, or in political terms as the Roman empire. Both Deuteronomy and the apocalypses fashion identity by constructing absolute, incompatible, contrasts. In the older literature, the contrast is ethnic and religious, but regional. In the apocalypses, it takes the form of cosmic dualism. In both cases, the absoluteness of the categories is guaranteed by divine revelation, and therefore not subject to negotiation or compromise. Herein lies the root of religious violence in the Jewish and Christian traditions.

Violence and Hermeneutics

"There is a time to kill," said Qoheleth, "and a time to heal . . . a time for war, and a time for peace."[84] Not all violence is necessarily to be condemned. The image of God the Warrior and the hope for an apocalyptic judgment have often given hope to the oppressed. Nonetheless, few will disagree that violence is seldom a good option and that it can only be justified as a last recourse. Most people in the Western world are rightly repelled by the idea that terrorists, such as the perpetrators of the attacks of September 11, 2001, could be inspired by religious ideals. The thrust of my reflections on violence and religion in the biblical tradition is that the problem is not peculiar to Islam, but can also be found in attitudes and assumptions that are deeply imbedded in the Jewish and Christian scriptures. The material of which I have been speaking is what Gerd Lüdemann has called "the dark side of the Bible."[85] The issues it raises are not just academic. These texts have had a long effective history, and there is no reason to believe that it has run its course. What are we, as biblical scholars, to say about it at the beginning of the twenty-first century?

There is a long and venerable tradition of interpretation, going back through the Church Fathers to Philo of Alexandria and Hellenistic Judaism, that sees it as its task to save the appearances of the text. Luke Johnson has recently argued that modern interpreters have still much to learn from the Fathers: "Origen shows how much more passionately Scripture is engaged when the reader is persuaded of its divine inspiration, which implies that God's wisdom is somehow seeking to be communicated even through the impossibilities of the literal sense. If interpreters today were to learn from Origen, they would not rest easy with the practice of excising or censoring troublesome texts, but would wrestle with them until they yielded a meaning 'worthy of God.'"[86] But allegorical interpretation, of the kind practiced in antiquity, is hardly viable in the modern world. It is all very well to say that the Canaanites that we should root out are vice and sinfulness, but we still have texts that speak rather clearly of slaughtering human beings.

A more promising strategy is to note the diversity of viewpoints within the Bible, and thereby relativize the more problematic ones.[87] So, for example, we can emphasize the concern for slaves and aliens in Deuteronomy, or the model of the suffering servant, or the New Testament teaching on love of one's enemies. It is not unusual for

Christian interpreters to claim that "the biblical witness to the innocent victim and the God of victims demystifies and demythologizes this sacred social order" in which violence is grounded.[88] Such a selective reading, privileging the death of Jesus, or the model of the suffering servant, is certainly possible, and even commendable, but it does not negate the force of the biblical endorsements of violence that we have been considering. The full canonical shape of the Christian Bible, for what it is worth, still concludes with the judgment scene in Revelation, in which the lamb that was slain returns as the heavenly warrior with a sword for striking down the nations. In short, violence is not the only model of behavior on offer in the Bible, but it is not an incidental or peripheral feature, and it cannot be glossed over. The Bible not only witnesses to the innocent victim and to the God of victims, but also to the hungry God[89] who devours victims and to the zeal of his human agents.

And therein precisely lies its power. There is much in the Bible that is not "worthy" of the God of the philosophers. There is also much that is not worthy of humanity, certainly much that is not worthy to serve as a model for imitation. This material should not be disregarded, for it is at least as revelatory as the more edifying parts of the biblical witness. The power of the Bible is largely that it gives an unvarnished picture of human nature and of the dynamics of history, and also of religion and the things that people do in its name.[90] After all, it is only in the utopian future that the wolf is supposed to live with the lamb, and even then the wolf will probably feel the safer of the two. The biblical portrayal of human reality only becomes pernicious when it is vested with authority and assumed to reflect, without qualification or differentiation, the wisdom of God or the will of God. The Bible does not demystify or demythologize itself. But neither does it claim that the stories it tells are paradigms for human action in all times and places.

The least that should be expected of any biblical interpreter is honesty, and that requires the recognition, in the words of James Barr, that "the command of consecration to destruction is morally offensive and has to be faced as such,"[91] whether it is found in the Bible or in the Qur'an. To recognize this is to admit that the Bible, for all the wisdom it contains, is no infallible guide on ethical matters. As Roland Bainton put it, in his survey of Christian attitudes to war and peace, "appeal to the Bible is not determinative."[92] But historically people have appealed to the Bible precisely because of its presumed divine authority, which gives an aura of certitude to any position it can be shown to support; in the phrase of Hannah Arendt, "God-like certainty that stops all discussion."[93] And here, I would suggest, is the most basic connection between the Bible and violence, more basic than any command or teaching it contains.

Oliver Wendell Holmes, the great American jurist, reflected late in his career that he had entered the Civil War brimming with certitude over the righteousness of abolition, which surely was a righteous cause. By the end of the war he had drawn a different lesson, that certitude leads to violence.[94] The Bible has contributed to violence in the world precisely because it has been taken to confer a degree of certitude that transcends human discussion and argumentation. Perhaps the most constructive thing a biblical critic can do toward lessening the contribution of the Bible to violence in the world, is to show that that certitude is an illusion.

Notes

This chapter was presented as the presidential address to the Society of Biblical Literature, Toronto, November 23, 2002, and was previously published in the *Journal of Biblical Literature*, Volume 122, Number 1 (Spring 2003), 3–21. It is republished here by permission.

1. Mieke Bal, *Anti-Covenant: Counter-Reading Women's Lives in the Hebrew Bible* (Sheffield: Almond, 1989), 14.

2. Jan Assmann, *Moses the Egyptian: The Memory of Moses in Western Monotheism* (Cambridge: Harvard University Press, 1997), 1–6.

3. See, for example, Regina M. Schwartz, *The Curse of Cain: The Violent Legacy of Monotheism* (Chicago: University of Chicago Press, 1997).

4. See Manfred Weippert, "'Heiliger Krieg' in Israel und Assyrien: Kritische Anmerkungen zu Gerhard von Rads Konzept des 'Heiligen Krieges im alten Israel,'" *ZAW* 84 (1972): 460–493; Sa-Moon Kang, *Divine War in the Old Testament and in the Ancient Near East* (BZAW 177; Berlin: de Gruyter, 1989); Leo Bersani and Ulysse Dutoit, *The Forms of Violence. Narrative in Assyrian Art and Modern Culture* (New York: Schocken, 1985); Eckart Otto, *Krieg und Frieden in der Hebräischen Bibel und im Alten Orient* (Stuttgart: Kohlhammer, 1999), 13–75. More broadly, on the mythology of violence in world religions, see James A. Aho, *Religious Mythology and the Art of War: Comparative Religious Symbolisms of Military Violence* (Westport: Greenwood, 1981).

5. Craig L. Nessan, "Sex, Aggression, and Pain: Sociobiological Implications for Theological Anthropology," *Zygon* 33 (1998): 451. Compare Leo D. Lefebure, *Revelation, the Religions, and Violence* (Maryknoll: Orbis, 2000), 13.

6. David Riches, "The Phenomenon of Violence," in *The Anthropology of Violence* (Oxford: Blackwell, 1986), 1–7.

7. On the antiquity of the song, see Frank Moore Cross, "The Song of the Sea and Canaanite Myth," in *Canaanite Myth and Hebrew Epic* (Cambridge: Harvard University Press, 1973), 112–144.

8. G. von Rad, *Holy War in Ancient Israel*, trans. M. J. Dawn (Grand Rapids: Eerdmans, 1991), 71. On the reception of von Rad's study, see Ben Ollenburger's introductory essay, "Gerhard von Rad's Theory of Holy War," in the same volume, 1–33.

9. Israelite religion was not at all exceptional in this regard. See the works of Weippert and Kang, cited previously.

10. Contra Millard C. Lind, *Yahweh Is a Warrior* (Scottsdale: Herald, 1980), who argues that Israel depended on the miraculous power of YHWH, and that Israel's fighting was ineffective. Lind takes the Song of the Sea in Exodus 15 as the archetypical example.

11. Philip D. Stern, *The Biblical ḥerem: A Window on Israel's Religious Experience* (BJS 211; Atlanta: Scholars Press, 1991); Susan Niditch, *War in the Hebrew Bible. A Study in the Ethics of Violence* (New York: Oxford, 1993), 28–89.

12. A. Dearman, *Studies in the Mesha Inscription and Moab* (Atlanta: Scholars Press, 1989); Stern, *The Biblical ḥerem*, 19–87. For the text, see ANET, 320–321 (trans. W. F. Albright).

13. For an exhaustive discussion of proposed parallels, see Stern, *The Biblical ḥerem*, 57–87. Stern tries to show "that a specific cast of mind that was responsible for the ḥerem was also present at varying times and places elsewhere in the ancient Near East" (87), but admits that none of the parallels are perfect. Kang, *Divine War*, declares that "the idea of the ban is not attested in the ancient Near Eastern context except in the Moabite stone and in the Bible" (81). Kang follows the analysis of C. H. W. Brekelmans, *De ḥerem in het Oude Testament* (Nijmegen: Centrale Drukkerij, 1959).

14. The sacrificial character of the ban is argued especially by Niditch, *War in the Hebrew Bible*, 28–55.

15. G. F. Moore, *A Critical and Exegetical Commentary on Judges* (ICC; New York: Scribners, 1901), 299.

16. Niditch, *War in the Hebrew Bible*, 50. Compare the remarks of James Barr, *Biblical Faith and Natural Theology* (Oxford: Clarendon, 1993), 209. Stern, *The Biblical ḥerem*, 218–220, argues that the enemy is perceived as an embodiment of chaos.

17. Compare Dick Anthony and Thomas Robbins, "Religious Totalism, Violence, and Exemplary Dualism: Beyond the Extrinsic Model," in *Millennialism and Violence*, ed. Michael Barkun (London: Cass, 1996), 10–50.

18. Niditch, *War in the Hebrew Bible*, 50.

19. G. C. Heider, *The Cult of Molek: A Reassessment* (Sheffield: JSOT, 1985); J. Day, *Molech: A God of Human Sacrifice in the Old Testament*, University of

Cambridge Oriental Publications 41 (Cambridge: Cambridge University Press, 1989); J. D. Levenson, *The Death and Resurrection of the Beloved Son: The Transformation of Child Sacrifice in Judaism and Christianity* (New Haven: Yale University Press, 1993), 3–17.

20. Levenson, *The Death and Resurrection*, 13. On the sacrifice of Abraham see further my essay "Faith without Works: Biblical Ethics and the Sacrifice of Isaac," in *Recht und Ethos im Alten Testament. Gestalt und Wirkung. Festschrift für Horst Seebass zum 65. Geburtstag*, ed. S. Beyerle, G. Mayer, and H. Strauss (Neukirchen-Vluyn: Neukirchener Verlag, 1999), 115–131.

21. Levenson, *The Death and Resurrection*, 3–4.

22. Ahaz in 2 Kings 16:3; Manasseh in 2 Kings 21:6.

23. Mic. 6:6–8; Jer. 19:4–6.

24. Deut. 12:31, 18:10.

25. Niditch, "The Ban as God's Justice," *War in the Hebrew Bible*, 56–77. Compare Walzer, *Exodus and Revolution*: "There are signs in the text of some anxiety about the conquest commands—a search for reasons, lest God's wrath seem wholly arbitrary" (143).

26. Stern, *The Biblical ḥerem*, 221, argues that the connection with idolatry is primary. Exod. 22:19 says that anyone who sacrifices to gods other than YHWH must be devoted to destruction. This does not require, however, that prevention of idolatry was always the primary factor in the use of ḥerem in warfare.

27. Deut. 7:1–6.

28. This point is emphasized by Jonathan Boyarin, "Reading Exodus into History," *New Literary History* 23 (1992): 525.

29. Moshe Weinfeld, *Deuteronomy and the Deuteronomic School* (Winona Lake: Eisenbrauns, 1992), 282–297.

30. Deut. 15:15, 24:18, 22, and so forth. Compare Exod. 23:9: "You shall not oppress a resident alien; you know the heart of an alien, for you were aliens in the land of Egypt."

31. Some formulation of the Golden Rule is known to nearly every culture, East and West. See Hans Dieter Betz, *The Sermon on the Mount*, Hermeneia (Minneapolis: Fortress, 1995), 509–516.

32. Emmanuel Levinas, *Alterity and Transcendence* (New York: Columbia University Press, 1999): "I have already spoken much about the face of the other as being the original locus of the meaningful" (23).

33. On the Exodus paradigm see Michael Walzer, *Exodus and Revolution* (New York: Basic Books, 1984).

34. Edward Said, "Michael Walzer's Exodus and Revolution: A Canaanite Reading," *Grand Street* 5 (winter 1986): 86–106; Robert Allen Warrior, "Canaanites, Cowboys, and Indians: Deliverance, Conquest, and Liberation Theology Today," *Christianity and Crisis* 49 (1989): 261–266; Keith W. Whitelam, *The Invention of Ancient Israel: The Silencing of Palestinian History* (London: Routledge, 1996), 71–121.

35. William Foxwell Albright, *From the Stone Age to Christianity: Monotheism and the Historical Process* (New York: Doubleday, 1957), 280–281, cited by Whitelam, *The Invention of Ancient Israel*, 83. Albright noted several analogies to the Israelite treatment of the Canaanites, including the treatment of Native Americans.

36. George Ernest Wright, "The Old Testament," in *The Book of the Acts of God: Christian Scholarship Interprets the Bible*, ed. G. E. Wright and R. H. Fuller (London: Duckworth, 1960), 109, cited by Whitelam, *The Invention of Ancient Israel*, 93. On the vilification of the Canaanites, see the comments of James Barr, *Biblical Faith and Natural Theology* (Oxford: Clarendon, 1993), 214.

37. For a more positive view of the Canaanites, see Niels Peter Lemche, *The Canaanites and Their Land* (Sheffield: JSOT, 1991).

38. For up-to-date assessments, see Israel Finkelstein and Neil Asher Silberman, *The Bible Unearthed. Archaeology's New Vision of Ancient Israel and the Origin of Its Sacred Texts* (New York: The Free Press, 2001), 72–122; William G. Dever, "Israel, History of (Archaeology and the 'Conquest')," *ABD* 3.545–558.

39. George E. Mendenhall, "The Hebrew Conquest of Palestine," *BA* 25 (1962): 66–87; Norman Gottwald, *The Tribes of Yahweh. A Sociology of the Religion of Liberated Israel, 1250–1050 B.C.E.* (Maryknoll: Orbis, 1979).

40. Finkelstein and Silberman, *The Bible Unearthed*, 105–122.

41. Von Rad, *Holy War*, 52–73, argued that holy war was an institution for the defense of the amphictyony. The whole idea of an amphictyony in the period of the Judges is no longer accepted, but in any case the biblical accounts associate herem with the conquest, not with defensive actions.

42. Barr, *Biblical Faith*, 209.

43. See, for example, Gen. 21:33, 28:18. On sacred sites and ritual objects in ancient Israel see Philip J. King and Lawrence E. Stager, *Life in Biblical Israel* (Louisville: Westminster John Knox, 2002), 319–353; Patrick D. Miller, *The Religion of Ancient Israel* (Louisville: Westminster John Knox, 2000), 62–79.

44. Lori L. Rowlett, *Joshua and the Rhetoric of Violence: A New Historicist Analysis*, JSOT Supp. 226 (Sheffield: Sheffield Academic Press, 1996), 12–13.

45. The violence might be explained to a degree along Girardian lines, insofar as the Canaanites become scapegoats for the sake of the solidarity of Israel. Girard's views may be found in *Violence and the Sacred* (Baltimore: Johns Hopkins, 1977) and, with reference to the Bible, *Things Hidden since the Foundation of the World* (Stanford: Stanford University Press, 1987). For a balanced evaluation of Girard's theories, see Lefebure, *Revelation, the Religions, and Violence*, 20–23, 29–31.

46. On the circumstances that led to the revolt see J. J. Collins, "Cult and Culture: The Limits of Hellenization in Judea," in *Hellenism in the Land of Israel*, ed. John J. Collins and Gregory E. Sterling (Notre Dame: University of Notre Dame Press, 2001), 38–61.

47. 1 Macc. 1:26.

48. For a full analysis of the passage see Baruch A. Levine, *Numbers 21–36* (AB 4A; New York: Doubleday, 2000), 279–303. Verses 1–5, where the problem is of Moabite origin, are usually ascribed to J or JE. The remainder of the story, which concerns a Midianite woman, is Priestly.

49. Num. 25:10–15.

50. Waldemar Janzen, *Old Testament Ethics: A Paradigmatic Approach* (Louisville: Westminster John Knox, 1994), 108.

51. Niditch, *War in the Hebrew Bible*, 81. The Midianites lived outside the promised land and were not subject to eradication by the decree of Deuteronomy. The slaughter is justified in Num. 25:16–18 on the grounds that "they have harassed you by the trickery with which they deceived you in the affair of Peor."

52. Martin Hengel, *The Zealots: Investigations into the Jewish Freedom Movement in the Period from Herod I until 70 A.D.* (Edinburgh: Clark, 1989). Josephus uses the name Zealots for a faction that emerged in 67–68 B.C.E., but the ideology of zeal informed other revolutionary groups too. For a nuanced summary see David Rhoads, "Zealots," *ABD* 6.1043–1054; also Richard A. Horsley and John S. Hanson, *Bandits, Prophets and Messiahs* (Minneapolis: Winston, 1985), 190–243. On the ideological continuity with the Maccabees see William R. Farmer, *Maccabees, Zealots, and Josephus* (New York: Columbia University Press, 1956).

53. David C. Rapoport, "Fear and Trembling: Terrorism in Three Religious Traditions," *American Political Science Review* 78, no. 3 (1984): 658–77.

54. Roland H. Bainton, *Christian Attitudes toward War and Peace* (Nashville: Abingdon, 1960), 148–149.

55. Walzer, *Exodus and Revolution*, 3–4.

56. Bainton, *Christian Attitudes*, 151.

57. Ibid., 168.

58. Ibid.

59. Conrad Cherry, ed., *God's New Israel: Religious Interpretations of American Destiny* (Englewood Cliffs: Prentice Hall, 1971), 11–12.

60. Walzer, *Exodus and Revolution*, 6; T. Dunbar Moodie, *The Rise of Afrikanerdom: Power, Apartheid, and the Afrikaner Civil Religion* (Berkeley: University of California Press, 1975), chapters 1 and 2.

61. Boyarin, "Reading Exodus into History," 538–543, disputes the extent of the influence of the Exodus story on early Zionism but grants its increased importance after World War II. On the use of the Bible by contemporary right-wing Israelis, see the thoughtful comments of Moshe Greenberg, "On the Political Use of the Bible in Modern Israel: An Engaged Critique," in *Pomegranates and Golden Bells. Studies in Biblical, Jewish, and Near Eastern Ritual, Law and Literature in Honor of Jacob Milgrom*, ed. David P. Wright, David Noel Freedman, and Avi Hurvitz (Winona Lake: Eisenbrauns, 1995), 461–471.

62. Keith Whitelam, *The Invention of Ancient Israel*, 71–121, finds pervasive analogies with Zionism in the various reconstructions of early Israel by modern scholars. His argument is overstated, but it is not entirely without substance, at least in some cases.

63. Obviously, this is not always the case. For example, the story of the sack of Shechem in Genesis 34 is retold repeatedly in Second Temple literature: Reinhard Pummer, "Genesis 34 in Jewish Writings of the Hellenistic and Roman Periods," *HTR* 75(1982) 177–188.

64. On this passage see Paul D. Hanson, *The Dawn of Apocalyptic* (Philadelphia: Fortress, 1975), 203–208.

65. John J. Collins, "Apocalyptic Eschatology as the Transcendence of Death," in *Seers, Sibyls and Sages in Hellenistic-Roman Judaism* (Leiden: Brill, 1997), 75–97.

66. 1 Enoch 90:9–16. Judas Maccabee is represented as a ram with a large horn. See Patrick A. Tiller, *A Commentary on the Animal Apocalypse of 1 Enoch* (Atlanta: Scholars Press, 1993), 62–63.

67. John J. Collins, *Apocalypticism in the Dead Sea Scrolls* (London: Routledge, 1997), 108–109.

68. Adela Yarbro Collins, "The Political Perspective of the Revelation to John," in *Cosmology and Eschatology in Jewish and Christian Apocalypticism* (Leiden: Brill, 1996), 198–217.

69. Adiel Schremer, "Eschatology, Violence and Suicide: The Role of an Early Rabbinic Theme in the Middle Ages," a paper delivered at the Apocalypse and Violence conference at Yale University, May 5, 2002.

70. *Mekhilta de Rabbi Ishma'el*, Shirta, 5.

71. *Sifre Deuteronomy*, 325 (ed. Finkelstein). For the use of Deuteronomy 32 in an earlier, apocalyptic text, see the Testament of Moses 9–10, and John J. Collins, *The Apocalyptic Imagination*, 2nd ed. (Grand Rapids: Eerdmans, 1998), 131.

72. H. G. L. Peels, *The Vengeance of God* (Leiden: Brill, 1995), provides a thorough study of the motif in the Hebrew Bible, but deals with "the intertestamental literature" and the New Testament only in an appendix (306–312).

73. Rom. 12:19–21. The quotation is derived from Prov. 25:21–22.

74. Krister Stendahl, "Hate, Non-retaliation, and Love. 1QS X, 17–20 and Rom. 12:19–21," *HTR* 55 (1962): 343–355. The citation is from 344–345.

75. Adela Yarbro Collins, "Persecution and Vengeance in the Book of Revelation," in *Apocalypticism in the Mediterranean World and the Near East*, ed. David Hellholm (Tübingen: Mohr-Siebeck, 1983), 729–749.

76. Matt. 13:24–30, 36–43.

77. See the history of the interpretation of Revelation by Christopher Rowland in *NIB* 12.528–543, and his paper "Apocalypse and Violence: The Evidence from the Reception History of the Book of Revelation," delivered at the Apocalypse and Violence conference at Yale, May 5, 2002. On the traditional quietism of orthodox Judaism, in anticipation of eschatological sal-

vation, see Aviezer Ravitzky, *Messianism, Zionism, and Jewish Radical Religion* (Chicago: University of Chicago Press, 1996), 40–78.

78. On the notion of "forcing the end," which traditionally had negative implications in Judaism, see Ravitzky, *Messianism*, 18.

79. Norman Cohn, *The Pursuit of the Millennium* (New York: Oxford, 1970), 198–280; Robin Barnes, "Images of Hope and Despair: Western Apocalypticism ca. 1500–1800," in *The Encyclopedia of Apocalypticism* (New York: Continuum, 1998) 2:143–184.

80. Barnes, "Images of Hope," 163: "The most famous case of radical expectancy in this period was that of the Fifth Monarchy Men, who saw it as the responsibility of believers to help bring on the final and most perfect historical age through militant action." See also Christopher Hill, *Antichrist in Seventeenth Century England* (New York: Oxford, 1971).

81. See James D. Tabor and Eugene V. Gallagher, *Why Waco? Cults and the Battle for Religious Freedom in America* (Berkeley: University of California Press, 1995). On the interpretation of the Book of Revelation by David Koresh, see pp. 52–79.

82. On violence and latter-day apocalyptic movements see further Catherine Wessinger, *How the Millennium Comes Violently: From Jonestown to Heaven's Gate* (New York: Seven Bridges, 2000); Wessinger, *Millennialism, Persecution, and Violence: Historical Cases* (Syracuse: Syracuse University Press, 2000); and Thomas Robbins and Susan J. Palmer, ed., *Millennium, Messiahs, and Mayhem: Contemporary Apocalyptic Movements* (New York: Routledge, 1997).

83. Walzer, *Exodus and Revolution*, 144; Greenberg, "On the Political Use of the Bible," 469.

84. Qoh 3:3.8.

85. Gerd Lüdemann, *The Unholy in Holy Scriptures. The Dark Side of the Bible* (Louisville: Westminster John Knox, 1997). Lüdemann provides an extensive discussion of the ban in holy war (36–54).

86. Luke Timothy Johnson, "Lessons from Premodern Biblical Scholarship," Henry Luce III Fellows in Theology 2001 Conference, Princeton, November 9–11, 2001, conference abstracts, 4–5.

87. So, in very different ways, Niditch, *War in the Hebrew Bible*; Peter C. Craigie, *The Problem of War in the Old Testament* (Grand Rapids: Eerdmans, 1978), 97; Otto, *Krieg und Frieden*, 76–156; Greenberg, "On the Political Use of the Bible," 466–469.

88. So James G. Williams, *The Bible, Violence, and the Sacred: Liberation from the Myth of Sanctioned Violence* (San Francisco: Harper San Francisco, 1991), 243. Williams bases his approach on that of René Girard. Compare also William Klassen, "Jesus and Phineas: A Rejected First Century Role Model," SBL Seminar Papers (1986): 490–500.

89. The phrase of David Shulman, *The Hungry God* (Chicago: University of Chicago Press, 1993).

90. Compare Phyllis Trible, *Texts of Terror* (Philadelphia: Fortress, 1984): "If art imitates life, scripture likewise reflects it in both holiness and horror" (2).

91. Barr, *Biblical Faith*, 218.

92. Bainton, *Christian Attitudes*, 238.

93. Hannah Arendt, "To Save the Jewish Homeland: There Is Still Time," in *Hannah Arendt, The Jew as Pariah: Jewish Identity and Politics in the Modern Age*, ed. Ron H. Feldman (New York: Grove Press, 1978), 181–182, quoted by Marc H. Ellis, *Unholy Alliance: Religion and Atrocity in Our Time* (Minneapolis: Fortress, 1997), 7.

94. Louis Menand, *The Metaphysical Club: A Story of Ideas in America* (New York: Farrar, Straus & Giroux, 2001), 61.

CHAPTER 3

SEEDS OF VIOLENCE IN BIBLICAL INTERPRETATION

Charles T. Davis III

The art and science of biblical interpretation, or hermeneutics, takes its name from Hermes, a richly ambivalent deity who is both the messenger of heaven and the one who blinds those whom he leads into the realm of the dead. This metaphorical root of the term *hermeneutics* should alert us to the possibility that unconscious, archetypal structures may both positively and negatively influence the direction of our search for understanding. It is almost universally assumed that the so-called right hermeneutic would unlock the mystery of revelation in unambiguously positive terms—a fact that blinds us to the dark side of every hermeneutic. In accordance with the ambiguous nature of Hermes, hermeneutic theories divide into two types. First, the mimetic, objective, approach searches for an "original meaning" intended by an author or community (Smith, 1995, 416). Second, the transformative, or subjective, approach insists that the goal of interpretation is personal transformation since all meaning is shaped by the act of interpretation (Smith, 1995, 416). Each of these approaches is of great value but each harbors the seeds of violence.

The Archetypal Roots of Hermeneutics in the Hero Story

Lurking beneath the distinction between the mimetic and the transformative hermeneutic is the Archetypal Feminine, the *uroberos* image—the dragon that bites its tail to form the Great Round, the primordial womb. The mythology generated by the emergence of consciousness from this womb gives us three important images that may influence our hermeneutic: (1) the Great Mother who is the Queen of Nature, (2) the Terrible Father who is the Lord of Culture, and (3) the Hero/Son who successfully defies them both and thereby wins greater consciousness.

According to Neumann (1991), the Archetypal Feminine evidences a coincidence of opposites: the elemental or *conservative force* and the *transformative force*. In the early stages of the development of consciousness, the conservative force dominates as the Archetypal Feminine "tends to hold fast to everything that springs from it" (Neumann, 1991, 25). It works for stability and tends to thwart any movements toward consciousness by pulling such energies back into the womb, the unconscious (26). The archetypal image of the Great Mother, the female dragon who presides over all of nature, dominates the mythology of this phase in which instinct is the dominant force in life (Neumann, 1973, 186).

When the psychic energies driving toward consciousness are sufficiently strong, the transformative force increasingly dominates the conservative/transformative pair driving the hero toward the development of greater consciousness and individuation (Neumann, 1991, 28–29). Individuality can now challenge the collective, the embodiment of the unconscious mind. In mythology, the male hero—identified in both male and female persons with consciousness—confronts the devouring mother aspect of the feminine as a female dragon and by defeating her wins the treasure of consciousness (Neumann, 1991, 27–28).

With the appearance of cultural life, the Archetypal Feminine expresses itself as the Terrible Father—the male dragon, who is the spiritual counterpart to the phallic Great Mother (Neumann, 1973, 186). The Great Mother is one face of the Feminine, the Terrible Father the other face. The Great Mother conserves the realm of instinct against the emergence of consciousness while the Terrible Father is the guardian of culture and the opponent of social change. The Father seeks to capture and destroy the consciousness of the Son/Hero through a spiritual system that claims "the binding force of the old law, the old religion, the old morality, the old order" (Neumann, 1973, 187). The Great Mother kills by attracting us backward into the uncritical exercise of instinct. The Terrible Father kills through ego inflation—that state of consciousness in which one cannot separate one's own power (ego) from the power of the Father/Mother (Self) (Edinger, 1992, 7). Under his influence, the Son/Hero risks losing touch with his dual earthly/heavenly nature through an exclusive identification with the spiritual nature (Neumann, 1973, 187). The task of the Son/Hero is to defeat the male dragon that pulls consciousness back into the womb of tradition—the pool of solutions that are no longer adequate to the needs of the developing individual (Jacobi, 1974, 27). If we are unable to perform the heroic task of dissolving our conscious and unconscious identification with our community, we will tend toward a "national, communal and racial intolerance, the bias of self-appointed chosenness and a holier than thou attitude towards all outsiders" (Whitmont, 1997, 89).

The conservative and the transformative forces exist as poles in a field of force. In the hero story, the potential hero is challenged to step outside of tradition for a journey of self-discovery, but he or she is impeded by the voices of traditional authority that urge him or her to resist the call and to stand firmly within the community. If the hero is obedient to traditional authority, the community will suffer. It needs the gifts that the hero can bring back from the journey to revitalize the tradition. Successful cultures strike a balance between the need to protect the tradition from erosion and the need to foster heroic innovation.

The positive function of tradition as a guide for spiritual pilgrims is beyond dispute, but it has its dangers. No tradition is free from the influence of the unconscious since language and tradition are rooted in the unconscious—even the Western philosophical tradition (Brown, 1998, 71; Lakoff & Johnson, 1999, 3; Whitmont, 1997, 28–29). In *Text and Psyche*, Brown (1998) observes that religious texts have a surface that is rationalized and moralized, but below the surface meaning there is the "world of archetypal imagery" that mediates the mystery of the Sacred and evokes affective responses (26). This is true of tradition generally. Tradition is never just a collection of rationally comprehensible teachings and practices. Below the surface, there is the interplay of archetypal soul-plots or psychic dramas. Like a Mother, the tradition calls upon us to be archetypal Innocents (Pearson, 1989, 25–26) and to dwell within its protective enclosure; hence, we speak quite comfortably of Mother Church, of priests as our Fathers, and of ourselves as children, both sons and daughters. The tradition is our Mary Poppins sent to transform us, like Michael and Jane, into well-mannered children who become solid citizens. As St. Paul puts it: "the law [Torah] was our disciplinarian until Christ came" (Gal. 3:24, New Revised Standard Version [NRSV]).

There is a potentially dark side of this arrangement that makes tradition our guardian. We may become forever trapped in immaturity like the archetypal Innocent Peter Pan. We may also be moved to violence. From within the tradition, any deviation from the orthodox path can appear to justify violence against an Other perceived as the deviant or the heretic. In the movie *Mary Poppins*, George Banks, the banker father of Michael and Jane, is rendered impotent by his loyalty to the "fathers" of the firm. When he dares break with the ideology of the bank under the influence of Mary Poppins (the positive aspect of the Great Mother), his boutonniere, the emblem of life, is taken; his hat and umbrella, images of masculinity, are smashed as he is driven out of the firm.

Jesus Challenges the Pharisee Tradition of the Fathers

In Matthew's story of Jesus, we encounter an introverted hero who will challenge the Tradition of the Fathers and bring down the wrath of the religious community upon himself. Jesus' defiance of tradition leads him to a scapegoat's death. As Whitmont notes (1997), "in the form of righteous zeal, repressed violence becomes intolerant destructiveness . . . toward the wrongdoing others" (110). Ego inflation leads to intolerance of the Other.

Jesus' move from Galilee to Judea in search of John the Baptist begins his heroic journey. How did Jesus experience the call to adventure described by Campbell (1968, 49–58)? Miller (1997) argues in *Jesus at Thirty* that Jesus probably had deep seated conflicts occasioned by his illegitimate paternity—an argument loosely supported by Matthew's genealogy (1:1–17) and "birth story" (1:18–25). A similar argument could be made from Matthew's suggestion that Jesus was a refugee from Judea living in exile in Nazareth. We can imagine that the news of John the Baptist's work in the Judean desert along the Jordan River came to Jesus as a call to adventure, a call to reconnect with his roots, a call to uncover his Judean heritage if not the secrets of his paternity. Hearing of John's proclamation of the imminent end of the world motivated Jesus to leave Galilee and go to Judea so that he too might prepare for the End of Time, an act suggesting a sense of guilt in one who takes the Jewish religious tradition seriously.

The hero's calling into the unknown and unexplored depths of the psyche/soul is frequently announced by some primitive figure, the herald (Campbell, 1968, 53). For Jesus, the herald is the visionary Dove that descends from Heaven to drive him from the River Jordan into the wilderness to meet Satan. Through a transformative experience precipitated by baptism, Jesus is forced to make the heroic inner journey into the wilderness, into the unconscious, where he must confront his own demonic aspects. Like all heroes, Jesus is called into a contest with the dragon for the prize beyond price. It is in keeping with his nature as an introverted hero—the "redeemer and savior who discovers inner values" (Neumann, 1973, 220)—that Jesus battles the Terrible Father, the guardian of tradition.

Jesus' heroic test is focused upon hermeneutics, upon the proper interpretation of the words of the Divine Voice: "This is my son" (Matt. 3:17, NRSV). Satan proposes three alternatives rooted in Jewish tradition. First, the appellation "the Son of God" could be interpreted as a call to be a miracle-working rabbi. Second, it could mean that one is called to found a new school of biblical interpretation. Third, the appellation "the Son of God" could mean that one is called to be the Messiah, the final Davidic king who would rule the world at the End of Time. Each of these possible mimetic interpretations would call Jesus' awareness from within himself back into the external, social world as the locus of his calling. To affirm any one of the three interpretations would cancel the heroic journey of individuation, would trap Jesus in the womb of tradition while winning him social acclaim.

Jesus replies to each of the mimetic interpretations suggested by Satan by moving his focus into the spiritual realm guided by his understanding of scripture. First, spiritual food, the Word of God, is more important to the life of the psyche/soul than food for the body. Second, Jesus refuses to accept the literal, or historical, interpretation of Psalm 91:11–12 proposed by Satan, but he does not offer a symbolic interpretation as an alternative. He simply refuses to make an interpretation. He will not tempt God to side with either the literal hermeneutics of the School of Shammai or the progressive hermeneutics of the School of Hillel. Jesus will wait for God to reveal the correct interpretation. The third temptation—the temptation to be the Christ, the Warrior King—is rejected in favor of being a servant of God. In the story, God reveals his interpretation of Psalm 91 by sending the ministering angels to serve Jesus as the true king. From God's perspective the Servant is the Christ.

Matthew presents Jesus in chapter 5 as proposing a new, transformative hermeneutic to challenge the Tradition of the Fathers, the oral

Torah of the Pharisee Party. Jesus attempts to replace the Tradition of the Fathers with a new interpretation of the Torah, but he does not condone the alteration of even the most insignificant mark on a Torah scroll (Matt. 5:17–20). The Torah Book is valid as God's revelation until the End of Time. Men cannot legitimately alter it.

Jesus' exhortation that his hearers exceed the righteousness of the scribes and Pharisees in their legal practice poses a paradox. How could one be more attentive to scripture and its application to practice than the Pharisees? Jesus' examples resolve the apparent paradox. The traditional formulation is: "You shall not murder," and "whoever murders shall be liable to judgment" (Matt. 5:21, NRSV). The new and more radical formulation is: "But I say to you that if you are angry with a brother or sister, you will be liable to judgment; and if you insult a brother or sister, you will be liable to the Sanhedrin; and if you say, 'You fool,' you will be liable to" Gehenna (Matt. 5:22, NRSV). Jesus shifts the context for the interpretation of the specific commands from the external-social realm to the inner-psychic realm.

The social act of murder arises from the presence of anger in the individual psyche/soul. The commandment of the Torah has not been fulfilled if you only abstain from giving your inner anger social expression. You must overcome anger at its source, in the psyche/soul. In a similar vein, the social act of adultery arises from the lustful image in the imagination. Refraining from adultery alone does not satisfy the command of God; you must police your imagination.

In all of his statements, Jesus calls for a change of attitude—a change of one's social posture vis-à-vis one's neighbor as well as one's psychic orientation. Traditionally, both love of neighbor and hatred of one's enemy are determined primarily by forces outside the psyche/soul; they are determined by forces present in the social world that threaten to usurp divine authority. Jesus calls upon men to imitate God and live according to the forces within the psyche/soul (Matt. 5:43–48). What does God do? He disregards his children's relative virtues and faults because his primary motive is love. He sends the rain on the religious and the nonreligious without distinction. The command to be perfect as God is perfect is synonymous with the call to enter the strange new world of God. For Jesus, interpretation that binds one to the historical, external social world is Satanic (Matt. 16:21–23). The Torah always calls one inward and upward (or downward) to the Kingdom of God (Matt. 6:19–20).

The shift of the locus of interpretation from the outer social world to the inner world of the psyche/soul is what distinguishes Jesus from the Pharisees. He compares them to "whitewashed tombs, which on the outside look beautiful, but inside . . . are full of the bones of the dead and of all kinds of filth" (Matt. 23:27, NRSV). The internalized Tradition of the Fathers is nothing more than a collection of interpretations that were living expressions of the Fathers' psyche/souls but are now dead. They block the Pharisees from having their own authentic experience of reading the scripture. The result is that the Pharisees "on the outside look righteous to others, but inside . . . are full of hypocrisy and lawlessness" (Matt. 23:28, NRSV).

Jesus' hermeneutical challenge to the Pharisees is positively formulated as a parable: "And he said to them, 'Therefore every scribe who has been trained for the kingdom of heaven is like the master of a household who brings out of his treasure what is new and what is old'" (Matt. 13:52, NRSV). In the act of interpretation, the good exegete does not abandon the Torah; he or she merely views it from a contemporary existential perspective. The result is that many old insights are preserved (responding to the conservative force) even as radically new ones (responding to the transformative force) are discovered. A balance is struck between the conservative pull of the unconscious that keeps us safely anchored in tradition and the transformative pull that calls us into individuation through heroic experience. If we uncritically neglect either tradition or transformative experience, we invite a disastrous ego inflation that blinds us to our own capacity for evil.

From Jesus' perspective, the Tradition of the Fathers gives evidence of men replacing revelation with human interpretation. Jesus challenges the Pharisees: "Why do you break the commandment of God for the sake of your tradition?" (Matt. 15:3, NRSV). Any element of the Tradition of the Fathers that negates the Torah given by Moses, however rational the innovation may be, cannot claim to be a valid interpretation of Moses' intentions. This is the basis of Jesus' argument. He insists that the Torah be honored as the telling word, the primary story. Interpretation must not be allowed to replace revelation.

How did Jesus discover the new approach to the Torah that is both like and radically different from that of the religious parties? According to Matthew, the answer lies in Jesus' mystical experience of wrestling with Satan over the proper interpretation of the words "This is my son" received in his baptismal vision. Jesus meets every temptation in terms of his own understanding of the Bible as the Word of God, and he is victorious over Satan. This accounts for his

Supper in the House of the Pharisee, by Peter Paul Rubens. Scala/Art Resource, New York.

hermeneutic shift from social interpretation to an interpretation grounded in the inner life of the psyche/soul. Jesus experienced the proper balance between the conservative pull of tradition and the transformative call of the Spirit through his postbaptismal vision. This leads Jesus to oppose the Tradition of the Fathers.

The Pharisees respond to Jesus solely in terms of the conservative pull that opposes deviation, apparently having no sympathy for the transformative force that would lead a scribe to discover new things in the ancient revelation. Jesus is regarded as a dangerous deviant. In Jesus' trial, the interpretation of the appellation Son of God is central. The assembly convicts Jesus on the interpretation that the phrase makes him "the Messiah" (Matt. 26:63)—one of the three interpretations rejected by Jesus. In the name of defending both God and society, Jesus is tried and executed for being a blasphemer (Matt. 26:63–66). Jesus makes no effort to avoid this fate because he identifies with the archetypal hero pattern of the Martyr (Pearson, 1989, 98–115) . He understands himself to be called into the Jewish role of the Suffering Servant.

The religious opponents of Jesus, following the conservative pull of tradition, condemn him to death as a heretic. This action should not be condemned too quickly. Johnson (1986) points out in *The Writings of the New Testament* that every society has its symbolic world, its "system of meanings that anchors the activities of individuals and communities in the real world" (12) and functions as "a system of shared meaning" enabling people "to live together as a group" (13). Tensions inevitably arise between the group and individuals threatening the symbolic world by deviation. Johnson reminds us that "the ritual of excommunication reveals the fragility of social life and how it depends on a concerted commitment to a certain way of knowing the world" (15). This is the challenge. How does a community distinguish between individuals whose deviation threatens the community's symbolic world with erosion and the prophets, those charismatic figures "who seek to renew or reinterpret the group's commitment to its primordial symbols" (15)? Failure to successfully solve this dilemma can lead the proponents of tradition into perpetrating violence, psychic and physical, on those who legitimately challenge the current interpretation of the primary symbols of the group's symbolic world. To the degree that we are unaware of the archetypal forces involved in such judgment, we will tend to reject any view or person who is apparently Other.

The prophet refuses to renounce his or her transformative mission in the face of the abuse heaped upon him, or her, by the defenders of tradition. Pearson (1989) shows that the Martyr willingly embraces pain and suffering as the path to redemption for himself and others (98–115). The purer the motivation, the more emphasis there is upon saving others. Fake or shallow martyrs use sacrifice as a way to manipulate the gods or other people. True martyrdom requires a commitment to the primacy of life over despair, a faith that the universe is ultimately on the side of life, growth, redemption, and transformation.

Traditions are rooted in the Father archetype. The Cultural Father, the earthly representative of the Terrible Father enshrined in the tradition, is "the leader, the voice of collective authority" (Whitmont, 1991, 181–182) whose will is absolute. As we have seen, Matthew's Jesus appears as the Son of God Hero who challenges the Terrible Father embodied in the Tradition in the name of discovering inner values that bring new life into a dying kingdom of the Fathers. We are immediately tempted to view Jesus from only one side. The moment Jesus is defined as the Son of God, we are unconsciously, and thus uncritically, attracted to view him in solely positive terms as the one who breaks the hold of the Mother Goddess/Terrible Father and begins the process of individuation. This inclines us to view the guardians of the tradition, the Pharisees, as negative. They easily become the targets of psychic abuse. If we can withdraw the projection of the Son archetype upon Jesus and the Shadow archetype upon the Pharisees, we will see the dangers in the transformative experience of saints like Jesus and Paul.

Christians tend to ignore the negative side of Jesus' experience, especially stories that suggest ego inflation. According to Matthew, Jesus brutally attacks the guardians of tradition as hypocrites who revel in religious posturing, as teachers who see the gates to the Kingdom but fail to go in themselves and actively prevent others from entering, and as missionaries who seek to inflate the party roster without any regard for a convert's spiritual quality (Matt. 23:5, 14, 15). Jesus further characterized the Pharisees as blind fools (Matt. 23:17)—a fact that violates his own teachings about anger and language abusive of one's fellowman (Matt. 5:22). This abusive language is followed by public violence as Jesus enters the Temple to drive out the merchants selling sacrificial animals and to disrupt the changing of money into temple coin (Matt. 21:12–13). Jesus engages in acts that are illegal—both then and now. The reason is clear. An unconscious identification of the ego with the God/Self archetype leads one into ego inflation. One's own action appears to be justified as the will of God. One's own enemies become the enemies of God. Ego inflation can only be countered by deflation. The Pharisees arrange for the deflation of Jesus' ego even as they act to preserve the true religion of the Fathers. Hanging on the cross, Jesus is mocked by the religious authorities for claiming that he is God's Son (Matt. 27:41–43). There are no traces of ego inflation in Jesus' last words, "My God, my God, why have you forsaken me?" (Matt. 27:46, NRSV). In Jesus' moment of humility, the centurion and his party recognize that Jesus is the Son of God (Matt. 27:54).

By failing to recognize the psychic violence that Jesus hurled at the proponents of the Tradition of the Fathers, we also fail to recognize their strength. A few decades after Jesus' death, Rabbi Johanan ben Zacchai (Ben-Sasson, 1976, 319–322) would found that religion that we know as Orthodox or Rabbinic Judaism. Two great religions, Christianity and Judaism, arise from the roots of the Pharisee party—a powerful testimony to its spiritual vitality.

Paul: Transformative Hermeneutics as an Instrument of Violence

St. Paul was a Pharisee defender of the Tradition driven by a zeal to destroy Stephen, the first Christian, as a threat to the Tradition (Acts 8:1–3). He is possessed unconsciously by the conservative force. On the Damascus Road, Paul is set free of this murderous possession by the transformative pull when he has the vision of God speaking to him through the body of Christ (Acts 9:1–9). Paul takes his nemesis Stephen's place as a missionary and becomes a major force in creating the Church. There is, however, a negative side of the experience.

We cannot say that Paul was a simple victim of ego inflation. He writes of having this experience in Second Corinthians 12:7–9. His elation over the vision of God as Christ is deflated by the prick of a thorn, a messenger of Satan sent by Christ to teach him that spiritual power is construed by the world as powerlessness. A chastened Paul, like Jesus, identifies with the Martyr plot. The negative side of Paul's experience arises almost accidentally as he struggles to make the Jewish Bible relevant to a pagan, or Christian, audience.

With Paul, we see the rise of a Christian transformative hermeneutic that is rooted in the inner mystical experience of the mature Christian. Paul repudiates not only the Tradition of the Fathers but even the mimetic interpretation of the Torah Book itself. The Torah is a dead letter to be revived through allegorical interpretation. According to Paul's allegory in Galatians 4:24–31, Sarah is the mother of the Christians, the child of promise, and the Heavenly Jerusalem. Conversely, the Jew is a descendent of Hagar, the Egyptian maid and concubine. Through allegory, Paul deprived the Jewish community of its biological Fathers! He goes even so far as to deprive the Jewish community of its right to interpret its own scriptures authentically. Based on the Pauline allegorical interpretation of Exodus 34:33–35, the Jewish person is regarded as one having a veil over his or her understanding that prevents the true understanding of scripture (2 Cor. 3:14) (Davis, 2002, 172–173).

Paul's ahistorical, transformative hermeneutic laid a foundation for Christian violence against non-Christians (Davis, 2002, 176). His exegesis was used, for example, in the Middle Ages to justify the crusade against the Muslim as the offspring of Hagar. In the eighth century, the Venerable Bede argued that the Saracens were children of Hagar and should be driven out (Mastnak, 2002, 104–105). In the

ninth century, Pope John VIII built upon this understanding to justify action against the Muslim as an enemy of the Cross (107–108).

By focusing unambiguously upon the Story of the Cross—the story
of the ultimate scapegoat—Paul connected Jesus to a new archetypal
root. The Jewish-Christian experience found in Matthew connects
Jesus with the Father archetype as the Son who defied the Terrible
Father and founded a new tradition of Torah interpretation that
defines the prefect manner for living the commandments. Had Jewish
Christianity survived, Jesus would have been revered as a founding
father of a new Torah tradition.

In Pauline Christianity, the archetypal image of the Son/Hero who
renews his Father's kingdom gives way to the archetypal story of the
Martyr. Salvation through death, an archetypal soul-plot rooted in
the Great Mother archetype, takes center stage. The crucified Jesus
is now comparable to Osiris and other dying and rising gods found in
the fertility religions centered on the Great Mother—as the name
Easter indicates. The Virgin Mary will later be transformed into the
Christian counterpart of the Great Mother Goddess. Western culture
will inherit an obsessive preoccupation with the scapegoat.
Whitmont (1997) notes that "as man is now declared a sinner before
God, we all have become scapegoats . . . weighted down with guilt
and self-rejection" (106) with the result that we project our guilt
upon others as we pursue our scapegoat psychology.

The Mimetic Hermeneutic as an Instrument of Power and Control

The image of the Terrible Father reappears with Marcion. In the
name of Paul, Marcion claims that the angry God of the Old Testament
has been replaced by a strange new God of love who accepted his Son's
sacrificial death as the purchase price for liberating Christians from the
oppressive God of the Old Testament. Marcion forced the Christian
community to face the task of gaining power and control over deviation
within the Christian community.

The Christian canon was born of the struggle to determine who
would exercise power and control in the Church. The Marcionite
effort to make the transformative hermeneutic of Paul the sole basis
for the interpretation of Christian experience led quickly to the coun-
teraffirmation of a mimetic hermeneutic that insisted upon the continuity of the "old" and the "new" covenants. Christianity insisted that
it had an essentially historical and nonmythological base that was

unique among religions (May, 1991, 24). The Bible was declared the only authentic history of the world—a claim rooted in the mythology of the Father archetype. Blindness to its own mythological foundation allowed Christians to discredit arbitrarily non-Christian religions as mythological and thus false. Non-Christians, especially Muslims and Jews, took on aspects of the Shadow archetype and became potential targets of violence as did all the mystics and intellectuals who dared to challenge the claims of Mother Church and the Apostolic Tradition.

The guardians of the new orthodox, or apostolic, tradition were the bishops. Tranformative mystical experiences of individuals, like the Gnostics and the Medieval saints, would be considered orthodox only if they did not conflict with the claims made by the mimetic hermeneutic. Christian tradition established by the Church Fathers became the new norm of Truth, with the danger that the collective mind would take precedence over self-conscious rationality. The Church's actualization of this potential led to the humanistic revolt.

The Middle Ages came to an end under the impact of a new mimetic hermeneutic. In the fourteenth century, Petrarch declared that the age of the Church was the Dark Age as he proclaimed a humanistic hermeneutic for writing history. Petrarch would look back to Greece and Republican Rome as the Golden Age of Light (Gay, 1966, 74; Mommsen, 1959, 111, 129). In the sixteenth century, Luther also challenged the Christian tradition of the Fathers when he, following Petrarch's lead, declared the Post-Chalcedonian Tradition to be the product of the Dark Ages and rejected it as a source of guidance in favor of a return to the Golden Age of the Early Church (Rosenstock-Huessey, 1969, 363).

Luther also restored the Pauline transformative hermeneutic in his doctrine of the priesthood of all believers. Every person can become a saint as they work out their salvation immediately with God through the Bible. The nature of the Church was redefined. The Protestant Congregation was the assembly of all who had worked out their salvation in terms of the norms of by grace alone, by scripture alone, and by faith alone.

The conservative force has strongly reasserted itself in a popular Protestant mimetic hermeneutic in which the Bible becomes the sole archetype of divine revelation. No hermeneutic is required, it is thought, since one need only read what is written in a true and univocal history. Doctrine is increasingly reduced to historical fact. For example, the Doctrine of the Virgin Birth is reified into the *fact* of the virgin birth. The doctrine could be debated; the fact cannot. Candidates for teaching in seminaries can be asked, "Do you believe in the virgin birth of Christ?" Only assent or denial of this fact is possible. Refusal to give assent to a self-interpreting Bible, God's true history, increasingly becomes a justification for treating others violently, as in the Christian bombing of abortion clinics and/or the murder of the attending physician—the extreme examples.

The Apostolic Tradition is the Christian replacement for the Jewish Tradition of the Fathers. It too embodies the demands of the Terrible Father. The possibility of castration by the Father through ego inflation is an all too real danger for the custodians of this tradition. From their perspective, any who step outside the fence of tradition will become Other and legitimate targets for psychic if not physical abuse. The Crusades, the Inquisition, the burning of witches in Salem, and the bombing of abortion clinics confirm this. Such is the effect of ego inflation. The humanistic revolt against Christianity is not unjustified.

The Scientific Revolt and Revolutionary Violence

Following the humanistic lead, the French Revolution gave rise to a scientific mimetic hermeneutic that challenged the Christian claim that the Bible is in any sense a true history. To "tell it as it really was" came to mean writing scientific history relying only upon naturalistic and nonarchetypal criteria. Tradition was uniformly rejected in favor of so-called modern knowledge.

There is no doubt that the new secular hermeneutic served to free thought and practice from the dogmatic strictures of Medieval Christianity. As Hall (1998) notes in *Reading Scripture with the Church Fathers*,

> positively, many Enlightenment thinkers, horrified and repulsed by years of religious warfare, championed religious toleration, freedom of conscience, the expansion of political liberty, democratic principles and philosophy, legal reform and humane punishment. (21)

Certainly, we would not want to return to the conditions of the Middle Ages, but the tradition of secular scholarship has its own dark side.

The revolutionary hermeneutic pitted natural science, or knowing, against a supernatural science rooted in revelation. The Revolution began with the Deistic assertion that there was a Supreme Being expressing itself in creation that could be apprehended by the disciplined, rational mind. Today, this proposition has been revised. The Modern affirmation is that revealed religion is impossible since the hypothesis that there is a god, or gods, has been shown to be incorrect and replaced by a more viable scientific explanation of the natural order. Religion is now explained as a neurotic fixation upon the Father that is projected upon the universe—Freud in *Future of an Illusion* (1928); or as the result of group dynamics—Durkheim in *Elementary Forms of the Religious Life* (1954); or as an opiate of the people used by the socially powerful to manipulate those not privileged to control knowledge—Karl Marx in "Contribution to the Critique of Hegel's Philosophy of Right" (Bottomore, 1963, 43–59).

Revolutionary violence was the method of the Terror of 1792 for dispensing with tradition (Jung, 1933, 97–98). Science even produced a new and humane method of execution for this purpose—the guillotine. The Terror used the guillotine to mercifully dispatch selected clergy, and nobles, who were vilified as the lying priests who had held people in bondage to superstition since the age of the apostles.

The mythology of the guillotine is informative. Schama (1990) in *Citizens: A Chronicle of the French Revolution* explicates an engraving of the newly designed death machine in which the instrument is depicted in a bucolic setting far "from the spectacle of the gutter mob" (621). The executioner "has been transformed from a brawny professional into a sensitive soul required to avert his eyes as he slashes the cord with his saber" (621). This is natural execution à la Rousseau. It is Reason's antiseptic alternative to the street violence of the Terror.

As external invasion threatened the Revolution, revolutionary violence was directed toward any suspected of being traitors. Schama (1990) reports that one placard proclaimed: "In the towns let the blood of traitors be the first holocaust, literally, *le premier holocauste*, to Liberty" (630). The goddess Liberty is the new manifestation of the Great Mother Goddess who demands death as the price for renewal. Whitmont (1997) articulates the mythological meaning of this turn toward violence in *Return of the Goddess:*

> At the low point of a cultural development that has led us into the deadlock of scientific materialism, technological destructiveness, religious nihilism and spiritual impoverishment, a most astounding phenomenon has occurred. A new mythologem is arising in our midst. . . . It is the myth of the ancient Goddess who once ruled earth and heaven before the advent of the patriarchy and of the patriarchal religions. (vii)

Ironically, Science has given us a new religion rooted in the Great Mother archetype while claiming to free us from ignorance and superstition. Such is the fruit of ego inflation.

Revolutionary violence was justified as a means to rid France, and the world, of the pernicious conspiracy said to have been perpetrated by priests and royals. Following the Revolution, the Quest for the historical Jesus, the true natural Jesus, began as a first fruit of the Revolution. Science would show that the true Jesus was the very fountainhead of French-style democracy. The revolution would be shown to be a courageous protest of reasonable humanity on behalf of freedom of the spirit. Without such a demonstration of the true Jesus to prove the gospels to be lies concocted by priests, the Terror would stand out simply as a thing of madness and murder (Emerson). The Life of Jesus movement, quite unwittingly today, is building upon this revolutionary program. Why do professionals keep up this quest? Why not accept Schweitzer's 1906 demonstration of the impossibility of ever writing a life of Jesus in view of the absence of sources other than the Gospels? Is it possible that the failure of the Life of Jesus movement would reveal the madness of revolutionary violence—its possession by the Great Mother archetype?

Science cannot produce the historical Jesus. What has been produced is the demonstration that the Bible is deeply enmeshed in mythology, as are most religious texts. As a result, the battlefront of the Revolution shifts to demythology. If the Revolution could not produce the natural Jesus, it could demonstrate that the gospel was intertwined in a tissue of pre-scientific understandings of the cosmos that needed to be discarded in favor of a philosophically articulated kerygma (Bultmann).

The psyche/soul is a victim of the Revolution. All metaphysics and transcendental religion have become the Shadow for a scientific culture. One eschews the use of words like *cult* and *myth* since they conjure up images of fanatics drinking poisoned soft drink with a cleric in Guyana, Heaven's Gate nerds committing suicide as the way to enter a Christ-sent cosmic space vessel, or the messianic holocaust at Waco. Serious academic investigations of the psyche/soul such as those of Carl G. Jung are forced to exist in institutes apart from the Scientific University that is the product of the Revolution; they are regarded as reversions to an outmoded, metaphysical explanation of the cosmos. Westerners have come to accept this state along with Rousseau's distinction between civic and personal religion. In the privacy of a religious community, one may advocate a personal religion, but in the workplace and the voting booth he or she is expected to put religion aside for scientific values.

Jung (1989) observed in 1932 that "with the decline of religious life, the neuroses grow noticeably more frequent" (335). The result of the loss of faith in revealed religion is the "shattering of our faith in ourselves and our own worth" (Jung, 1933, 203). As our culture has shifted from the Christian Middle Ages to the Modern Scientific World, we have not voided religion but, in the words of Whitmont (1997), "we have . . . secularized our religion" and "turned to new gods: technology, production of goods, greater physical wellbeing" with the result that "we feel like homeless aliens in a senseless, soulless universe" (99). Frattaroli (2001) writes in *Healing the Soul in the Age of the Brain* of a modern rationalization that "goes like this: 'Descartes was wrong. There is no mind-body problem. Mind, soul, and brain are really all the same thing' " (21). The result of this reduction of all personality to an epiphenomenon of brain chemistry is that we lose all that is unique to the individual. May (1991) in *The Cry for Myth* concludes:

> When we in the twentieth century are so concerned about proving our technical reason is right and we wipe away in one fell swoop the "silliness" of myths, we also rob our own souls and we threaten to destroy our society as a part of the same deterioration. (19)

It cannot be argued seriously that the scientific humanistic hermeneutic is an unalloyed good. We have gained power and control over the material dimension of our existence at the price of losing our psyche/soul. As a price for our ego inflation, we are unconsciously living the myth of Faust!

In *The Bible in Human Transformation*, Wink (1973) describes the Faustian plight of scientific biblical scholarship in terms of possession by the unconscious:

> It has been all too easy for us scholars to deceive ourselves about our situation . . . If we are bankrupt, it is not because we have not tried, but because we have continued to try too long in the wrong way. For we are dealing with not simply false notions but an alienating ethos: a principality and power which shapes not only our thoughts, but our lifestyles, self-images, ambitions, commitments and values. No simple shift of categories will touch that. We are possessed, and we require exorcism. . . . And are there those who say they are not possessed? Very well. But those who know their possession and have fought to become free speak differently. *They* say: no longer possessed. (81–82)

Conclusion

Every hermeneutic has a shadow side that is capable of inflicting psychic harm. We need to consider the archetypal roots of each hermeneutic. A mimetic hermeneutic tends to connect us with the conservative archetypal force that binds us to the community and its tradition while the archetypal transformative hermeneutic encourages us to break away and risk the journey of individuation. Each of these approaches has great strengths. Both are needed by the individual and the community. Unfortunately, the practitioners of either the transformative or the mimetic hermeneutic may fall victim to an ego inflation that leads them to absolutize their particular approach with the result that they attack the proponents of the other hermeneutic. We need to rethink our hermeneutical assumptions and the degree to which they are being driven by archetypal forces leading us into intractable positions that defy all challenges from other experience and philosophical positions. As we dissolve our equation of ego with the God/Self archetype and withdraw our Shadow projections, we may discover that as good scribes we can bring forth from our treasure both what is old and what is new.

References

Ben-Sasson, H. H. (Ed.). (1976). *A history of the Jewish people.* (G. Weidenfeld, Trans.). Cambridge: Harvard University Press.

Bottomore. T. B. (Ed., Trans.). (1963). *Karl Marx: Early writings.* New York: McGraw-Hill.

Brown, S. (1998). *Text and psyche.* New York: Continuum.

Campbell, J. (1968). *The hero with a thousand faces.* Princeton: Princeton University Press.

Davis, C. T. (2002, November). The evolution of a Pauline toxic text. *Pastoral Psychology, 51*(2), 165–176.

Durkheim, E. (1954). *The elementary forms of the religious life* (J. W. Swain, Trans.). Glencoe: Free Press.

Edinger, E. F. (1992). *Ego and archetype.* Boston: Shambhala.

Frattaroli, E. (2001). *Healing the soul in the age of the brain: Becoming conscious in an unconscious world.* New York: Penguin.

Freud, S. (1928). *The future of an illusion* (W. D. Robson-Scott, Trans.). New York: H. Liveright.

Gay, P. (1966). *The enlightenment: An interpretation, the rise of modern paganism.* New York: Knopf.

Hall, C. A. (1998). *Reading the scriptures with the Church Fathers.* Downer's Grove: InterVarsity Press.

Jacobi, J. (1974). *Complex/Archetype/Symbol in the psychology of C. G. Jung* (R. Manheim, Trans.). Princeton: Princeton University Press.

Johnson, L. T. (1986). *The writings of the New Testament.* Philadelphia: Fortress.

Jung, C. G. (1933). *Modern man in search of a soul* (W. S. Dell & C. F. Baynes, Trans.). New York: Harcourt Brace Jovanovich.

Jung, C. G. (1989). *Collected works: Psychology and religion: East and West. Vol 11* (R.F.C. Hull, Trans.). Princeton: Princeton University Press.

Lakoff, G. & Johnson, M. (1999). *Philosophy in the flesh: The embodied mind and its challenge to Western thought.* New York: Basic Books.

Mastnak, T. (2002). *Crusading peace: Christendom, the Muslim world, and Western political order.* Berkeley: University of California Press.

May, R. (1991). *The cry for myth.* New York: Bantam Doubleday Dell Publishing Group.

Miller, J. W. (1997). *Jesus at thirty: A psychological and historical portrait.* Minneapolis: Fortress.

Mommsen, T. E. (1959). *Medieval and renaissance studies.* Ithaca: Cornell.

Neumann, E. (1973). *The origins and history of consciousness* (R.F.C. Hull, Trans.). Princeton: Princeton University Press.

Neumann, E. (1991). *The great mother* (R. Manheim, Trans.). Princeton: Princeton University Press.

Pearson, C. S. (1989). *The hero within: Six archetypes we live by.* San Francisco: Harper SanFrancisco.

Rosenstock-Huessey, E. (1969). *Out of revolution.* Norwich: Argo Press.

Schama, S. (1990). *Citizens: A chronicle of the French Revolution.* New York: Vintage.

Smith, J. Z. (Ed.). (1995). *The HarperCollins dictionary of religion.* San Francisco: HarperCollins.

Whitmont, E. C. (1991). *The symbolic quest: Basic concepts of analytical psychology.* Princeton: Princeton University Press.

Whitmont, E. C. (1997). *Return of the goddess.* New York: Continuum.

Wink, W. (1973). *The Bible in human transformation.* Philadelphia: Fortress.

CHAPTER 4

"The Bible Made Me Do It": Text, Interpretation, and Violence

D. Andrew Kille

Following every flare-up of religiously oriented violence there is a flurry of debate regarding the role of sacred texts in fomenting, supporting, or guiding violence. Charges and countercharges are thrown out, to be met by apologetic explanations on all sides. For every violent image or prescription in religious writings, one can easily find both a corresponding violent manifestation in another tradition and a mitigating text in one's own tradition.

This exchange of text and countertext is most pointed in relation to conflicts involving those religious communities that share the name of "People of the Book," Jews, Christians, and Muslims. In each of these traditions, written scriptures hold a central position. Jews honor the Tanach: the Torah, the Prophets, and the Writings. Christians also esteem these scriptures as the "Old" Testament while adding to it their own scriptures, the "New" Testament. Muslims regard the Qur'an as the direct revelation given to Muhammad by Allah.

Critics highlight "toxic texts," scriptures that seem to codify violent and destructive behavior. The assumption is that a straight line can be drawn from the text to violent behavior. As a familiar bumper sticker succinctly phrases it: "God Said It. I Believe It. That Settles It." If a text contains violent imagery or commands, those who take the text as authoritative will simply act violently, will they not? The reality is, of course, far more complex. Alongside destructive images and models there are other texts that express a different and even opposed viewpoint within the same tradition. They stress mercy, reconciliation, and peace. How does one decide which is more determinative? In any given situation, which is more likely to shape behavior and attitudes?

Each of the three traditions of the Book has a slightly different approach to understanding its sacred scriptures as authority. Within each tradition exists a wide range of possible responses to the images, worldview and pronouncements within sacred texts. Although one book occupies a central and privileged status, it is found only in the context of a complex of interpretation that includes other texts, interpretative communities, and structures of teaching and organization that seek to guide individuals' understanding and application of the text. From the Talmud in Judaism with its layers of commentary to Christianity with its creeds, affirmations of faith, commentaries and liturgy, to Islam with the Hadith, sacred texts are never found in isolation.

To understand the role of sacred scriptures in shaping violent attitudes and behavior we must recognize that texts do not do anything in themselves. It is only in the dynamic encounter between the text and a specific reader, in a specific community, in a particular historical and cultural context that individuals engage, interpret, internalize and ultimately act on those texts.

Let's return to our car with the "God Said It" bumper sticker as it approaches a stop sign at an intersection. What will happen? What seems at first glance to be a simple everyday occurrence proves in fact to be a highly complex example of behavior influenced by the interpretation of a text. In order for the driver to stop, she must first recognize the text presented by the sign. She must determine what behavior is being called for, what behavior is appropriate (not necessarily the same thing), what the current situation might be, and then she must act in a way to produce the desired outcome. Many factors other than the plain meaning of the text on the sign will go into her decision. What level of authority does she accord the sign or those who posted it? Where will she rank the authority of the sign in a hierarchy of values? Will she obey the letter of the law and come to a full stop? Will she observe the "spirit" of the law, slow down and hesitate just long enough to check for oncoming traffic? Will she decide that another concern demands more attention, a critically sick child in the back seat? Will she be distracted by a cell phone, by a frustrating encounter with an imperious official, or by road rage?

Let us take another example. Following the September 11, 2001, attack on the World Trade Towers in New York, one individual wrote to a conservative Catholic newspaper the following reflection:

The Sunday after the 9-11 attack on America I entered my church an angry man. My pastor spoke to the congregation of Matthew's Gospel. He was sensitive as he explained Matthew's message of forgiveness: "Love your enemies, do good to those who hate you and pray for those who persecute you." I thought, "Yes, Jesus forgave his executioners for they know not what they do." Therefore [I thought] "as we strive toward the perfection of Christ we should do likewise and do good to those who hate and persecute us." As a Catholic I understand that. I thought how much I love my dog. If that beautiful animal created by God should go mad and hurt others, I would show my love for it and "do good" to my dog. I would destroy it. In fact, I would have a moral obligation to destroy it to protect others from its madness. And by destroying it I would be forgiving the poor creature for its madness.

I left church convinced that there is an appointed time for everything. This is the time for moral clarity, not moral confusion. Now is the time for "overturning the tables" in the temple of the terrorists. Now is the time for "the terrible swift sword." (DeNunzio, 2001)

What has happened here? This individual is not ignorant of what the Gospel reading says, nor of how it has been understood in his community. One might justifiably presume, given the venue of the letter, that he considers both the Bible and the Church's teaching to be authoritative. How does he reduce the conflict between his personal anger and frustration and his understanding of what the Gospel text demands? He redefines the meaning of *love*, dehumanizes the enemy to the level of his dog, and musters alternate texts from Ecclesiastes, the Gospels, and the "Battle Hymn of the Republic." He entered the church an angry man; he apparently left in the same way, but now finding justification in the scripture for his anger. In this brief encounter with the text it is clear that it has been the text that has been converted, rather than the reader.

Much has been written on the political, historical, cultural and other factors that underlie violent conflicts with religious overtones. I focus on the encounter between a reader and a sacred text that might provoke violent attitudes or actions. What is needed to transform a reading into a deadly reading? Is it possible to identify characteristic distortions or tendencies that might lead to violence? What psychological factors come into play in reading sacred texts, and what significance do they have for action?

The examples below are primarily drawn from the Christian tradition and experience; this reflects my own location and my familiarity with it. However, my own experiences in interreligious dialogue among religious leaders of traditions including not only the People of the Book but also Buddhists, Sikhs, Baha'i, Gnostics, Neopagans, and others, have convinced me that psychological dynamics, while certainly influenced by culture, experience, and environment, are essentially similar across human experience. This intuition is supported by cross-cultural psychological studies.

In the Beginning: Object Relations

We begin our exploration of the encounter with sacred texts with reference to the earliest stages of human development. Psychologists of religion have long recognized the close connection between early childhood development and later religious images and behavior. In the earliest experiences of mother and care lie the roots of God images and emotionally charged attitudes and reactions to spirituality and religious thinking. Adequate childhood development lays the foundation for mature adult spirituality and, conversely, disruptions of early development may distort later religious life. Object relations theory traces the development of the child from the earliest stage of fusion and identification with the mother through the process of differentiation and identity formation. The "objects" of object relations theory are not external things in themselves, but internalized psychological representations of others, significant people or things in the surrounding world. These object representations are invested with emotional force and associated with images and attitudes that continue to influence the individual throughout his or her lifetime (St. Clair, 1994).

Internal object representations are developed through characteristic psychodynamic mechanisms. The task is to develop a coherent ego or identity that is able to relate appropriately to the world. In order to achieve this goal, the developing individual engages in processes of integration and differentiation, identifying with desirable traits and rejecting undesirable ones. People and things in themselves are always ambiguous, displaying both positive and negative aspects, but the young child has not as yet developed the perspective or ego strength to deal with that ambiguity. Thus, in the early stages, the psyche employs a strategy of splitting, separating the "good" qualities from the "bad." These elements are integrated through processes of identification and introjection or rejected and projected onto others (Hamilton & Gregory, 1987).

Internalized objects and the process of their formation continue to affect individuals throughout their lifetimes. In healthy development, the individual gradually becomes able to deal with ambivalence and ambiguity in significant others. If, however, the normal course of development is disrupted, adults may continue or revert to immature strategies of splitting and projection.

Idealization and Religion

How is it that religion is able to be at one and the same time the source of profound human transformation and maturity and a source of hostility and aggression? James W. Jones suggests that part of the answer can be found in the psychological dynamic of idealization (Jones, 2002). Idealization enables a child to defend himself or herself against the perceived failure of the mother to provide adequately for his or her needs by splitting the good and bad aspects of the mother and internalizing the bad while projecting the good outward onto the mother. This psychic relationship between the needy and vulnerable self and a wholly good external object provides the psychic energy for later distinctions of sacred and profane in religious experience.

Every experience of the sacred, be it sacred experience, sacred mountain, sacred image, or sacred text, is linked to and colored by this archaic experience of idealization. The difference between transformative encounters and destructive encounters lies in whether the individual can move beyond idealization to genuine encounter or whether he or she remains caught in the grip of idealization and projection.

In healthy development, the child eventually develops a positive enough self image to be able to deal with the inherent ambiguity of life. Without sufficient nurturing or opportunity to compensate in later development the individual will continue to react to the world through idealization and splitting as an adult. Idealization is unavoidable; it is an essential dynamic of human relating to the world. It is the same dynamic that we see in romantic relationships. The giddy feeling of being in love may provide an emotional high and initially one sees one's partner as lacking any faults. In a mature relationship, one eventually comes to see the other as more fully human, encompassing both positive and negative qualities. A deeper and more encompassing relationship develops. Some people, however, cannot move beyond that initial stage. They may expend tremendous energy in maintaining the idealization, filtering out any perceptions that might contradict their idealized image of their partner. Or, at the first indication that their partner is not perfect, they may decide that he or she is entirely unworthy and move on to the next idealized relationship, "addicted to love."

The idealization of a sacred text can offer the opportunity for personal transformation. A new perspective or possibility may be offered through reading and responding to the text. One has the opportunity to step outside one's own perceptions and to be addressed through the text. If the idealization of the text does not move into a more complex and realistic understanding, it may lead to religious fanaticism instead. If one's own text is perfect and all-good, without regard for inconsistencies, varied interpretations, and contextual factors in its development and transmission, then all the weaknesses, negativity and inadequacy that might otherwise be discernable in the tradition are projected on others.

Given its deep roots in object relations and incomplete development, archaic idealization affects more than just the relationship with a sacred text. Although the text may be an important component of a religious tradition, it is only part of that tradition. An individual who idealizes the text is likely to bring the same dynamics to the whole life of the religious community—to its ideology, its leaders, and its self-identifications.

Group Identity Formation

Scriptures may provide a particularly potent tool for supporting aggression and hostility to others due to the significant role sacred texts play in developing group identity and setting group boundaries. Formation of a group identity is essential in the creation and sustaining of a religious community, or any other human community. W. W. Meissner identifies this process of identity formation, especially when it involves a new group's emergence from a previously existing movement, as the "cultic process." Although in some ways it may appear to be a conscious endeavor, what undergirds it is an unconscious dynamic of individual and intergroup relationships that Meissner dubs the "paranoid process." The term *paranoid* here does not indicate necessarily a pathological condition. Rather, Meissner employs the term technically to refer to a dynamic of attitudes, perceptions, and unconscious strategies that serves to consolidate and clarify identity, both individual and group. These dynamics are common to all group identity formation, and when they allow a transition into a more mature and fully functioning identity they are creative and necessary. It is when they become detached from reality or resort to archaic defenses that they can become pathological (Meissner, 2000).

The elements of the paranoid process correspond to mechanisms we have already encountered at work in the early stages of object relations development, now operative in adult behavior. The process of group identity formation is analogous to the process of individual development, and involves the same processes of integration and differentiation. Human relationships are both positive and negative; they can be created and strengthened by positive feelings of affiliation and connectedness and they can be prevented or inhibited by feelings of hostility and aggression. The paranoid process provides several means for cementing relationships with those within the circle of positive relations and limiting affiliation with those outside.

In group formation, the most visible manifestations of the paranoid process are the idealization of the in-group and projection of negative perceptions on outsiders. Meissner suggests that the cultic process serves as a means of bolstering members' self-esteem and enabling them to cope with a sense of vulnerability and powerlessness. The paranoid process enables adherents to deal with these feelings of inadequacy and inferiority by splitting them off and projecting them on the Other. "We" become the Children of Light; "they" are the Children of Darkness. These idealizations of the inner group and projections onto outsiders are consolidated and supported through a development of a belief system and ideology, often contrasted sharply with the beliefs of others.

When sacred texts develop to express and define group identity in a context of conflict, they often crystallize these idealizations and projections and preserve them in written form. While these formulations may be appropriate in the formative stages of the religious community, it sets the stage for future distortions. As Paul Ricoeur has observed, something significant happens when communication moves from speech to text. In dialogue, it is possible to clarify ambiguity by direct reference to the surroundings. Once a communication moves into text, however, the direct referential context is lost, and the multiple significances inherent in written language make a variety of interpretations possible.

Sacred texts that preserve the originating conflict through the expressions of the paranoid process can serve creatively to guide believers through present situations of conflict or persecution. The reader can project his situation onto the imagined world of the text, identify with those who were able to endure, and thus begin working through to a healthier and more integrated way in the world. In the case of individuals and groups whose sense of persecution is excessive or heavily shaped by archaic reaction mechanisms, it is a simple thing to project their present feeling of vulnerability and powerlessness onto the scriptural images, and to reframe the (now decontextualized) language of good and evil to fit their perceived situation. Indeed, what often happens in a violent religious movement is an insistence on recontextualizing the sacred text to fit a new situation. In its cultic formation, the new group not only rejects previously conventional interpretations of sacred text, it forms precisely around its claim that it understands the text better than anyone else.

Take, for example, the hostile characterizations of Jews in the Christian scriptures. In their struggle to define themselves over against Second Temple Judaism, Christians claimed that they had the correct interpretation of the scriptures they shared with Jewish tradition. In the context of increasingly antagonistic relationships with other emergent Jewish groups, the gospel writers cast the leaders of those other groups, Scribes and Pharisees, in the role of primary antagonists, ultimately laying the blame for the (Roman) crucifixion on "the Jews." In generation after generation these words, lifted out of their first-century context and remapped into entirely different political, economic, and social contexts, have served religious and political leaders as a justification for anti-Semitism, crusades, pogroms, and the Holocaust.

Does this lead us to the conclusion that scripture causes violence? Does a toxic text necessarily trigger paranoid reactions? Does it always support hostility and aggression? Which comes first, paranoia in the text or paranoia in the reader? Idealizations of the in-group and outward projections of aggression onto others developed during the beginnings of a religious movement provide only potential stimuli for violence. Scriptural justifications are far more likely to be secondary phenomena, mustered to support a worldview, attitude, and ideology that are already hostile and aggressive.

Illusion Processing

Another way to understand psychological interaction with a sacred text is through Paul Pruyser's concept of "illusion processing." Building on D. W. Winnicott's exploration of the "transitional object" in childhood development, Pruyser suggested that, even as adults, human beings carry forward that object relations dynamic and thus experience the world in three dimensions. Between the world of external, objective reality (the "realistic world") and the internal psychic world of the child (the "autistic world"), there is a middle state, the "illusionistic world," characterized by playfulness, imagination, and creativity. The realistic world comprises sense perceptions, hard facts, and logic, while the autistic world is a private world of random fantasy, free associations, and private needs. The illusionistic world is the arena of shared experience, of culture, art and religion, and engages the individual in imaginative exploration guided by cultural values and esteemed tutors. Relations with transitional objects in the illusionistic world allow for creative reevaluation of group values, innovation, and personalization of community resources.

Pruyser describes his own relation to the Bible as a transitional object. His mother would read an illustrated children's Bible to him and his siblings as they sat together. The Bible book itself was overlaid by the emotional power of the feelings of motherly love and warmth and the fact that the Bible sat on the mantel next to a picture of his dead father. These personal associations offered imaginative inroads to enable his own identification with biblical characters and the development of his religious life (Pruyser, 1991a).

Threats to the illusionistic world come from both sides. Realistic distortion treats the playful potentialities of the illusionistic sphere as if they are hard facts and unquestionable reality. Autistic distortion resulting from immature psychological development pulls an individual toward hallucination and inability to relate to others. In relation to the Bible, autistic distortion gives rise to the characteristic apocalyptic splitting into paradisiacal images of heaven and aggressive fantasies of slaughtered enemies. Realistic distortion takes the form of fundamentalist concretizing of symbolic language and the doctrine of inerrancy of scripture. This shift demands increasingly complex gymnastics to deal with challenges to the factual reliability of the text (Pruyser, 1991a, 1991b). Once again we see that how the individual approaches the text and what developmental and emotional resources he or she brings to the reading and interpretation of the text will have a large bearing on how he or she will understand and interpret the text.

As a Person Thinks: Cognitive Theory

Alongside the relational development described by object relations theories, there is a gradual development of cognitive functioning, the ability to think and make choices. Despite broad similarities in the stages of development, the ways in which individuals conceptualize, organize and respond to the world display great variety. Religious life is not exempt from this diversity. Some people seem simply to be inherently more literal than others; some are more attuned to the world around them while others march to the beat of a different drummer . . . or no apparent drummer at all.

In a seven-year study of the religious attitudes of adult Christian seminarians, H. Edward Everding and his associates analyzed patterns of cognition, patterning, and development in the subjects' religious perspectives. They discovered that, despite the variation and complexity of interrelated factors, four significant clusters of attitudes and perspectives on religious faith emerged, which they designated as "viewpoints" (Everding, Wilcox, Huffaker, & Snelling, 1998).

Perspective A (Affiliating) is characterized by concern for personal relationships, feelings, and mystery. These individuals are not interested in rationality or institutions and view authority as being external to themselves, in the group or in individuals who express qualities confirmed by the group. Scripture is one of those external authorities, having absolute authority, and interpreted in terms of universal guidelines for life. There can be only one true interpretation.

In contrast, perspective B (Bargaining) is aware of the diversity of religious approaches; authority is rooted in individual preferences shaping one's relationships to the divine and to others. Images in the Bible may have different meanings for different people, depending on their needs. Interpretation is not critical; its aim is to discover useful guidance for the individual that may not be universally applicable.

Perspective C (Conceptualizing) is characterized by rationality and concern for systems and institutions. People of this orientation have less concern for feelings or relationships. Often, they will reject or remain skeptical of mysterious or irrational phenomena that cannot be reduced to rational criteria. From this perspective, the authority of scripture may be derived from the authority of the group or institution that sanctions it, or it may be internalized in the form of logical truths derived from an abstract and analytical reading of the text. A concern for balance between the multiple dimensions of human religious experience is the mark of perspective D (Dialectical). Here, the individual seeks to take into account the rational and mysterious, personal and institutional. Authority of scripture is determined by weighing the claims of the text against those of other individual and corporate authority figures, as well as one's own internal sense of commitment and truth. These viewpoints are descriptive of approach, rather than content. People of the same cognitive orientation will appear quite similar to each other regardless of their religious identification. It often appears that a Christian fundamentalist may have more in common with an Islamic terrorist than with other Christians.

The Affiliating perspective comes closest to the "God Said It. I Believe It. That Settles It." attitude. Looking to an absolute external authority and a tendency toward black and white thinking, this perspective is most open to manipulation by others. If drawn into a community by a sense of personal inadequacy or hunger for an idealized religious experience, such a person may accept identification with a particular interpretation of sacred text and religious life, and be willing to act aggressively against those perceived as a threat. This is not to say that perspectives B, C, or D are immune to religiously based violence. A Conceptualizing person might find what he or she considers to be objective justification for taking violent action to establish or preserve justice. Bargaining and Dialectical individuals are more concerned about relationships in general and persons with a Dialectical viewpoint are more likely to be found in peacemaking work, having a greater capacity for living with ambiguity.

These categories are abstractions from observations of actual human beings. Most people do not operate purely out of one viewpoint alone but display a mix of different factors. What is relevant here is to note the diversity of perspectives. No matter what a sacred text may say objectively, equally faithful readers of that text will bring different cognitive structures to their reading, structures that will shape and organize their understandings of those texts and thus their behavior in response to them.

Just as I Am: Personality Theory

Everding concentrated on cognitive structures of religious perspectives, evidenced in conscious expressions of faith and belief. Unconscious factors also come into play. No matter what someone might say their attitude or approach may be, their actions may demonstrate something quite different, even though they may not at all be aware of the contradiction.

We have already considered unconscious dynamics related to object relations theory. Another way of looking at patterns of human behavior is through personality theories such as the Myers-Briggs personality theory based in the work of Carl Jung. The Myers-Briggs

Personality Inventory (MBTI) organizes human behavior in terms of four sets of polarities: Introversion-Extroversion, Sensing-Intuition, Thinking-Feeling, and Judging-Perceiving (Myers, 1998). Various writers have developed each of these factors in depth; only two of the polarities are pertinent to our discussion here: Sensing-Intuition and Thinking-Feeling. Sensing and Intuition have to do with how a person tends to take in information about the surrounding world. Sensing individuals are attuned to sensory input in this moment; they notice color and sound, texture and taste. They observe facts and details, and tend toward the concrete and specific. In the extreme, they truly can't see the forest for the trees. Intuitive individuals, on the other hand, grasp possibilities, interrelationships, and wholes. They are future-oriented, imaginative and, in the extreme, can be unrealistic.

Thinking and Feeling describe how a person evaluates the information that has been taken in either through Sensing or Intuition. Thinking types value logic and reason, based on objective observation and analytical thinking. They seek fairness, justice and equality. Feeling types, on the other hand, value people and relationships. Note that *feeling* is not used here in the sense of emotional states, but of relational states. Feelers will evaluate how something affects others; they seek harmony, tact, mutual appreciation, and sympathy. The four possible combinations of these factors define the core "temperaments": Intuitive-Thinking, Sensing-Feeling, Sensing-Thinking, and Intuitive-Feeling.

Peter Richardson found the Myers-Briggs temperaments useful in identifying clusters of religious sensibilities (Richardson, 1996). His study of diverse religious expressions in Buddhism, Christianity, Hinduism, Islam, Judaism and others led him to formulate four "ways" that find expression across religious groupings and to correlate them to the Myers-Briggs temperaments: the Journeys of Unity (NT), of Devotion (SF), of Works (ST), and of Contemplation (NF). Each of these journeys represents a cluster of attitudes, perceptions and goals for religious life and practice. Of the four, the Sensing-Thinking individual pursuing the Journey of Works is most likely to look to sacred scriptures as a central guide for behavior. Attuned to structures of law, order, and covenant, he or she approaches the world with a deep concern for discerning and maintaining rules governing righteous conduct. Knowing the right and doing the right are fundamental to the Journey of Works and by attending to recognized authority and living according to righteousness an individual shapes and maintains his or her sense of identity. Recognized authorities may include other forms of writing, teaching, or individuals, but for People of the Book, scripture is bound to be included.

These individuals may also have a sense that their individual commitment has cosmic implications. Living the righteous life is not only an individual struggle but is part of a dramatic global, eternal conflict. The Christian book of Revelation and the "Battle Hymn of the Republic" are expressive of this cosmic battle. Sensing-Thinking types have a tendency toward black-and-white categorization, which can draw them toward apocalyptic thinking.

To say that Sensing-Feeling spirituality is perhaps more prone to scripturally based religious violence is not to imply that the other three types cannot be violent; it is only to highlight the role that the religious text may play as an impetus to violence. Sacred writings play a role in the other three journeys, but an individual's approach to them is likely to be less directly linked to behavior. The Sensing-Feeling Journey of Devotion, with its central attention to community and relationships, may lead to violent conflict, but motivation is more likely to arise out of perceived threats to one's own community or faith and the declarations of community leaders. Both of the Intuitive approaches, the Intuitive-Thinking Journey of Unity and the Intuitive-Feeling Journey of Harmony, tend toward a more universalized perspective on religious life and seeking the commonalities that may bring individuals and communities together. Conflict can arise in the Journey of Unity in relation to one's demand for clarity and justice (these individuals can be blunt and tactless), but at the same time one is more likely to believe that ignorance is at the core of the problem and can be addressed better through education than through coercion.

Of the four, the Journey of Harmony is the least likely to result in violence at all, much less violence prompted by sacred texts. Intuitive-Feeling individuals are inclined to seek ways to bring people together, to seek unity, even if it may blur distinctions between communities and traditions. They bring a flexibility to their interpretation of symbols and traditions, and a concern for human relationships that transcends particularities. Many individuals involved in interfaith dialogue and peacemaking are likely to take this approach.

Not only do personality types shape the way individuals lead their religious lives and approach their sacred texts, they also suggest characteristic ways that religious approaches may become destructive. While making no direct reference to personality types, Vernon Ruland identifies three religious ways, which he asserts have Christian, Hindu, and Jewish manifestations, as well as expressions in Neoplatonic thought and the psychological approach of Karen Horney. These three are the Way of Action, the Way of Affectivity, and the Way of Contemplation (Ruland, 1994). It takes no great leap of imagination to see that these three correspond well to three of Richardson's four Journeys: Works, Devotion, and Unity. It can be argued that the remaining Journey of Harmony represents a universalizing and unifying perspective that seeks to balance and incorporate the other three into a whole.

Ruland explores the strengths and concerns of each religious way, but also offers insight into what happens when a religious way becomes a "detour." Each way has a particular tendency to certain characteristic forms of distortion, different from the others. In only one of the Ways, the Way of Action, are sacred texts likely to play a significant role in fomenting violence toward others. Distortions in the other two ways may lead an individual to become a part of a violent religious group, but the motivations are not primarily based on scriptural authority. For example, one common unhealthy manifestation of the Way of Contemplation tends toward a heightened asceticism and withdrawal from life. Such an individual seeks to abdicate responsibility for his or her life by "renouncing" what he or she does not wish to tend. One way of doing this is to hide oneself in a group, and to cede all responsibility to an idealized leader. In the case of the Way of Affectivity, a person may be drawn to a religious group out of an immature dependency in which the individual feels unlovable and desperately seeks approval and affirmation from others. Many of these individuals find the desired acceptance and inclusion in religious cults, groups with rigid boundaries separating members from the outside world, demanding total commitment and often having charismatic leadership.

Two of the distortions related to the Way of Action seem most pertinent in relation to sacred writings, the tendency toward religious self-assertion and the tendency toward religious paranoia. These represent two inadequate responses to the disjunction between desired perfection and lived ambiguity. The Way of Action focuses on identifying and doing the righteous thing, and those inclined to this approach seek to live pure lives in the midst of a less than pure world. Religious self-assertion eliminates doubt and contradiction by asserting that my will and God's will are one and the same, my understanding is God's understanding and my interpretation of God's sacred text is the same as

God's voice. God exists to fulfill my needs and desires. If I do what God wants, God is compelled to do what I want. In the Christian and Jewish Bibles, this attitude seems to be validated by the Deuteronomy code with its promise of direct reward for righteous conduct.

Religious paranoia, on the other hand, deals with the disjunction of desire and reality by the now familiar defense mechanisms of splitting and projection. In order to sustain a sense of purity in situations of real or perceived persecution in which an individual feels limited control over his or her circumstances, the individual idealizes himself and his community and devalues the Other. Those on the inside are viewed positively as bearers of truth and righteousness. Those on the outside become the enemy, the agents of the devil, the Evil Empire, or the Axis of Evil. We have already noted the attraction of this apocalyptic thinking evidenced in The Revelation of St. John and other apocalyptic writings in Jewish and Christian traditions. Someone caught in the dynamics of religious paranoia tends toward rigid and unchallengeable attitudes and is seldom open to other points of view. "Those who are not with us are against us" is a clear expression of this attitude. Unfortunately, the most widely known manifestation of Christianity in the United States today, televangelism, is deeply influenced by this way of thinking.

Each of the religious Ways has definite strengths and the potential for guiding healthy religious life. Distortions generally arise when one or another Way is absolutized to the exclusion of the others. Although each individual will be naturally drawn to one of the religious Ways, the key to health is through understanding and appreciating the gifts of each. Once again we see that response to a religious text is based not so much on what the text says, but on the interpretative framework in which it is read, a framework that is molded by developmental issues, personality types, cognitive structures, and interpersonal relationships. While groups may use scripture to justify their hostility and to undergird their legitimacy and authority, we see that these strategies have persuasive power because they activate and manipulate psychological dynamics having to do with identity, authority, relationship, perception and cognition.

Group Identity: Social Psychology

Let's revisit that car nearing the stop sign. Our attention so far has been on the driver and individual factors that may influence his or her response to the sign, but seldom is a vehicle on the road by itself. It is surrounded by other vehicles, other drivers, all deciding how they will react to the signals around them. Under normal circumstances, most drivers will at least make some effort to obey the law, if only out of a sense of self-preservation; but let us imagine further that our car is not on the road alone, nor merely one more car on the road, but that it is part of a convoy moving together and led by someone in authority. It becomes less possible to predict how the individual driver will act, since the sense of group identity and purpose becomes a strong factor, likely even more powerful than the individual's own inclinations.

Social psychologists studying the phenomena of intergroup conflict note that analogies between interpersonal relationships and intergroup relationships, such as those between differing religious groups, are of limited usefulness. When the individual identifies with a group, individualities become depersonalized and relations with outsiders are likely to be shaped by intergroup struggles for power, status, and the like, more than by personal preferences (Hewstone & Cairns, 2001). In fact, what appear to be religiously based conflicts may mask or at least incorporate sources of conflict other than aggressive relationships to other religious traditions. Sudhir Kakar observed of the Muslim-Hindu conflicts in India that they reflected less a resurgence of religion than social, economic, and political interests that included religious affiliation as one component. Threats to individual and communal identity, presented by globalization and modernization, coupled with a sense of vulnerability and helplessness due in part to migrations from rural to urban settings, set the stage for regressive coping mechanisms. The sense of identity developed in childhood through introjection, identification, idealization, and projection includes an inner sense of group identity and belonging. There is a wide spectrum of behavior within the group, from those who are able to maintain a sense of individual identity in the midst of a group to those who feel constantly under attack by the outside and insistent on defending group identity at all times, even in times of peace or the absence of visible threat.

An outbreak of violence is occasioned by a sense of threat so great that communal identifications overwhelm personal identity, strengthening affilliative bonds with the group and intensifying the hatred toward the out-group. In this situation of identity threat and violent self-defense, religion may serve to intensify the emotions and motives of the group, bringing justifications from idealized sacred history and imagery that connects powerfully with deep inner passions. Religious ritual, which developed in part to consolidate and strengthen group identity, is often conducive toward breaking down boundaries within a group. In times of crisis and fear, such rituals can serve to create violent mobs (Kakar, 1996).

The Bible Made Me Do It: Concluding Observations

It must be clear by now that there is no simple line to be drawn between sacred text and religious violence. As much as religious leaders might want to believe that people base their lives and actions directly on sacred texts, the reality is not that simple. While sacred writings may well be employed by religious (and political) leaders to bolster and defend a course of action or set of attitudes, they generally do not in themselves give rise to those attitudes or actions.

In *When Religion Becomes Evil*, Charles Kimball, expert in comparative religions and the Middle East, identifies five factors that may indicate a propensity for religiously based violence: absolute truth claims, blind obedience, establishing the "ideal" time, the end justifying any means, and declaring holy war (Kimball, 2002). None of these factors depends on whether violent images or expressions appear in the group's scriptures. Three of the factors, however, may hint at how sacred scriptures could enter the mix.

When a group makes absolute truth claims, it will often make them with reference to sacred writings. Yet it is important that truth is claimed not only for the writings themselves, but for how leaders and authoritative teachers interpret those writings. As we noted in reference to the cultic process, teachings considered authoritative may not only depart from other accepted interpretations, but the strength of the group's sense of identity may be reinforced precisely by that departure. We can easily recognize the dynamics of extreme idealization at work, an inability to deal with ambiguity and imperfection.

Establishing an ideal time and declaring holy war are often closely linked and likewise have their roots in the tension between an idealized perfect world and the actual world. A group declares that it is their religious responsibility to realize on this earth the envisioned perfect city, state, or community. Such a task is likely to be appealing to individuals who approach the world with the qualities of the Way of Action. When frustrated by their inability to achieve perfection these people can potentially move toward religious paranoia and apocalyptic thinking. The blueprint for this envisioned world is usually derived from sacred texts that have been yanked from the illusionistic world of symbol and image into concrete distortion in the realistic world. Images and symbols of hope and completion are decontextualized, concretized, and remapped onto the present day.

Calls to holy war are likewise often buttressed by reference to sacred text, making use of scriptural images and their profound power to stir up deep, early emotions and a sense of group identity. These citations can often be entirely self-serving, used less as expressions of religious fervor than as tools to whip up group cohesion and hostility toward the so-called enemy. Whether this is the case, scriptures used in this way are not truly concerned with a rational process of reading, understanding and debate, but function as idealized objects, stirring up archaic psychological defense mechanisms. It is not about what the texts mean rationally and cognitively, but what they trigger unconsciously.

The recurring debate about what images in religious texts are violent, and whether someone who holds that text as sacred must hold certain attitudes or beliefs regarding religious violence misses the point. It can itself be manifestation of the idealization/projection dynamic, especially when I can see no potential negativity in my own text, but am overly sensitive to such images in another's. In the situation following September 11, it is neither sufficient nor helpful to focus on sacred texts in isolation. It is vital that we be sensitized to the complex interactions of text, reader, community, and context. We must be attentive to where and how it is that religious communities are likely to head down a destructive road.

Is there hope? Is there a way to preserve the power and meaning investing religious texts without bringing with them the defenses and mechanisms that lead to religious violence? Paul Pruyser once commented that the psychological function of the god-image is to remind us that we are not god. Our survey has suggested some specific areas in which we need to be reminded of that fact. We need to preserve a sense of humility in our religious affirmations and heartfelt commitments. This means the willingness to see and acknowledge the limitations of our human formulations of the divine, the willingness to see and acknowledge the ambiguity of life, and the willingness to see and acknowledge the value and contributions of other ways.

References

DeNunzio, M. (2001, November). Time for war. *San Francisco Faith*, 2.

Everding, H. E., Jr., Wilcox, M. W., Huffaker, L. A., & Snelling, C. H., Jr. (1998). *Viewpoints: Perspectives of faith and Christian nurture*. Harrisburg: Trinity Press International.

Hamilton, M. D., & Gregory, N. (1987). *Self and others: Object relations theory in practice.* Northvale: Jason Aronson.

Hewstone, M., & Cairns, E. (2001). Social psychology and intergroup conflict. In D. Chirot & M.E.P. Seligman (Eds.), *Ethnopolitical warfare: Causes, consequences, and possible solutions* (319–342). Washington, DC: American Psychological Association.

Jones, J. W. (2002). *Terror and transformation: The ambiguity of religion in psychoanalytic perspective.* New York: Taylor & Francis.

Kakar, S. (1996). *The colors of violence: Cultural identities, religion, and conflict.* Chicago: University of Chicago Press.

Kimball, C. (2002). *When religion becomes evil.* New York: Harper Collins/Harper SanFrancisco.

Meissner, W. W. (2000). *The cultic origins of Christianity: The dynamics of religious development.* Collegeville: The Liturgical Press.

Myers, I. B. (1998). *Introduction to type* (6th ed.). Palo Alto: Consulting Psychologists Press.

Pruyser, P. (1991a). The seamy side of current religious beliefs. In H. N. Maloney & B. Spilka (Eds.), *Religion in psychodynamic perspective: The contributions of Paul W. Pruyser* (47–65). New York: Oxford University.

Pruyser, P. (1991b). The tutored imagination in religion. In P. Pruyser (Ed.), *Changing views of the human condition* (101–115). Macon: Mercer University Press.

Richardson, P. T. (1996). *Four spiritualities.* Palo Alto: Davies-Black Publishing.

Ruland, V., SJ. (1994). *Sacred lies and silences: A psychology of religious disguise.* Collegeville: The Liturgical Press.

St. Clair, M. (1994). *Human relationships and the experience of God: Object relations and religion.* Mahwah: Paulist Press.

CHAPTER 5

Scenes of Sex and Violence in the Old Testament

Simon John De Vries

It is surprising how many scenes of sex and violence we find in the Bible and the Qur'an, the sacred scriptures of the dominant Western religions. Serious believers in Judaism, Christianity, and Islam read these sacred scriptures regularly, devotedly, and through the eyes of faith. They interpret them, as they read, in terms of theological perspectives that reflect the believer's understanding of and quest for a meaningful relationship with God. The numerous narratives of sex and violence constantly nag the reader in the back of the brain, even if he or she is able to repress their impact upon the central message of sacred scriptures and, in effect, delete them from devotional experience and from the ideology it evokes. Nonetheless, these repressed or unconscious memories can have a significant effect upon our sense of things, and upon personal and cultural values and behavior.

The trouble is not with the Bible, but with the misuse of the Bible by Fundamentalists and other exploitive ideologists. In the present discussion I define a *Fundamentalist* as one who may claim to cling to the earliest form of a religion but who in fact has selected a feature that may not be essential, and who makes it centrally significant at the expense of what turns out to be, upon careful and unbiased investigation, the truly central and basic point of the faith. The present, well-designed project, *The Destructive Power of Religion*, is largely concerned with the results of abuses and misinterpretations of the otherwise nobly conceived, humane, and uplifting scriptures of the major religions. This has been done, and is still being done, either by dominant individuals and groups or by those on the fringe, including Islamic terrorists carrying on a holy war against Western culture, Israeli triumphalists dispossessing native Palestinians, and of course Christian literalists over many centuries viciously persecuting the Jewish people as though they were enemies of God.

Many of the contributors to this project will be assessing the damage done by this long prevailing pattern of destructive Fundamentalism, but that is not my task in this chapter. I intend to provide a historical point of reference for the entire discussion by evaluating how violent the people of the Bible—those of the Old Testament in particular—actually were. This will require a sympathetic but critical examination of a representative selection of passages, those especially that have stimulated or appear to justify extreme replications in the behavior of pious but misguided followers. In light of the fact that the New Testament, apart from the Apocalypse of John, is notably a quietistic, or peace-teaching, book, Christians have turned for fuel for their aggressions to their Older Testament, also the Bible (Tanach) of the Jews. Islamists have texts to inspire them as well, but I leave an examination of the Islamic scriptures and holy books to those more qualified than I, trusting that the results of my Old Testament evaluations will have appropriate parallels there as well.

In what follows I offer what I consider to be a critical yet sympathetic interpretation of selected scenes from the Old Testament in which drastic or unjustified violence, including violent sex in particular, provides the theme. I shall be biased neither toward censure nor toward finding excuses. The first thing I shall do is to exegete the text through the application of sound historical and literary method in the light of the most up-to-date and relevant information. Then I shall evaluate the ideological (including theological) assumptions and implications of the text. And, finally, I shall assess the moral and spiritual authority of the text, initially for the faith community that produced it, and by extension for those who stand, or claim to stand, within the tradition of the text. Within the framework of the volume as a whole, this discussion must be succinct yet adequate for the purpose. Being aware, as I am, of the extensive scholarly literature on each of these passages, I aim only to show the way to better understanding for those who may have little training in this field of biblical study.

Exposition

Revenge and Hatred for Enemies

Biblical Texts

O daughter of Babylon, you devastator,
Happy be he who pays you back for what you have done to us!
Happy be he who takes your nursing babes and smashes them on a
    rock! (Ps. 137:8–9)
Do I not hate them who hate you, Yahweh?
And do I not loathe them who rise up against you?
With perfect hatred shall I hate them,
Counting them as my sworn enemies. (Ps. 139:21–22)

Exegesis

These texts may seem especially shocking because they are exceptional within the Psalter, the Book of Psalms. Passionate expressions of lust for revenge can be found elsewhere in the Old Testament, notably in the short "prophetic" book of Obadiah, which excoriates Judah's brother-state, Edom, for gloating and abetting when the Babylonians sack Jerusalem in 586 B.C.E. Nevertheless this must be acknowledged as an authentic expression of a very human emotion. Not only is there bitter lamentation—a form of submission—but denunciation and the cursing of the enemy—a form of defiance.

It seems certain that Psalm 137 was composed early, and Psalm 139 late, in the exile period (586–539 B.C.E.), and their circumstances differ. The first is a cry of rage and resentment, while the second is a calm and trusting testimonial. Psalm 137 has the form of a communal lament that is styled in the first-person plural, passionately rejecting the Babylonians' mocking demand to sing of Zion (homeland and city), vowing instead to keep Zion in remembrance while imploring the Lord to keep in his own memory the gloating of the Edomites. This is followed by a curse upon the children of those who have butchered the little children of those in captivity. In spite of its intense individuality, this probably served in a liturgy of public sorrow. Psalm 139 is quite different. It is styled in the first-person singular and is in the form of the meditation of an individual, but it too may have served in liturgy as a testimonial or sermon. Judged thematically, the entirety of verses 1–16 is a rehearsal of "God's precious thoughts" (v. 17; cf. v. 23) as they come to manifestation in the human mind and heart, throughout the universe, and within the human organism. Its intention is to unite the speaker with God in his entire being and throughout his entire earthly existence, which he enthusiastically embraces as token and assurance of a perfect union with God in the unknown destiny prepared for him.

Verses 19–24 within this psalm must be understood with this in mind. It is a pragmatic effort on the speaker's part to ward off the contrary ill effects of his daily exposure to some who would disturb his peace and sense of unity with God. The terms for these disrupters and corrupters are "the wicked," "bloody men," "the defiant," and "schemers of evil" (vv. 19–20). The Hebrew behind some of these expressions is uncertain and perhaps corrupt, but it may be assumed that the terms refer to incompatible individuals or groups within the exile community—those whose attitude and behavior threaten the speaker's and community's trust and security because they ally them with the captors in exploiting the helplessness and passivity of the captives. Perhaps all these terms are metaphorical variants or poetic synonyms for "the wicked one." In verses 19–20 the speaker invokes God's curse upon these disrupters and corrupters. In verse 21 he makes his oath of clearance (cf. Job 31:4–40), vowing (v. 22) to repudiate the wicked categorically ("reject/hate them with a complete rejection/perfect hatred and count them as my enemies") while calling (vv. 23–24) upon an omniscient and omnipresent God to monitor the Psalmist's thoughts and motives for conformity to these emotions. The speaker ends by asking God to continue to lead him in the "way" that leads to everlasting truth and authentic reality.

Ideology

The ancient Hebrews had a strong sense of corporate solidarity based on their distinctive covenant with their god. To remain attached to one another, they knew that they had to remain attached to Yahweh. The promise that they adhered to was that this solidarity with God and with one another would bring blessing, a good life, and peace. The time came, however, when empires began to overrun their world, sweeping them into desperation and chaos. All that made life worth living seemed lost as they were subjected first to the extreme harshness of the Assyrians, next to the more moderate bondage of the Babylonians, eventually to the more humane treatment of the Persians.

It should be kept in mind that both these psalms contain curses against Israel's enemies, yet how different they are! In Psalm 137 the enemy is the captor and tormentor, but in Psalm 139 the enemy (so v. 22b) belongs within the captive community itself as a potentially even more destructive enemy. Psalm 137:8–9 is a bitter imprecation lyrically addressed to "the daughter of Babylon" in the form of a mock double blessing, "Happy be . . . happy be" (cf. Ps. 1:1), first calling upon a violent person to do the same to her that she has done to her helpless captives, then calling upon an avenger to do to her what she has done to the captives from Zion—dash the tormentor's little children against a rock as she has dashed the little ones belonging to these captives. The recognition that the speaker does not claim to have authorization or the means to do this bloody deed himself takes away from the impression of raging personal revenge and places the matter in the hands of someone more powerful and more authoritative than the vaunting Babylonians. Yet the curse's bitterness is palpable, certainly understandable under these dire circumstances.

Verses 19–20 of Psalm 139 are also in the form of an imprecation, but it lacks both the bitterness and the passion of Psalm 137:8–9. Here the speaker is calling upon God to carry out the appropriate action to ensure covenantal harmony, which is to "slay" the wicked and drive away, or do away with, the "men of blood." It is not quite clear from the other Old Testament occurrences of this root, those in Job 13:15, 24:14, and Obadiah 9, that this rare Aramaic loan-word involves a literal killing. Since God is the one who is called upon to do this, it is difficult to assess the contemplated violence. Certainly there is firmness and even intolerance in this imprecation, but little passion, showing that it is probably meant schematically and programmatically. It is notably different from Psalm 137:9 in that it seeks not to redress individual victims but to protect the covenant community, whose survival and well-being are endangered, from some who threaten it from within their fragile and still tentative social setting.

This interpretation is based on the recognition that the main concern of Psalm 139 continues to be that of verses 1–18, inculcating a trust that the god of Israel has not, after all, been conquered by the gods of their captors, and that the rules of his covenant continue in effect. The speaker rehearses unshakable truths undergirding the faith that God may still be counted upon in all trials, temptations and adversities whatsoever. Some had given up on God and had begun to walk in the way of wickedness. The speaker utters his curse upon such apostacizing, swearing his own innocence while vowing to repudiate in his own mind and heart every form of deviation and disloyalty from faith in God. He concludes with the prayer that God may scrutinize his own heart for any inclination toward this evil path, and may lead him safely onward in the path of eternity, thereby transcending all historical dilemmas and disturbances in order to pre-serve an ideal union with his people and an all-knowing, all-caring, all-powerful God.

Authority

It is understandable that the final editors of the Old Testament found no need to censor either of these two passages. The Jewish people have often been the victims of internal strife and foreign aggression. We can only imagine what the closing words of Psalm 137 could have meant to the modern-day victims of the unimaginable pogrom conceived and carried out by the Nazis. Nothing but the dashing of little ones could ever expiate for this sin! Most of those who were directly implicated in this monstrous crime have by this time received personal punishment, but the German nation that allowed or ignored it has suffered, and we know that most Germans are deeply serious about making such amends as are still possible, or at least symbolically meaningful. How wrong it is, in balance, that present-day zealots among the generations that have survived the horror are tempted to capitalize upon this resentment and defensiveness to the point of sabotaging peace and the cause of international brotherhood, particularly in the Near East.

The New Testament took an opposite path with regard to retribution, eschewing violence and leaving vengeance to God (Rom. 12:19; but cf. Deut. 32:35). Christians have grown accustomed to hearing that violence and personal revenge are unworthy. One effect of this shows up in the refusal of many lectionary editors to include in their lessons verses 21–22 with the rest of Psalm 139. It is only right to try to do better justice to controversial passages of Scripture. Is it too much to ask why the Psalmist included such words of hate and loathing in his long and almost classical meditation on God's healthful ways? This would no doubt call for some explaining on the part of any liturgist who chooses to take these words as a valid and expressive part of Scripture. It should be made very clear that the words as they stand are appropriate only within their immediate ancient context.

It might be well, in seeking to understand what is behind the fierce words of Psalm 137, to read it aloud, and with feeling and emphasis, so that, when coming to verse 8, a special inflection would be on the word *your.* No sentiment could be more germane to this situation than "May the God who judges all things requite this terrible outrage by smashing little ones!" We may not like these words and may not feel that we can approve them, yet they are honest and real to the situation. The ultimate problem with revenge is that it tends to breed revenge upon the avenger. Both sides may take turns claiming the right to say, "Happy be he who takes little ones and dashes them against a rock!" The system of revenge or retribution, just as the system of "preemptive defense" merely seems to justify in the mind and heart of the perpetrator, some further self-righteous violence against the hated enemy.

The Standard of Retribution

Biblical Texts

Then Yahweh said to him, "Not so!
If anyone slays Cain, vengeance
Shall be taken on him sevenfold."
And Yahweh put a mark on Cain,
Lest any who came upon him should kill him. . . .
Lamech said to his wives:
"Adah and Zillah, hear my voice,
You wives of Lamech, hearken to what I say,
I have slain a man for wounding me,
A young man for striking me."
If Cain is avenged sevenfold
Then Lamech seventy-sevenfold. (Gen. 4:15, 23–24)
If any harm follows,
Then you shall give life for life,
Eye for eye, tooth for tooth, hand for hand, foot for foot,
Burn for burn, wound for wound, stripe for stripe. (Exod. 21:23–25)

Exegesis

Scholars have identified the probable composer of Genesis 4 as J, the Yahwist, that is, a writer/editor who regularly uses the historical name of Yahweh for Israel's ancient god, instead of using the generic name, Elohim (gods/God), which other large parts of the Bible use. That writer is responsible for composing the more ancient of the two biblical tales of creation, 2:4b–3:24. To be correct, one would say that J received this tale from his tradition substantially as it appears in the biblical text. We know this because in 4:25 the generic word for man, Adam (man, mankind), regularly employed in chapters two and three, abruptly shifts to the proper name for the specific person, Adam. As is suggested by the Greek Septuagint, it originally appeared also at 4:1 but has been normalized there by a scribe to the form appearing within the two previous chapters. J is directly responsible for the aetiological genealogy in 4:1–2a, a nonformulaic connecting link in 4:16–17a, and

Engraving by Lucas van Leyden of Cain killing
Abel, 1529. Library of Congress.

another aetiological genealogy in 4:25–26a. Properly speaking, these
three items together conceive of only two genealogical successions: (1)
that from Adam-Eve to Cain-Abel and (2) that from Adam-Eve to Seth.
J is, however, composing around two major blocks from his tradition,
which are the tale of Cain and Abel in 4:2b–16 and the genealogy of
Lamech in 4:18–23. All of this gains special significance when one tries
to interpret the declaration about a sevenfold reparation for Cain in
4:15a and that about Lamech's seventy-sevenfold reparation in verse
24. Without the recognition that it is J as a redactor rather than the
boasting Lamech who is speaking in verse 24, one is left in the dark
concerning why the killing of a single man should provide the basis for
magnifying Cain's hypothetical sevenfold vengeance into the seventy-
sevenfold vengeance claimed by Lamech.

One should observe how J's redaction restructures his traditional materials. The Cain account is actually a folk-saga for the Kenites, probably a guild of smiths living on the fringe of the cultivated land and dependent on the early Israelites. In Hebrew and in the cognate Semitic languages, the root upon which the proper name is based refers to metallurgy and the name probably means "smith." Cain is eponymous in the present account for a guild or clan of smiths, and the tale is not actually about two brothers, but about two groups who originally enjoyed a close alliance with each other but fell out over an act of unjustified or unrequited violence. Yahweh, guardian god of the Israelite settlers, condemns the Kenites to a fugitive existence outside his land, but when the Kenites complain that this renders them defenseless against random attack, he places a taboo mark upon them so that would-be attackers may recognize them, adding the solemn declaration that sevenfold vengeance shall be visited on anyone who slays one of them. The numeral seven is schematic and the threat may be rhetorical rather than programmatic or prescriptive. It should, however, be interpreted on the basis of this people's occupation as smiths, and as such it may imply that, because they possessed weapons of metal, they enjoy a sevenfold advantage over more poorly equipped attackers.

Verse 16 is J's redactional or editorial conclusion to the saga material, while verse 17a is his redactional introduction to an independent genealogy for the succession, Enoch-Irad-Mehujael, Methushael, Lamech. It will be observed that this tradition stands in competition with that of the Priestly genealogy in chapter 5, which has the succession of Kenan, Mahalalel, Enoch, Methuselah, and Lamech between the opening link in verses 6–11 (Seth to Enoch) and the closing link in verse 32 (Noah). Here as there, all names are eponymous, that is, they stand symbolically for larger categories or communities, rather than individual persons. As in numerous examples from Genesis and Chronicles, the direct line from Enoch to Lamech (v. 18) gives way to a lateral arrangement and is itself followed by a fragment of aetiological narrative. Lamech's first subordinate line is through a wife who becomes ancestress of tent-dwellers, on the one hand, and of musicians, on the other. The second subordinate line is through a wife who becomes the ancestress of those who forge instruments of bronze and iron. It is this aetiological item that gives an important clue for interpreting Lamech's boastful words to his two wives. The theme of differentiation and expansion in human inventiveness is similar to that of J's aetiological tale in Genesis

11:1–9, where humankind becomes a menace through its ability to cooperate in the erection of a high tower. Because Lamech has now obtained through his son Tubal-Cain iron as well as bronze weapons, he boasts to his wives in a poetic couplet that he has prevailed in the retaliatory slaying of a would-be attacker. With this, the aetiological couplet is concluded. It is J himself who makes the assessment, "If Cain is avenged sevenfold, so Lamech seventy-sevenfold." What is meant is that civilization has now advanced so far that a single man has the means to do eleven times more murder with a single blow than previously (cf. Samson's similar boast in Judg. 15:16).

An important conclusion to this line of analysis is that the selected verses in Genesis do not intend to regulate the taking of revenge as such. Lamech is not claiming to have avenged Cain (who is not identified as Lamech's ancestor in the aetiological fragment). He has not been seeking revenge, but merely defending himself with more power and effectiveness because he possesses weapons of iron and not just of wood, stone or bronze!

The law of the Talion (Latin for *tooth*) in Exodus 21:23–25 is juridical in nature and offers a rule for punishing those who intentionally or innocently do harm to another. There are modified examples of this saying in Leviticus 24:20 and Deuteronomy 19:21, but this passage shows a more primitive, though not necessarily the original, lapidary form. The Deity speaks directly, unconditionally, and hypothetically regarding the case in which one man has injured another. Although the injuries involved may vary somewhat from passage to passage, the phrases, "eye for eye" and "tooth for tooth" are found in the identical order both in the Leviticus and the Deuteronomy passage and in Matthew 5:38. This is evidence that these two items stood together at, and in identical order, in the most primitive formulations.

The sequence found in Exodus is important. First, the Exodus formulation functions as a gloss upon a casuistic rule concerning injuries done to the pregnant wife of one of two struggling men. If only a miscarriage results, the man causing it must pay whatever the husband requires, as confirmed by judges, but if serious or even fatal harm is done to the woman herself, the law of reparation must apply, "life for life." Without stating precisely how this is to be administered, the rule goes on to state less serious circumstances: "eye for eye, tooth for tooth, hand for hand, foot for foot," and so on, each of which might be appropriate in particular cases. It is probable that all of verses 24–25, including the phrase, "As the judges determine," may be secondary within this context because the list as such takes a noticeable step back from the more serious "life for life" situation and because elsewhere the formula, "eye for eye and tooth for tooth," appears at the beginning of lists and does not follow another item, as here. Furthermore, the mention of judges conflicts with the designation of the husband as arbiter. It is also probable evidence of later restructuring, incorporating a more formal judicial setting. With these modifications, the passage becomes part of an early casuistic series of rules (vv. 12–14, 15, 16, 17, 18–19, 20–21, 22–25, 26–27, 28–32, 33–35), some of which show still later expansion within their individual structures. This becomes one of several blocks of rules taken up into the pre-Deuteronomic law book known as the Book of the Covenant in Exodus 21–23.

Ideology

The Covenant Code in Exodus appears to be earlier than the law book of Deuteronomy 12–26 and the variegated collections found in Leviticus-Numbers. The fact that the individual rules may not always be in harmony with one another has provided the ancient Jewish Bible scholars, known as the Midrashic and Mishnaic traditionists, with much to discuss and worry about. A more modern way of handling the text's disparity is to apply historical criticism, which involves taking note of individual stages of literary growth within the Pentateuch (the first five books of the Bible, Genesis through Deuteronomy). This kind of study has been enriched by the recovery and study of extrabiblical law codes from neighboring cultures that are contemporary with, and in some cases even more primitive than, those of the Old Testament.

It happens that similar rules are found in the Code of Hammurabi deriving from (second millennium B.C.E.) Babylonia that show sporadic traces of the Talion formula, often referred to today by the Latin phrase *Lex Talionis*, or sometimes in popular English as the "law of the jungle" (see G. R. Driver and J. C. Miles, *The Babylonian Laws*, Oxford: Clarendon, 1955, 77–78). This code is composed almost entirely in the casuistic form, "If . . . then," and the general theory throughout is that if damage or an injury has been done, a retaliatory payment may be levied on behalf of the injured party. A striking change in style appears in columns 196–97 and again in column 200: "If a man has put out the eye of a free man, they shall put out his eye. If he breaks the bone of a (free) man, they shall break his bone . . . If a man knocks out the tooth of a (free) man equal (in rank) to him(self), they shall knock out his tooth." These occurrences are sporadic and appear to have been glossed into the dominant casuistic framework. It is important to observe that the rule of equality pertains only to injuries done to full citizens who are male. For injuries done to villeins, slaves and women, a payment of money is to be substituted. Thus a quid pro quo reparation is the rule only among equals. Elsewhere equivalent retaliation is demanded. The clear implication is that where men are politically free and socially equal, injuries cannot be paid for with money and property, but must be avenged in kind and in full proportion.

Authority

This insight from the Hammurabi Code supports our study of Exodus with regard to the origin of the more stringent rule of Talion. In both contexts, this is relatively primitive and shows modification toward a more nuanced situation, one in which there are judges and in which property may be substituted, instead of equivalent injury being done to the offender. At the very least, the biblical form of this principle represents a less severe reparation, demanding only a one-for-one substitution rather than Cain's sevenfold retribution and the seventy-sevenfold retribution of Lamech. Careful study of the Pentateuchal law codes reveals notable efforts in the direction of humaneness and fairness, an example being Exodus 21:23's decree that legally appointed judges and not just husbands shall determine the penalty. A few verses further it is stated that Hebrew male as well as female slaves shall be set free if their master blinds one of their eyes or knocks out one of their teeth. This is an amazingly humane provision in light of the hapless condition of slaves in general. The rule of eye for eye, tooth for tooth, and even life for life, seems cruel and excessive both in biblical and in Islamic law; but it must be conceded that it is more merciful than the haphazard, barbaric, rough-and-ready rule of brutal and hasty death, for minor as well as major offenses, which some societies of the present as well as of the ancient world have inflicted.

Jesus declared that the Pentateuchal rule is superseded and inappropriate within his new kingdom and urged his followers to substitute kindness and generosity in the place of retaliation (Matt. 5:38–42). Jesus was not so much a revolutionary as a creative adapter and extender of biblical law. He was himself, alas, the victim of an excessive and drastic travesty of justice, less that of the book of Moses than one imposed under a harsh and cruel foreign power, the Roman Empire. It takes greater courage and determination to live by the rule he proposed than by the misdirection of political power under which he suffered.

Two Bloody Rituals

Biblical Texts

At a lodging place on the way Yahweh met him (Moses) and sought to kill him. Then Zipporah took a flint and cut off her son's foreskin, and touched Moses' feet with it [probable original reading was "foot," euphemism for penis], and said, "Certainly you are a bridegroom of blood to me!" So he let him alone. It was then that she said, "You are a bridegroom of blood," because of the circumcision. (Exod. 4:24–26)

Moses stood in the gate of the camp and said, "Let whoever is on Yahweh's side come to me." And all the Levites gathered themselves together to him. And he said to them, "Put every man his sword on his side, and go to and fro in the camp, and slay every man his brother, and every man his companion, and every man his neighbor." Then the Levites did according to the word of Moses, so that there fell of the people that day about three thousand men. And Moses said, "Today you have devoted yourselves ["been ordained," "filled your hand"] to the service of Yahweh, each in place of his son or of his brother, that he may bestow on you today a blessing." (Exod. 32:26–29)

Exegesis

Both of these passages preserve fragments of ancient ritual, the first in Zipporah's statement, "Certainly [or "verily, indeed"] you are a bloody kinsman for me!" (4:25b) and the second in Moses' words of invitation, "Let whoever is on Yahweh's side come to me" (32:26), followed by his declaration, "today you have devoted yourselves to the service of Yahweh, . . . that he may bestow on you today a blessing." Though both passages feature an element of blood-shedding, in Exodus 4 the passage seems original to the narrative, while in Exodus 32 it apparently belongs to a secondary and later level of composition.

Exodus 4:24–26 requires first to be isolated from its literary context, and once isolated, needs to be untangled for its original meaning. In the earliest J layer underlying the Hebrew text of chapters 3 and 4, Yahweh reveals himself to Moses on Mount Sinai and then commissions him to confront the Egyptians with a demand to let the Hebrew people go. But according to 4:18–20, Moses goes first to his father-in-law (better: kinsman), Jethro, to fetch his wife and sons. In 4:27–31 Aaron and Moses go together to Egypt. This is the narrative context into which Exodus 4:24–26 has been inserted. As it stands it is thematically jarring because it presents in the place of a self-giving, saving God, a dark numen (only later editing identifies him as "Yahweh") who threatens to kill Moses and is conjured away

by Zipporah's ritual act of touching Moses' sex organ with the pre-
puce of her son, followed by her declaration, "Certainly you are a
bloody kinsman to me!" These words imply a primitive ritual in
which infant circumcision is substituted for adult circumcision.

The second passage is Moses' reaction to the Israelite idolatry in
worshiping the golden calf. In this narrative, bloody retribution is not
thematically present at an early stage in the writing of the golden calf
narrative of Exodus 32. Of course, Moses and Yahweh seem very
angry, and Moses goes so far as to force the sinning people to drink
the residue of the golden calf, reduced to powder, with water (v. 20);
but, according to verse 30 and following, Moses is quite willing to
supplicate to God for forgiveness on behalf of the sinners, and how
could he do that if he had just slaughtered three thousand of them?
Absolutely unbelievable is the immediately following report that he
calls for volunteers to pass through the Hebrew camp, indiscriminately murdering victims, and without regard to rank or affinity.

This image is, however, not what J intended, but what the redactor
(later editor) makes of it. An important clue is the fact that the expression, "son and brother," in verse 29 becomes "brother . . . companion . . . neighbor." This approximation is the clear sign of literary
alteration in verse 27, which contains the command that Moses purports to have received from Yahweh, but is actually a later editorial
invention.

A *hieros logos* (sacred teaching) belonging to the primitive Levites
may well have contained verse 29's ritual call for loyal service,
"Whoever is on Yahweh's side, come to me!" along with words of
solemn ordination, "You have today devoted yourselves to the service
of Yahweh, seeking a blessing from him." The blessing to be enjoyed
by one who volunteered would no longer be expected from a son or
a brother, but from Yahweh himself.

This rings true to the scattered biblical traditions concerning the
Levites. They possessed no tribal heritage in spite of the fact that their
eponym (Levi) is honored within the ancestral lineage as a senior, and
therefore high-ranking, son of Jacob. As partial compensation for this,
the Levites were given special cities to dwell in. Within the Old
Testament they seem often to be grasping for recognition and a better
share, and eventually they came to be closely identified with the priesthood and served in the administration of the temple. While avoiding
any attempt to discuss the numerous problems associated with their
special history, it may reasonably be conjectured that these words of
sacramental actualization do indeed echo a solemn memorialization of
the Levites' special devotion to Yahweh's service and worship.

In this light, the Moses of this text should not be understood as calling for indiscriminate slaughter among the calf worshipers, but for a decision toward complete devotion to Yahweh within a special group, or office, that had declared their willingness to be cared for henceforth only by Yahweh himself rather than by family and relatives. Apart from the fact that, according the biblical record, the Levites eventually did receive the task of guarding the temple precincts, there is no hint that their initial service was constabulary or military in nature. The Pentateuchal record as it stands distorts their tradition by adding to it a reputation as a rough and ready band of religious fanatics.

Ideology

The roots of the strange narrative in Exodus 4:24–26 are to be found within early Midianite traditions not merged with complete success into the main Exodus narrative about a theophany and covenant at Sinai, including that of Moses' marriage to a Midianite woman in Exodus 2:15b–22 and that of a festive reunion with his Midianite kinsmen in Exodus 18:1–12. Moses is a name eponymous for a people known as Mushites (cf. Num. 26:58), a Levitical group eventually assimilated into Israel, and Zipporah and Jethro are eponymous for clans belonging to the people known as Midianites. Taken together, these passages have two implications, (1) that the Moses people are related by blood (i.e., a ceremony involving blood) to the Midianites, and (2) that through the Moses people the Israelites came to be at a time in the remote past cultically associated with Midianites at a shrine somewhere in their eastern-desert territory, though not necessarily in the worship of Yahweh as such (cf. 18:12, which mentions Elohim, God, within a literary context featuring the name Yahweh). The special nature of the bond between these two peoples is that they have become kinsmen, but Moses has been endangered because he has received the wrong rite: adult circumcision rather than infant circumcision. To placate the angry numen, Zippora circumcised her son and touched Moses' penis with the foreskin while declaring, "Certainly you are a kinsman to me by blood!" In this fragment of a primitive cult legend, she performs the symbolic act of connecting the token of the child's circumcision with the locale of Moses' wrongly performed circumcision, in order to validate the substitution and thus the kinship.

If we are to judge by the biblical record as it stands, the earliest Israelites, or only some of their primitive elements, must have practiced adult circumcision rather than infant circumcision. Alongside the evidence provided by the present text, we may refer to the account of the forced circumcision of the adult Shechemites in Genesis 34:14–24. Even in the prescriptive postexilic passage, Genesis 17, it is adult male members of Abraham's patriarchal family who are circumcised, and the only son that Abraham has acquired to this point, the thirteen-year-old Ishmael, is certainly not an infant. Nevertheless, the twelfth verse of Genesis 17 specifically does require that it is on a male child's eighth day, and not later, that he is to be circumcised, and this became the definitive rule for the Jews (Lev. 12:3; cf. Luke 2:21).

It should be deduced that infant circumcision did not supplant adult circumcision until long after the formation of Israel as a nation. The shift from adult to infant circumcision must have occurred in connection with the development of Israel's more mature understanding of the covenant with Yahweh in which male infants (and by implication, female infants as well) were included. In this process the primitive notion concerning circumcision was all but completely lost. In the light of Exodus 4:14–26, it had originally been a rite of protection against an angry deity, in this case a pre-Yahwistic fertility god, who required the fleshly token along with the blood, as proof of submission. The only thing that specifically memorialized this primitive element was the flint knife by which the ceremony was traditionally performed, a token of its origin in the stone age, before metal tools were invented.

It seems a pity that the earliest tradition behind the rise of the Levites was allowed to subside into obscurity, to the point of encouraging the Pentateuchal redactor to rewrite the story of their call to special ministry in Exodus 32. A desire for special recognition is behind the textual alteration by which they march through the camp of their fellow-Israelites, slaying indiscriminately. Whose desire was this, that of the Levites themselves or that of a non-Levite who was angry enough at idolaters to credit a group claiming special sanctity with the performing of a bloody work to take the place of the repentance and divine mercy that the original narrator intended? Psychoanalytic psychology would suggest that we have here a mythic or confessional report of an historical event or a subconscious wish, on the part of the disenfranchised Levites, to destroy the male authorities of the other twelve tribes who had gained special privileges of land and power by depriving the Levites of both. The mass slaughter is a fancied wish fulfillment ideation or an actual event of jealousy-induced mass murder. As Quinones indicates (*The Changes of Cain*, Princeton, 1991; cf. also his chapter in this series), it is a passage in any case, which expresses the perpetually present cultural Cain-Abel myth of the brother-sacrifice as resolution of societal imbalance and potentially lethal internal turbulence. Another form of this symbolic myth that prevails throughout history is the scapegoat method of resolution of social conflict.

Authority

There is no evidence that either of these two tales of ritual violence influenced the mainstream of biblical tradition. Exodus 32:26–29 is a fake and Exodus 4:24–26 preserves nothing but a fossil that has brought little light for understanding the Pentateuchal story as a whole. In view of the fact that circumcision has been no less than a founding rite for postbiblical Judaism, the sparsity of biblical evidence for its origin is astounding. Apart from the passages cited, there is no biblical witness for this but a brief aetiological legend in Joshua 5:2–3 recording Yahweh's command and a report of the people's compliance. It is little wonder therefore that circumcision has not gained acceptance in Christian practice, but what is a wonder is that Judaism has made the bloody violation of the human body so important and so indispensable. Unquestionably, this divergence in practice is more important for defining the two religions than the great body of agreement that both share as heirs of the biblical tradition.

Amid all the discussion and controversy concerning the proper place of circumcision within a religious system, the one thing that remains central is the blood. Blood is a synecdoche or metaphor for violence, but while the rite of circumcision requires no more than a token wounding, and certainly does not endanger life or threaten serious harm, it does remind us that the ritual laceration of the flesh has been practiced by some religions for expressing repentance and for turning one's life seriously toward Deity, in the same manner that it is used by some psychotics to express their self-punishment and death wish because of their dysfunctional notions of reality. Certainly the biblical record provides no justification for using it as a means of appeasing God or as a price to be paid for entrance into an elite group.

Cruel and Violent Sex

Biblical Texts

Two angels appearing as men are welcomed by Lot into his house, verses 1–3; the entire adult male populace ("both young and old, all the people to the last man") of Sodom surround the house and demand, "Where are the men who came to you tonight? Bring them

Flight from Sodom, by Raphael. Scala/Art Resource, New York.

out to us that we may know them," verses 4–5. Lot implores them
"not to act so wickedly" and offers his two daughters "who have not
known man," if they will do no wrong to the guests "who have come
under the shelter of my roof," verses 6–8. The men of Sodom inso-
lently threaten Lot and join together to break down the door, verse 9.
The angels reach out to rescue Lot, after which the men of Sodom are
struck blind and are unable to grope their way to the door, verses
10–11. Lot warns his relatives ("kinsmen," as in Exod. 4:25–26 [who
have married other daughters of his]) that Yahweh is about to
destroy the city, but they just laugh, so at dawn he flees with his wife
and two unmarried daughters (Gen. 19:4–11).

A Levite and his concubine, on their way from Bethlehem to the hill
country of Ephraim, lie down in the public square of Gibeah, but an
old farmer coming from the fields invites them into his house, verses
10–21. As they are enjoying themselves, base fellows from the town
surround the house and beat on the door, demanding that the man
who came as guest to the old farmer's house should be given up to
their lust, verse 22. The old farmer implores, "No, my brethren, do
not act so wickedly . . . do not do this vile thing. Behold, here are my

virgin daughter and his concubine. Let me bring them out instead. Ravish them and do with them what pleases you, but against this man do not do so vile a thing," verse 24. When the men at the door refuse this offer, the Levite thrusts his concubine outside the door for them to rape and abuse all night, and in the morning he finds her lying motionless outside the door, verses 25–27. When she fails to get up, he realizes that she is dead and places her body on his donkey to continue the journey home, verse 28. He then divides her body into twelve parts, sending one to each of the tribes of Israel, urging vengeance against Gibeah and the tribe of Benjamin that are responsible for this horror (Judg. 19:10–28).

Amnon, the eldest of David's sons, is infatuated with Tamar, David's virgin daughter by another wife. Amnon pretends illness so that he might ask the king to send Tamar to his house to prepare food for him, verses 1–7. When she places cakes she has baked before Amnon, he instructs her to bring them into his private room and feed them to him by hand, verses 8–10. He seizes her and demands, "Come, lie with me, my sister!" but she refuses, verses 11–12; she implores him not to allow himself to become one of the wanton fools in Israel by disgracing her, and she even promises to become his wife if David will give his permission, verse 13. He will not yield to her imploration but forces her to have sex with him, verse 14. Immediately he hates her with a hatred exceeding his "love," puts her out of his room, and bolts the door, verses 15–17. Placing ashes on her head, Tamar rends the long-sleeved robe betokening her virginity and lays her hand on her head as she goes away weeping, verses 18–19 (2 Sam. 13:7–19).

Exegesis

Each incident of sex or attempted sex, as summarized here, is but a single element within a longer and more complex tale. In all three narratives, the main concern lies beyond the cruel and violent deed in itself. In the Genesis passage, the incident, in which a raging gang of men and boys demands though in this case does not acquire access to helpless guests, is employed as full and final proof of the need for Sodom's overthrow. The tale goes on to depict the flight of Lot with his wife and two virgin daughters from the imminent destruction of the city. In the Judges passage a strikingly similar tale of brutal lust is told, not for its own inherent interest, but to legitimize a summons to the tribal union to join in punitive war against Gibeah and the Benjamites. In the chapter from 2 Samuel the incident of Amnon's rape of his half sister, and refusal to marry her in order to make amends for violating her virginity, is employed as the crucial narrative link to Amnon's assassination and Absalom's revolt. There is a notable progression among all three of these narratives from a lesser to a greater sophistication, both in literary style and in the depth and complexity of psychological motivation.

Textually there is little problem with these three passages, and the vocabulary is standard to Israelite narrative from the early monarchy period. The Genesis passage belongs to the J document, which was probably composed during or soon after the reign of Solomon. The Judges passage belongs to a collection of tribal sagas composed shortly prior to the emergence of the monarchy (cf. Judg. 21:25, "In those days there was no king in Israel; every man did what was right in his own eyes"). The story of Tamar is an integral part of the "throne-succession narrative," probably dating from the time of Solomon, whose right to rule this story seeks to legitimize.

Ideology

It is useful to examine these three stories together because of the common theme of sexual exploitation. In all three, even though it does not become the dominant theme of the document into which it has been incorporated, this sin is severely censured. The story about Lot shares with the Levite narrative the theme of gang rape upon a male stranger (or strangers) lodging in the home of a fellow citizen. In the case of Lot and the men of Sodom, this crime is not carried out, serving instead as final and conclusive evidence of the city's incorrigible wickedness. However, in the case of the Gibeahites, even though the crime is not carried out against the male stranger in question, it is perpetrated against his concubine. This motif is what links it with the story of Tamar in the throne-succession document, in which a single male with deceptively acquired access, a half brother rather than a gang of strangers, is the perpetrator, and a princess rather than a lowly concubine is the victim.

The pitiful story of Tamar is almost classic in its poignancy, but that of the Levite's concubine is also profoundly touching. In each story, but not in the Genesis narrative, there is development of the victim's personality, even though this is not the main point of attention in either. In the case of the concubine, this begins already in an opening episode in which the Levite's concubine is said to be angry with her master, without a statement of the reason why, and goes home to her father in Bethlehem. This explains why this Levite from the Ephraimite hill country is in Bethlehem at the start. He has gone there to recover his concubine. After an extensive sequence of implorations from the woman's father to remain his guest, a contrast between the hospitality of the woman's father and the Levite's unconcern for her, he begins his return journey by way of Gibeah, a Benjamite town not far from Jerusalem. Here the outrageous incident occurs. Exasperation is suggested as the possible motivation of the Levite's willingness to gain his own safety by abandoning this pitiable woman to gang rape and murder. In any case it is no justification for it. It is a tragic disappointment that this biblical narrative expresses neither pity nor concern for the woman.

In contrast, the narrative about Tamar provides an intimate and authentic portrayal of female psychology and behavior, with the result that Tamar stands out as far more real and believable than the Levite's concubine, who remains little more than a type or figure. The Genesis 19 narrative of Lot and Sodom, on its part, merely mentions who the intended victims are. Set phrases such as "both young and old, the men of the city to the last man" and "both small and great," which seem to come out of folklore, are employed to create the overarching aura of the imminent and catastrophic judgment that is the main theme of this narrative. All males in the city, even graybeards and juveniles, join in this folly, showing that Abraham's interview with Yahweh in Genesis 18 had indeed pointed to the proper conclusion: "I will go down to see whether they [the evil Sodomites] have done altogether according to the outcry which has come to me, and if not, I will know" (18: 21). It was as Yahweh suspected.

Two important differences between the ruffians of Genesis 19 and those of Judges 19 are that the Sodomites demand sex with other males while refusing desirable females, but end up with neither when they are stricken, first with blindness and soon afterward with smoke and brimstone. Whereas those of Judges 19 are demanding sex with a male while likewise refusing the females who are offered, ending up outrageously brutalizing the guest's concubine in place of her master.

It is likely that the implication here is that the offenders were sufficiently enraged by the insult to their homosexual interests that they wreaked their rage upon the "property" of the guest, namely, his concubine, because they were deprived of the opportunity for sex with him. Thus their sexual sadism wreaked upon the concubine is less sexual behavior and more the typical abusive power and violence of consciously contrived rape and murder. This smells of the psychopathology and terrors of the "snuff films" made in Mexico and Thailand during the 1960s and 1970s.

The abominable and abusive royal personage in 2 Samuel 13 obtains the heterosexual satisfaction he has sought by stealth and violence. Here the abused female is no speechless, passive victim. Tamar protests with passion and eloquence the wicked thing that is being perpetrated upon her. She makes it clear that this sin affects the entire kingdom of Israel, not just one hapless female.

Authority

It would be a disservice to leave the discussion of these three stories without saying something on the issue of homosexuality. Some argue that the wickedness of the men of Sodom lay in its violence, coerciveness, and flagrant disregard of the social norms of Near Eastern hospitality codes, rather than in the perpetrators' sexual orientation. A counterargument might be that the Sodomites turned down the offer of Lot's virgin daughters. An important factor in weighing this issue is that the biblical text clearly sees the Sodomites' greatest sin to be their disregard of the rules of hospitality, just as in the incident of Judges 19. Respect for this rule was so great that Lot was willing to sacrifice his own daughters, precious as they must have been to him, in order to protect his guests from abuse. It seems that hospitality had more urgency in the society that produced these two narratives than sexual safety and integrity within the family. This viewpoint fits a threatened, seminomadic society in which travelers needed to be able to count on finding food and lodging, and in which virgin daughters might tend to be viewed as burdens or as chattels.

Of course, Lot's guests were not actually human; they were what we might call angels, a point that proved to the narrator of this story that the Sodomites were indeed depraved beyond redemption. Thus Genesis 19 makes no straightforward condemnation of homosexuality as such, but it most certainly does condemn social delinquencies in which sexual violence is likely to occur. This is the main issue as well in Judges 19. It is striking that both passages tell about a gang of males in connection with the violation of the rules of hospitality. The most likely reaction among modern readers to these stories will be strong sympathy for the women who were threatened and abused. The cruel act of the Levite in exposing to almost certain rapine and murder, the helpless concubine whom he had the duty to protect, seems just as reprehensible as the gang rape. This seems especially true in view of his taking her a second time from her father's house. The Levite is craven beyond belief, throwing his concubine out the door to save his own skin.

The question is whether this was also the narrator's main point of concern. All three stories agree in demanding extreme retaliation for such wanton acts, yet in Judges 19, neither the gang of malefactors nor the uncaring Levite receives condemnation or punishment. This large gap in the narrative development of this story is clear evidence that it is a tribal saga rather than a moral anecdote. Far from lamenting the sad fate of his abused concubine, the Levite severs her body into twelve pieces to be sent to each of the tribes for retribution upon Gibeah and Benjamin. As a saga, this account is concerned about errant, nonconforming political entities, such as the "crazy and uncooperative Benjamites who are not fitting into the tribal unity of ethical political codes." Thus it is less a story about wicked individuals. This is, of course, a viewpoint that has lost all relevance in modern societies, unless one were to see something similar to the nonconformist Benjamite behavior in the behavior of the Islamic Fundamentalist terrorists who conduct themselves in a manner counterproductive to the best interests of the family of Islamic nations in the Middle East, from Egypt to Pakistan.

Conclusion

The major religions that derive directly or indirectly from ancient Israelite religion, either as derivatives from it or reactions against it, are faith traditions that depend heavily upon the sense of their historical rootedness that seems to be implied in all of their sacred scriptures. Judaism, as we know it today, arose during the first centuries of the Common Era and consolidated itself, as we know it today, under the great Rabbis of 300–600 C.E. Christianity came into its own during the same period. Islam arose in the seventh century C.E., coincident with the final demise of the Western Roman Empire. All are rooted in ancient Israelite religion in the sense that they derive their metaphors and much of their narratives from the images of the Hebrew Bible, the Tanach.

As J. Harold Ellens has indicated in his introductory essay for this work, the Hebrew Bible and its purportedly historical narratives formulate a picture that calls humankind to action and responsibility. Even in their reprehensible passages these ancient scriptures tend to be action oriented. This is quite different from some forms of Eastern spirituality that tend to promote a more interior quest for meaning and the sacral possibilities for human existence. Thus Islam, Judaism, and Christianity tend to be religions that take action on theological, ethical, moral, and political issues. In each case these action-oriented modes of life reflect a worldview that is shaped by that particular twist that each religion gives to its sacred scriptures, its sense of historicity, and its consequent philosophy of life.

In each of these three religious traditions there have been those devotees of irenic spirit who have seen in scripture and history the options of grace and mercy. On the other hand, each tradition has also produced those sick souls who have translated God's call into the creation of hellish terror for humanity. In those cases in which our sacred traditions have been screened through psychopathological minds and spirits to create violence and horror, rather than grace and goodness, there are regrettable but readily available elements in all our sacred scriptures, the Hebrew Bible, the New Testament, and the Qur'an, to inflame and reinforce such dastardly deeds as those of which sick and evil folk are capable.

I have attempted, in this chapter, to wade into the lion's den and address those reprehensible passages in my own sacred tradition, tease them out into the open where they can be seen in their historical and literary context, and interpret them so that the truth about them may be viewed clearly. This is crucial so that we may ensure that they are put in their place, so as not to obstruct the main stream of grace and peace in this tradition of faith, and so that they may never be employed by us, consciously or unconsciously, to evoke or justify the abusiveness of which every human individual and culture, as we all know from experience with ourselves, is thoroughly capable of generating all on our own.

Note

Unless otherwise noted, all translations are my own from the original Hebrew.

CHAPTER 6

HUMAN SACRIFICE IN THE OLD TESTAMENT: IN RITUAL AND WARFARE

Simon John De Vries

In the foregoing chapter I addressed a number of passages from the Hebrew Bible, the sacred scripture of Judaism, which present violent narratives. Since the wholesome and the destructive elements in the religious traditions of Islam, Christianity, and contemporary Judaism derive to some degree from the Hebrew Bible and its narratives of ancient Israelite religion, it is important that we understand these roots of our modern ideas and values.

Some violent narratives in sacred scripture are not problematic because they present a context in which God's abhorrence of such abusive behavior is clearly expressed. Other violent passages are very problematic because they describe horrific human behavior and make no ethical judgment, human or divine, about it. Such a text is the story in Judges 19 of the man who allowed the rape and horrible murder of his concubine, to ensure his own safety. Neither he nor the rapist gang is judged or disciplined in the story. Such passages in our sacred scriptures must be faced head-on, so to speak, in an effort to see them in their historical and literary context and understand their function as part of the ancient believing community's report on how they saw God in their history.

In this chapter I wish to give my attention to even more terrifying and more potentially toxic sacred texts. I wish to address the issues at stake in those scriptures that confront us with scenes of human sacrifice, many of them perceived by the narrator of the story to have been overtly commanded by God. How are we to understand these reports? How can we tolerate them in our sacred books? How can they be part of the mainstream of our faith tradition? Are they accidental and peripheral legends, erroneously collected into these ancient books; are they somehow existential descriptions of the worst humans can imagine; or are they to be taken as instructive in some way, forthrightly or conversely?

The passages I will attend to here are of two types: those that are narratives of ritual human sacrifice and those that are stories of the monstrous massacres of warfare. The former usually have to do with the sacrifice of one or more individual persons in an act of worship of, or obedience to, some god, sometimes even Yahweh, the God of Israel. The latter deal with the sacrifice of hosts of people, sometimes entire communities or nations, combatants and noncombatants, militants and unarmed civilians, in what the perpetrators were sure were divinely required acts of war.

It is difficult in our time to imagine such a concept of God, but it does not seem far removed from us when we realize the religious motivation apparently driving a great deal of the mayhem and terrorism that is afflicting our immediate moment in history. Therefore, it is imperative that we look at the inner dynamics of these passages from our sacred scriptures and discern wisely how we must handle the destructive power that some of these religious narratives and metaphors can have in our lives and cultures.

Exposition

Ritual Human Sacrifice

Biblical Texts

Then Abraham put forth his hand and took the knife to slay his son. But the angel of Yahweh called to him from heaven and said, "Abraham, Abraham!" And he said, "Here am I." He said, "Do not lay your hand on the lad or do anything to him; for now I know that you fear God, seeing you have not withheld your son, your only son, from me." And Abraham lifted up his eyes and looked, and behold, behind him was a ram, caught in a thicket by its horns; and Abraham went and took the ram, and offered it up as a burnt offering instead of his son. (Gen. 22:10–13)

The firstborn of your sons you shall give to me ... Every [human] firstborn among your sons you shall redeem. (Exod. 22:29b [Heb. 22:28b], Exod. 13:13b, Exod. 34:20b)

And Jephthah made a vow to Yahweh and said, "If you will give the Ammonites into my hand, then whoever comes forth from the doors of my house to meet me when I return victorious from the Ammonites, shall be Yahweh's, and I will offer him up for a burnt offering." . . . Then Jephthah came to his home at Mizpah, and behold, his daughter came out to meet him with timbrels and with dances. She was his only child; beside her he had neither son nor daughter. And when he saw her, he rent his clothes and said, "Alas, my daughter! you have brought me very low and have become the cause of great trouble to me, for I have opened my mouth to Yahweh and I cannot take back my vow." . . . And she said to her father, "Let this thing be done for me: let me alone two months, that I may go away and come down upon the mountains, bewailing my virginity, I and my companions." And he said, "Go." And he sent her away for two months; so she departed, she and her companions, and bewailed her virginity upon the mountains. And at the end of two months, she returned to her father, who did with her according to his vow that he had made. She had never known a man. (Judg. 11:30–31, 34–35, 37–39)

When the king of Moab saw that the battle was going against him, he took with him seven hundred swordsmen to break through, opposite the king of Edom; but they could not. Then he took his eldest son, who was to reign in his stead, and offered him for a burnt offering upon the wall. And there came great wrath upon Israel; and they withdrew from him and returned to their own land. (2 Kings 3:26–27)

Ahaz was twenty years old when he began to reign . . . and he did not do what was right in the eyes of Yahweh his god, as his father David had done, but he walked in the way of the kings of Israel. He even burned his son as an offering, according to the abominable practices of the nations. (2 Kings 16:2–3a)

With what shall I come before Yahweh,
   or bow myself before God on high?
Shall I come before him with burnt offerings,
   with calves a year old?
Will Yahweh be pleased with thousands of rams,
   with ten thousands of rivers of oil?
Shall I give my first-born for my transgression,
   the fruit of my body for the sin of my soul?
He has showed you, O man, what is good;
   and what does Yahweh require of you
but to do righteousness and love faithfulness
   and walk humbly with your god? (Mic. 6:6–8, RSV)

Etching by Rembrandt Harenszoon van Rijn, *Abraham Caressing Isaac*, 1638. Library of Congress.

Exegesis

The famous story of Abraham sacrificing Isaac is a *hieros logos* or cult legend, for the ordination of animal sacrifice in the place of human sacrifice. Abraham does not in fact sacrifice his son, but is stopped in the act of sacrificing him. The knife is poised, but the angel of the Lord stops him and immediately a substitute is found, a ram caught in a thicket. This passage has been ascribed to the Pentateuchal work of the Elohist, or E, and is not found in the parallel strand, J. Within the E narrative as a whole, the episode has the function of confirming Abraham as one who truly stands in awe of God (v. 12b). Far from representing Abraham as a practitioner of child sacrifice, it depicts him as one who acts in absolute obedience to

God and not out of his own desire or preference. The lad is entirely complaisant, voicing the question about a sacrificial lamb (v. 7), which elicits Abraham's trustful reply that God would provide it (v. 8).

The only other speech is placed in the mouth of Yahweh's angel, commanding Abraham to desist from killing the boy, and explaining that his willingness to go through with the sacrifice has proven his true devotion to God (vv. 11–12). Abraham sacrificed the ram caught in a thicket in the place of his son. A naming aetiology for the shrine-site (place) where this happens ends the account (v. 14), but the identity of such a site remains uncertain in spite of the notation in verse 2 that Abraham was to go to the land of Moriah and make this sacrifice "upon one of the mountains of which I shall tell you." Although 2 Chronicles 3:1 equates the temple site in Jerusalem with Moriah, there is no early evidence to confirm this and the statement may be meant as typological rather than literal.

These cited partial verses from scattered law codes in Exodus pertain to the legitimacy or nonlegitimacy of human sacrifice within early Israel. The fact that these are almost buried in surrounding cult-legislative materials, and that the second and third conflict with the first, suggests that at one time this was controversial but eventually became unimportant because a proper substitute had gained acceptance. The basic rule was that the victim chosen for sacrifice, supposedly either animal or human, must be a choice object, an especially high-quality entity, hence in Exodus 22:29, where child sacrifice is demanded, it must be an unblemished male and it must be the firstborn that is offered. This single biblical statement approving human sacrifice survives in spite of the complete revulsion that eventually drove it into obscurity. It may at one time have been promulgated in the name of Yahweh, but far more likely, it was pre-Yahwistic groups who practiced it. The ordinance that provided for a substitute sacrifice indicated that firstborn human males could be ransomed by the substitution of a suitable animal sacrifice.

It is possible to conceive of the story of Jephthah's sacrifice of his daughter as a product of pre-Yahwistic Israel in spite of the fact that it does present Yahweh as Jephthah's god. Chapter 11 of Judges contains saga materials of various kinds from Transjordan, only imperfectly integrated and normalized into the dominant Cisjordanian, that is, later Israelite tradition. Jephthah is identified as a mighty warrior from Mizpah in Gilead. He attributes all his victories to Yahweh, the god of Israel (Judg. 11:21, 23–24). When the Ammonites refuse to make peace with him, he makes a powerful vow, powerful because extreme, in order to get Yahweh's backing for an attack. It has the effect of a wager, and this alone explains why he is so reckless in his bargain. It has the conditional form, "If you will give the Ammonites into my hand, then . . . I will offer. . . ."

What Jephthah asks of Yahweh is so unreasonable and extreme that he dares offer something out of the ordinary on his side of the wager, something that he certainly does not expect to have to fulfill and beyond all that is reasonable, a sacrifice, a human sacrifice, the sacrifice of the first suitable victim to greet him at the moment of his triumphant return home. It is not expressly stated that the victim has to be human, but Jephthah's wording leaves this as a possibility. The tale is full of irony, for the first living being to greet him as he returns home from his victorious campaign is his daughter, his only child, a virgin in her purity.

Jephthah's first word is that her greeting causes him great sorrow and trouble, for she must now bear the consequences of his reckless vow. The young woman agrees that he must keep his vow, and after spending two months wandering among the mountains with her companion virgins, she returns to her father to be dealt with according to his vow. Driving home the point about her innocence in contrast to his willful folly, the narrator adds, "which he had made." Pious commentators have sometimes avoided the difficulty of explaining why it should be necessary and right to fulfill such a vow by suggesting that the conclusion leaves open the possibility that Jephthah may have found an adequate alternative to actually burning the girl as a whole offering to Yahweh. To sacrifice her in this awful way was literally what he promised in verse 31. Commentators, hoping to soften the import of this text, have suggested that an alternative might have been simply consigning her to a monastic life among a primitive group of nunlike recluses, her fellow virgins. This clever alternative may explain why a notation about the daughters of Israel going each year on a pilgrimage to her shrine is added as a conclusion. Its weakness is that it remains conjectural.

The second passage cited above, 2 Kings 3:5b–25, is an exceptionally sophisticated prophet legend that features the prediction with two separate elements, the second of which comes to fulfillment through the fulfillment of the first. The armies of Judah, Israel, and Edom have moved together to the eastern desert to attack Moab but are out of water and are about to die of thirst. When Elisha is summoned, he predicts two things, (1) a vast amount of water at early morning and (2) victory over Moab caused by this water. At dawn, this water mysteriously comes in sufficient quantity to fill the land, and when the Moabites see the red dawn reflected in it, they imagine that it is a vast pool of blood caused by the death of a great many warriors. When they rise up from their positions to finish off the survivors, they expose themselves to a counterattack from the allied armies, as a result of which they are slaughtered, their capital is destroyed, and their land is plundered.

A redactor, an editor, was however not satisfied with this formulation and adds retroactive details of the fighting and then indicates that because the king of Moab sacrificed his eldest son, a mysterious "great wrath" comes upon "Israel," causing them to return home. A conclusion from this analysis is that the reference to the human sacrifice is not an integral element of the prophet legend but was inserted by a later Israelite editor. His motive for inserting this additional element, including the child sacrifice by the king of Israel's enemies, is very difficult to discern. Was he saying that it was a great wrath from God that sent the Israelites home, because God was enraged that they had driven this campaign so far as to have caused the Moabite king to kill his only begotten son? That would be interesting in every way. Or was the editor motivated to claim that the Israelite army was sickened by this wanton ritual act by the king of Moab and so they went home; or that they were enraged by the king's reverting to the old-fashioned and primitive ritual of child sacrifice in order to persuade the gods to undo Israel, so they considered that the king was not playing fair in invoking this unusual manipulation of the gods, and out of fear that he now had the upper hand they went home in a rage? Probably the latter. Why else would they have preserved this in their sacred traditions about how God is in their history?

The famous words of Micah 6:6–8 are almost certainly from the prophet himself. This passage is lyrical in style and takes the form of a catechism, or prophet torah (teaching). The speaker represents himself as one who intends to present himself before Yahweh in his temple (cf. Pss. 15 and 24). Verses 6 and 7 display his rising anxiety in a series of rhetorical questions leading to a definitive answer in verse 8: "Shall I bring burnt offerings, year-old calves, thousands of rams, ten thousand rivers of oil—is that what Yahweh wants? How about my firstborn, fruit of my body?" The answer is something that has long been known among human beings, namely, that Yahweh requires justice, personal devotedness and a humble walk with God. Micah's words are the ultimate conclusion in Israelite religion and history that seals the truth that God is against child sacrifice, indeed, desires devotion and not sacrifice. God is for kindness and mercy.

Ideology

In 2 Kings 3:5–25 Elisha is not the main character, as he is in the other Elisha legends, but seems to appear casually from some mysterious place in the desert as a roving ecstatic capable of strange predictions (v. 15). The most important thing to realize is that it is not the original storyteller, but the early redactor, who brings in the human sacrifice, and he mentions this only as the Moabite king's final resort, after having failed with a phalanx of seven hundred swordsmen to break the allied lines. This redactor is chiefly interested in the idea that the Moabite king is willing to make so extreme a sacrifice as a final appeal to Deity in order to bring sufficient divine wrath upon Israel, to drive them back to their own land.

Whether this event actually happened, and whether it represents the Moabites' actual ideology, or is just the fancy of the storyteller, is impossible to say. The least that needs to be said is that the storyteller must have witnessed it or heard about it as something that actually happened in his time. Certainly for him it was something so horrible that it seemed destined to bring divine wrath as Moab's ultimate defense against the allied attack.

The Deuteronomistic redactor (after 586) is probably well informed in his accusation of child sacrifice against king Ahaz of Judah, the southern kingdom, in 2 Kings 16:3. In 2 Kings 17:17 he claims that the northerners, from the kingdom of Israel, burned their sons and their daughters as sacrificial offerings, but there is some question about the possible bias against the northerners on the part of this editor. Whatever the explanation for this may be, it is clear that child sacrifice did flourish, at least underground, at certain times in Judah, very probably under the influence of their two nearest neighbors, Ammon and Moab.

Leviticus 20:2–5, 2 Kings 23:10, and Jeremiah 32:35 condemn the practice of causing sons and daughters to "pass through the fire" in honor of Milcom (Melek, "King"). Milcom, Melek, or Molek, was the god of the neighboring Ammonites, originally introduced into Judah/Jerusalem at the time of Solomon. 1 Kings 11:4–7 tells that Solomon went so far as to build shrines for Ashtaroth of the Sidonians, Milcom of the Ammonites, and Chemosh of the Moabites, as accommodation to his numerous foreign wives. This fact the author of the Books of the Chronicles of the Kings of Israel, a pro-

Davidic line propagandizer, conveniently chooses to ignore when he tells the story of his hero Solomon.

It is speculative to try to relate the Jephthah and Abraham stories to this pattern, yet it is interesting that Jephthah was from Transjordania, which might make his resort to child sacrifice more understandable. The unmistakable polemic against child sacrifice in the Abraham story, on the contrary, may become more meaningful if it is correct, as many have claimed, that the E (Elohist) document arose within the northern kingdom, whose kings, bad as some of them were, are not accused, except in a dubious accusation found in 2 Kings 17, of this most dreadful of crimes, sacrificing children.

Authority

In primitive societies there was a pervasive dread of the supernatural, which could lead, under the direction of priests, to the offering of animal sacrifices as appeasement. When societies became militarily strong, and in societies where human captives were eaten, such captives could readily be forced to serve as sacrificial victims, as well. Where cannibalism was no longer tolerated, it could happen that worshipers might offer their own children, and by preference even their sons. The choicest form of child sacrifice would be the sacrifice of a king's own eldest son and putative successor.

Without surveying the whole range of practices in ancient and contemporary cultures that reflect this practice, it may be noted that there is scarcely a trace of tradition about human sacrifice within the Old Testament. When Micah does raise the question of the acceptability of sacrificing one's own son as a last resort for expiating sin, it is clear that for him at least this is no more than a rhetorical consideration. What he intends to say is that salvation from sin does not ask anything so extreme or self-serving. It requires only the universal moral and spiritual requirement that God lays on every human: to be fair, equitable, and honest; faithful; and humble toward God.

Fighting and Warfare

Biblical Texts

Then came Amalek and fought with Israel at Rephidim. And Moses said to Joshua, "Choose for us men and go out and fight with Amalek. Tomorrow I will stand on the top of the hill with the rod of God in my hand." So Joshua did as Moses told him and fought with Amalek. And Moses, Aaron and Hur went up to the top of the hill. Whenever Moses held up his hand, Israel prevailed, and whenever he lowered his hand,

Amalek prevailed. But Moses' hands grew weary, so they took a stone, put it under him, and he sat upon it, while Aaron and Hur held up his hands . . . so that his hands were steady until the going down of the sun. And Joshua mowed down Amalek and his people with the edge of the sword. (Exod. 17:8–13)

Joshua's army besieges Jericho. Joshua follows Yahweh's instructions for a ceremonial march around the city. Seven priests blow on seven trumpets while armed men and the ark march around the city, doing this seven times on the seventh day. The walls fall down, the people attack, and the city is taken. "Then they utterly destroyed all in the city, both men and women, young and old, oxen, sheep, and asses, with the edge of the sword." saving only Rahab and her family and kindred. But the people of Israel broke faith in regard to the devoted things, for Achan the son of Carmi, son of Zabdi, son of Zerah, of the tribe of Judah, took some of the devoted things, and the anger of Yahweh burned against the people of Israel . . . And Joshua and all Israel with him took Achan the son of Zerah, and the silver and the mantle and the bar of gold, and his sons and daughters, and his oxen and asses and sheep, and his tent, and all that he had, and they brought them up to the valley of Achor. And Joshua said, "Why did you bring trouble on us? Yahweh brings trouble on you today." And all Israel . . . burned them with fire and stoned them with stones. And they raised over him a great heap of stones that remains to this day. Then Yahweh turned from his burning anger. (Josh. 6:1–16, 20–16, 7:1, 24–26a)

Ehud made for himself a sword with two edges, a cubit in length, and he girded it on his right thigh under his clothes. And he presented the tribute to Eglon . . . a very fat man. . . . He . . . turned back . . . and said, "I have a secret message for you, O king." And he commanded "Silence!" and all his attendants went out from his presence. And Ehud came to him as he was sitting alone in his cool roof chamber, and Ehud said, "I have a message from God to you," and he [Eglon] arose from his seat. Then Ehud reached with his left hand, took the sword from his right thigh, and thrust it into his belly, so that the hilt went in after the blade and fat closed over the blade, for he did not draw the sword out of his belly; and the guts oozed out. Then Ehud went out into the vestibule and closed the doors of the roof chamber upon him and locked them. When he was gone, the servants came, and when they saw that the doors of the roof chamber were locked, they thought, "He is only relieving himself in the restroom of the cool chamber." So they waited till they were utterly at a loss; but when he still did not open the doors of the roof chamber, they took the key and opened them, and there lay their lord dead on the floor. (Judg. 3:16–25)

[Deborah] sent and summoned Barak the son of Abinoam from Kedesh in Naphtali and said to him, "Yahweh god of Israel commands you, 'Go, gather your men at Mount Tabor . . . and I will draw out Sisera, the general of Jabin's army, to meet you by the river Kishon with his chariots and his troops, and I will give him into your hand'." . . . Then Deborah arose and went with Barak to Kedesh and Barak summoned Zebulun and Naphtali to Kedesh; and ten thousand men went up at his heels, and Deborah went up with him. . . . Sisera called out all his chariots, nine hundred chariots of iron, and all the men who were with him, from Harosheth Hagoiim to the river Kishon. Then Deborah said to Barak, "Up! For this is the day in which Yahweh gives Sisera into your hand. Does not Yahweh go with you?" So Barak went down from Mount Tabor with ten thousand men following him. And Yahweh routed Sisera, all his chariots, and his entire army before Barak. . . . But Sisera fled away on foot to the tent of Jael, the wife of Heber the Kenite. . . . Jael the wife of Heber took a tent peg and, taking a mallet in her hand, went softly to him [Sisera] and drove the peg into his temple, till it went down into the ground as he was lying fast asleep from weariness. So he died, and behold, as Barak pursued Sisera, Jael went out to meet him and said to him, "Come and I will show you the man whom you are seeking." So he went into her tent, and there lay Sisera dead with the tent peg in his temple. (Judg. 4:6–7, 9b–10, 13–15a, 17a, 21–22)

Samson went and caught three hundred foxes and took torches and turned them tail to tail so as to put a torch between each pair of tails. And when he had set fire to the torches he let the foxes go into the standing grain of the Philistines, and so burned up the shocks and the standing grain along with the olive orchards. Then the Philistines said, "Who has done this?" And they said, "Samson, kinsman of the Timnite, because he has taken his wife and given her to his companion." Then the Philistines came up and burned her and her father with fire. And Samson said to them, "If this is what you do, I swear I will be avenged upon you, and after that I will quit." And he smote them hip and thigh with great slaughter. (Judg. 15:4–8a)

David was the son of an Ephrathite from Bethlehem in Judah named Jesse, who had eight sons. . . . David was the youngest; the eldest three followed Saul . . . And Jesse said to David his son, "Take for your brothers an ephah of this parched grain and these ten loaves and carry them quickly to the camp for your brothers. . . . See how your brothers fare and bring some token from them." . . . Then David rose early in the morning, left the sheep with a keeper, took the provisions, and went as Jesse had commanded him. And he came to the encampment as the host was going forth to the battle line, shouting the war cry. And Israel and the Philistines drew up for battle, army against army. Then David left the things in charge of the keeper of the baggage, ran to the ranks, and went to greet his brothers. While he was talking with him, behold, a champion . . . came up from the ranks of the Philistines. . . . All the men of Israel, when they saw the man, fled from him and were much afraid. Then the men of Israel said, "Have you seen the man who has come up? Surely he has come up to defy Israel; and the man who kills him the king will enrich with great riches, and will give him his daughter, and will make his father's house free in Israel." . . . Then the Philistine came on and approached David with his shield-bearer in front of him. . . . David ran quickly toward the battle line to meet the Philistine, . . . and David defeated the Philistine by striking him with sling and stone, killing him. There was no sword in his hand. . . . When Saul saw David go forth against the Philistine, he said to Abner the commander of the army, "Abner, whose son is this youth?" Abner said, "As you live, O king, I cannot tell." And the king said, "Inquire whose son the stripling is." So as David was returning from the slaughter of the Philistine, Abner took him and brought him before Saul with the head of the Philistine in his hand. And Saul said to him, "Whose son are you, young man?" And David answered, "I am the son of your servant Jesse, the Bethlehemite." And Saul took him that day and would not allow him to return to his father's house. (selected verses from 1 Sam. 17:12–18:2)

Now the Philistines fought against Israel and the men of Israel fled before the Philistines and fell slain on Mount Gilboa. And the Philistines overtook Saul and his sons. And the Philistines slew Jonathan and Abinadab and Malchishua, the sons of Saul. The battle pressed hard upon Saul and the archers found him, and he was badly wounded by the archers. Then Saul said to his armor-bearer, "Draw your sword and thrust me through with it, lest these uncircumcised come and thrust me through and make sport of me." But his armor-bearer would not, for he feared greatly, therefore Saul took his own sword and fell upon it. And when his armor-bearer saw that Saul was dead, he also fell upon his sword and died with him. . . . On the morrow, when the Philistines came to strip the dead, they found Saul and his three sons fallen on Mount Gilboa. And they cut off his head. . . . They put his armor in the temple of Ashtaroth and fastened his body to the wall of Beth-shan. But when the inhabitants of Jabesh-Gilead heard what the Philistines had done to Saul, all the valiant men arose and went all night and took the body of Saul and the bodies of his sons from the wall of Beth-shan, and they came to Jabesh and burnt them there. Then they took their bones and buried them under the tamerisk tree in Jabesh and fasted seven days." (1 Sam. 31:1–9a, 10–13)

So the army [of Judah] went out into the field against Israel; and the battle was fought in the forest of Ephraim. And the men of Israel were defeated there by the servants of David and the slaughter there was great on that day, twenty thousand men. The battle spread over the face of all the country; and the forest devoured more people that day than the sword. . . . And Absalom chanced to meet the servants of David. Absalom was riding upon his mule, and the mule went under the thick branches of a great oak, and his head caught fast in the oak and he was left hanging between heaven and earth when the mule that was under him went on. . . . Joab . . . took three darts in his hand and thrust them into the heart of Absalom while he was still alive in the oak, and ten young men, Joab's armor-bearers, surrounded Absalom and struck him and killed him. (2 Sam. 18:6–9, 14b–15)

The king of Israel disguised himself and went into battle . . . and when the captains of the chariots saw Jehoshaphat (the king of Judah) they said, "Surely it is the king of Israel." So they turned to fight against him; and Jehoshaphat cried out. And when the captains of the chariots saw that it was not the king of Israel, they turned back from pursuing him. But a certain man drew his bow at a venture and struck the king of Israel between the scale armor and the breastplate; therefore he said to the driver of his chariot, "Turn about, and carry me out of the battle, for I am wounded." And the battle grew hot that day, and the king was propped up in his chariot facing the Syrians until at evening he died, and the blood of the wound flowed into the bottom of the chariot. So the king died. . . . And they washed the chariot by the pool of Samaria, and the dogs licked up his blood, and the harlots washed themselves in it. (1 Kings 22:31–38)

When Jehu came to Jezreel, Jezebel heard of it; and she painted her eyes and adorned her head, and looked out the window. And as Jehu entered the gate she said, "Is it peace, you Zimri, murderer of your master?" And he lifted up his face to the window and said, "Who is on my side? Who?" Two or three eunuchs looked out at him. He said, "Throw her down," so they threw her down; and some of her blood spattered on the wall and on the horses, and they trampled on her. Then he went in and ate and drank; and he said, "See now to this cursed woman and bury her, for she is a king's daughter." But when they went to bury her they found no more of her than the skull and the feet and the palms of her hands. When they came back and told him, he said "This is the word of the Lord, 'In . . . Jezreel the dogs shall eat the flesh of Jezebel; and the corpse of Jezebel shall be as dung upon the face of the field . . . so that no one can say, "This is Jezebel" ' ." (2 Kings 9:30–35)

They shall beat their swords into plowshares
and their spears into pruning hooks;
Nation shall not lift up sword against nation,
neither shall they learn war anymore. (Isa. 2:4, Mic. 4:3, RSV)

On that day, when my people Israel are dwelling securely, you [Gog]
will bestir yourself and come from your place out of the uttermost parts
of the north. . . . You will come up against my people Israel like a cloud
covering the land. In the latter days I will bring you against my land,
that the nations may know me when through you, O Gog, I vindicate
my holiness before their eyes. . . . On that day there shall be a great
shaking in the land of Israel. I will summon every kind of terror against
Gog, says the Lord God, every man's sword against his brother. With
pestilence and bloodshed I will enter in judgment with him. . . . So I
will show my greatness and my holiness and make myself known in the
eyes of many nations, and they will know that I am Yahweh. (Ezek.
38:14–15a, 16, 19–23)

Prepare war,
　stir up the mighty men;
Let all the men of war draw near,
　let them come up.
Beat your plowshares into swords
　and your pruning hooks into spears,
Let the weak say, "I am a warrior." (Joel 3:9–10)

Zerah the Cushite came out against them (Israelites) with an army of a
million men and three hundred chariots and came as far as Mareshah,
and Asa went out to meet him. And they drew up their lines of battle
in the valley of Zephathah at Mareshah. Then Asa cried to Yahweh his
god, "O Yahweh, there is none like thee to help, between the mighty
and the weak. Help us, O Yahweh our god, for we rely on you, and in
your name we have come against this multitude. O Yahweh, you are our
God; let not man prevail against thee." So Yahweh defeated the
Cushites before Asa and before Judah, and the Cushites fled. Asa and
the people that were with him pursued them as far as Gerar, and the
Cushites fell until none remained alive. (2 Chron. 14:9–15 [Heb.
10–14])

Exegesis

Large books have been written about warfare in the Old Testament.
The passages reproduced here represent a judicious selection out of
the many examples that could have been chosen, ranging from primitive legend to apocalyptic. An account of actual fighting is rare in the
Pentateuch. The hero legend of Exodus 17:8–13, in which Moses is

credited with miraculous power to influence the course and outcome of battle against Amalek, seems to semideify him, with helpers to hold up his hands and a lieutenant to take care of the fighting. The narrative is sketchy and highly schematic. All four named figures, Moses, Aaron, Hur, and Joshua, are eponymous.

The books of Joshua and Judges, on the contrary, are largely occupied with tales of fighting and warfare, but some of them have to be judged as unhistorical on the basis of their highly ideological structure. Such an account is that of the conquest of Jericho in Joshua 6, which is notably schematic and artificial. A daily march around the city, climaxing in a sevenfold march on the seventh day, results in the collapse of the wall, the seizing of the city and the taking of booty.

However, there is a structural problem in the text with the mention, in verses 17, 18, and 21, of the devoted things, the sacral booty consecrated to God. In the first place, verses 17–19 destroy the literary connection between Joshua's command to raise the battle cry at the end of the seventh circuit of the city (v. 16) and the narrative of its immediate effect in verse 20. These intrusive verses are, moreover, cast in the form of an instruction that specifies that the city and its contents shall be dedicated as a sacrifice to Yahweh, leaving only Rahab and her household safe (17). This command also forbids the coveting of booty of any kind from whatever is devoted to God (18), and requires that any stocks of precious metals or metal vessels shall be held as sacred to Yahweh and be stored in Yahweh's treasury, wherever that was supposed to be. Verse 24 adds that these goods are to be stored in the temple of Yahweh, which, of course, did not exist for another 350 years or so.

Without these added items, the original narrative continues with the statement that they utterly destroyed all in the city with the edge of the sword, identifying what is meant by all in rhythmic pairs, men and women, young and old. Oxen, sheep and asses may be intrusive both here and in 7:24. Connecting back to chapter 2, which tells about Rahab and the spies, the original account concludes with a statement that Rahab was spared (vv. 22–23). In its received form the passage also incorporates incongruous verses at the end (vv. 25–26).

Another intrusive element may be the following story of Achan. If it were not for its direct juxtaposition with chapter 6 and the incorporation of the Ai narrative in verses 2–10, the original narrative of chapter 7 could have had almost any other literary setting than the one it has. Joshua is of course brought in from chapter 6, and a summarizing introduction at 7:1 states the two major matters of this new account: (1) the people of Israel have done wrong with regard to the devoted things, causing the anger of Yahweh to burn against them, and (2) Achan is found to be the culprit.

The main body of the narrative continues with a speech of Yahweh to Joshua accusing Israel of transgressing the covenant by hiding goods from the devoted things and keeping them for themselves (vv. 11–15). Then follows the narrative of Achan's identification and his confession of guilt (16–21), the uncovering of Achan's hoard (22–23), the confiscation of the stolen goods (24), the death sentence and its execution (25), and the raising up of a memorial (26). The concluding naming aetiology, "Therefore to this day the name of that place is called the valley of Achor," suggests that the entire Achan narrative may have been imaginatively conceived as an explication of the place-name Achor, even though a genealogy for Achan in 1 Chronicles 2:7 both mentions his sin and identifies him as a descendant of Judah through Perez and Carmi (omitting Zabdi), thus suggesting historicity for both Achan and the narrative about him.

In Judges 3 we encounter a gripping, bloody-minded anecdote that has been expanded into a battle account. This anecdote is full of the kind of architectural, anatomical, and geographical minutiae that cause vexation for lexicographers but guarantee originality. The people of Israel have been paying tribute to Eglon king of Moab for eighteen years. A Benjamite named Ehud is identified in the opening rubric in verse 15a as an anointed one and deliverer, and is described as having been deputed to bring the tribute money. This is typically received with great ceremony. On his way home, he turns back at a resting-place near Gilgal named The Sculptured Stones and returns to Eglon under the pretext of delivering a private message to him.

Contriving to approach the curious Eglon alone in his chamber, and while holding out his right hand in a gesture of peace, he uses his left hand to draw out the sword strapped on his right thigh and drives it deeply into Eglon's fat belly. He then goes out unobserved and escapes, after passing The Sculptured Stones and a place named Seirah, to the hill country of Ephraim. There he summons the people of Israel and leads them in seizing the fords of the Jordan and in killing a large number of Moabites. The text says 10,000, but battle reports almost always state huge, rounded-off numbers like this. Except for the casualty report, this narrative is entirely believable because of its clear logical development and appropriate details. Told with great enthusiasm where Hebrew warriors would have been gathered, it preserves an essentially reliable account of the kind of fighting that soldiers of all times and nations enjoy telling about.

Judges 4:6–15 is the first traditionally styled holy-war story that we encounter in the Old Testament. Interestingly, it is structured to include a complete and self-contained hero saga. Typical holy-war stories are more than just battle accounts because charismatic individuals are usually introduced in them at the crucial moment of summoning troops and issuing orders. This happens, for instance, in 1 Samuel 11:5, where another Benjamite, Saul, hears of the predicament of his kinsmen in Jabesh-Gilead and issues to all the tribes a summons to battle by cutting up the oxen with which he has been plowing and sending pieces of the flesh to each of them. Notice the similar act on the part of the Levite in Judges 19 who sends pieces of his concubine to each tribe of Israel to summon them to war against the abusive Benjamites.

In Judges 4, once the predicament of the people has been described, the narrator identifies a prophetess named Deborah, who summons the man Barak with ten thousand soldiers to prepare to meet the formidable army of a Canaanite king, whose general is Sisera. Barak and Deborah go together to the summit of Mount Tabor, from where they are able to observe Sisera's movements. When Sisera's army has been drawn up at the Kishon river, Deborah says to Barak (v. 14), "Up, for this is the day in which Yahweh has given Sisera into your hand. Does not Yahweh go out before you?" Barak rushes down with his ten thousand and routs both Sisera's chariotry and his infantry. Then Barak chases them out of the country, while, as the redactor adds, Sisera himself flees on foot and evidently in a different direction.

In contrast to the standard battle report as found in Judges 3, this is the way most early holy-war narratives end: with the dispersal of the attacking army rather than with the extermination of the enemy forces. The Deborah-Barak story is directly continued in that about Jael (vv. 11, 17–22). Here the narrator, possibly a woman, tells a heroic (or ethnic) saga about another heroic woman to go with Deborah. We have her name, but the mention of her husband's name and ethnic identity (the Kenites again!) shows that the story may first have been told among the Kenite people as an example of how they have stood, and still stand, ready to do the Israelites a favor. Much of the keen interest in bloody details seen in the Ehud anecdote is here as well: the deceptive friendliness, the sudden, surprising, and effective blow, the victorious outcome. There is now nothing supernatural, just the courage, deception, and resoluteness of a woman, with a mallet and a tent-pin in her hands, who is not afraid of blood.

The Samson story is full of fantasy but at the same time down-to-earth. Here again the problem is to decide whether the story is just about a man, or about the clan within the tribe of Dan from which he came. The form of the name Samson, from the same stem as the word for sun, seems to suggest that this heroic character may be somehow associated with sun worship. This might complicate the problem of viewing him as an authentic Israelite, were it not for the observation that similarly named heroes, such as Gideon and Solomon are good Hebrews and model Israelites. Like Till Eulenspiegel, Samson is a man endowed with an excess of mischievousness to go with his awesome strength. Those who read the anecdotes about him enjoy his exploits equally as much as he did who first told about them. It seems truly a marvel that these tales have been preserved more or less intact in a book that has been supposed by many to be straitlaced and somber.

In my article "David's Victory over the Philistine as Saga and as Legend" (JBL 92, 1973), I offer an extensive literary analysis of 1 Samuel 17:12–18:5. The result is the reconstruction of an early heroic/ethnic saga from a context that includes also a hero legend. Most of the biblical text belonging to the saga has been reproduced in the citation above. One observes that all the details about Goliath's armor, Saul's preparation of David, Saul's offer of his own armor, the stereotyped brags of the champions as they face each other, David's weapons and his use of them, and the flight of the Philistines before the victorious Israelites, belong to the hero legend and are on a conceptual level similar to that of the tale of Ehud, expanded into a full battle report.

The saga is much simpler in concept but David is equally as heroic. He is not even supposed to be in or near the battle. By chance or by design, the Philistine champion comes directly toward where he happens to be standing in the battle line. David reacts with the only weapon he knows: his sling. But he is deadly accurate and his first stone kills his attacker. Saul views this with amazement, but not knowing who David is, orders Abner to summon him. When the lad tells his name and family, Saul refuses to allow him to return to his father in Bethlehem, but takes him with honor into his own family by way of marriage, and installs him as chief of his army.

Although this tale is integral to the history of David's rise to power, its essential and original concern is to tell how, and why, a

Engraving of David holding the head of Goliath by Lucas van Leyden, 1517. Library of Congress.

rude Judahite/Bethlehemite shepherd-lad gained status within the then dominant tribe of Benjamin. Nowhere but among those who could sling a stone at a hair and not miss (Judg. 20:16) could David's exploit with a sling be held in such high admiration!

1 Samuel 31, which I have substantially reproduced here, has the form and ideology of another heroic/ethnic saga, in which a Transjordanian branch of the Benjamites centered at Jabesh-Gilead, sal-

vaged their champion Saul's honor at the time of his tragic death on Mount Gilboa. Far from casting opprobrium on Saul for taking his own life, this saga intends to applaud him for daring to fall on his sword in order to save himself from torture and disfigurement at the hands of the Philistines.

The text that I have drawn from 2 Samuel 18 is realistic and has a high probability of being historically accurate, which is not to say that it does not have a personal point of view. It tells of a very important battle in biblical history, one that is crucial to the role of David both in his own time and in later tradition. David draws the rebel army of Absalom into a thick forest. What happens here is very similar to what happened at two battles during the Civil War, within the area west of Fredericksburg, Virginia, known as the Wilderness. Here stronger armies lost their advantage when losing good communication and the ability to coordinate both offensive and defensive actions. The worst effect of Absalom's tactical defeat, according to the author of the throne-succession narrative, is the death of the rebel leader himself. In verses 9–15 an anecdotal report tells precisely how this came about. One of the most realistic actions is Joab's cynical assassination of Absalom as he hangs by his hair in the branches of an overtowering oak.

The battle scenes chosen from the book of Kings are realistic and bloody minded. Others could have been selected, but it is clear from the bitterness and gloating with which their deaths have been described that Ahab and Jezebel were especially despised in Judah. These narratives illustrate the truism that it is always the victors who get to write the history books. Occasionally the Chronicler, whose book was written long after the Hebrew kingdoms had ceased to exist, includes in his account items about historical events that are not included in the preexilic source document that he is following, in this case the so-called Deuteronomistic History running from Judges through 2 Kings.

Almost without fail, the writer of the Chronicles greatly exaggerates and at the same time theologizes such stories. Zerah attacks the kingdom of Judah with a million men but with only three hundred chariots, a ratio of 3,333 to one! Asa prays for help to Yahweh and is immediately answered by Yahweh, who himself defeats the Cushites. Precisely how this is accomplished is not clear. The reader is confused by conflicting details: "Asa and the people" pursue the Cushites, who fall until none remains alive; they are "broken before Yahweh and his army." Further redundant description completes the picture and confuses it. The men of Judah carry off much booty. They smite all the cities in the vicinity of Gerar. They plunder all the cities. They smite the tents of cattle-herders, in order to take possession of abundant sheep and camels.

The Chronicler, living during the fourth century B.C.E., has no clear idea of historical and geographical conditions in the border region during the ninth century. He inserts this confused and fragmentary narrative for the sole purpose of telling how mightily God sometimes answers prayer. Similar grandiose, schematic, and absolutely unhistorical battle accounts may be found in 2 Chronicles 20 and 28.

I have cited some verses from the Gog and Magog apocalypse in Ezekiel to show how battle imagery comes to serve a radically unhistorical image of the future. In 38:14–16 a mythical aggressor comes with many peoples, a great host, a mighty army, like a cloud covering the land, all in order to vindicate Yahweh's holiness before all nations, by the rescue of his people. In verses 19–23 a great earthquake is described, but this is not intended for bringing further dismay upon God's people, but to terrorize Gog and his horde. This example is representative of how the image of fighting and warfare is used in stock metaphors, employed in apocalyptic visions of the world's future (see Zech. 12 and 14, Joel 3, and the Book of Revelation in the New Testament).

Less extreme than the radically nonworldly and nonhistorical imagery of fully developed apocalyptic is the beatific vision of Isaiah 2:1–4 with its parallel passage, Micah 4:1–4. These passages include the well-loved words about turning swords into plowshares. In Joel 3:9–10 this is turned on its head; plowshares become swords. The reason for this disappointing alteration may simply be that Joel's idea of God's future consists entirely of a final reckoning upon enemy nations, rather than for sinners among Israel/Judah/Jerusalem. For him it is purely a matter of just retribution: "What are you to me, O Tyre and Sidon, and all the regions of Philistia? Are you paying me back for something? If you are paying me back, I will requite your deed upon your own head, swiftly and speedily" (vv. 4–5). Seemingly, there will always be a need both for swords and for plowshares, for spears as well as for pruning hooks!

Ideology

Like all people who ever existed on this earth, the people of Yahweh, with their predecessors and their successors, have been unable to avoid armed conflict. When they were not victors they

were likely to be victims. Battle and war passages in the Old
Testament range from the legendary and mythical, to the realistic
and immediate, from the schematic and ideological, to the bizarre and
apocalyptic. The persons who first heard or read these accounts were
not often left in the dark about their morality. They applauded the
exploits of the legendary heroes and, except when they recognized
that it was unavoidable, they deplored tales of blood. They knew that
violence may not be wrong in itself, but must be judged on circumstances and motives.

I have arranged my examples more or less chronologically to show
development in ideology and literary treatment in the Hebrew Bible.
Except in semimythical texts such as the *ex opera operata* story of
Moses' arms being held up to keep the Israelites fighting, the action
in early narratives is likely to be realistic as well as creditable. When
they are in a weak position, the people must avoid armed conflict
except when directly attacked. During the period of the monarchy,
when the Hebrew nations have become relatively strong, they have
few wars except with rebels in their own ranks or with each other.
This begins to change during the imperial age, when larger and
stronger nations constantly threaten their independence. Never again
until the epoch of the Maccabees and the Hasmonean kingdom is
there occasion to celebrate military exploits by Jewish heroes.
Instead, tales of military action become highly schematized or are
cast into an apocalyptic realm in which only God fights.

Thus the essential differences within the Old Testament are that
realistic fighting is described in early documents and imaginary
fighting in late documents. This horizontal trajectory is disturbed,
however, whenever the vertical dimension of sacrality intrudes. The
peoples of the ancient world tended to believe that God or the gods
led them into battle, but sacrality takes hold when the desire to grat-
ify God through the presentation of booty and captives becomes the
main motive of waging war, and not just the effect. Although the
most ancient holy-war stories explicitly draw in an aura of transcendence, they avoid this element of sacrality. That is because the conflicts they depict are defensive, reactive, and largely realistic. It is in
tales or reports of aggressive warfare that the issue of consecrating
the sacral booty intrudes. Sometimes Yahweh commands it, sometimes a person vows it. It may affect both animals and people, both
men and women. It may include material goods as well as living
beings. The Israelites carry it out so systematically within the conquest stories that it becomes a platitude.

The two passages, having an extensive and detailed element of narrative, show themselves to be more interested in the consequences of someone neglecting the sacral dedication of the devoted booty than in the booty itself. These two are the account in Joshua 6–7, including the Achan narrative, and 1 Samuel 15, which is a prophet legend. This latter one has received theologizing expansions that argue against Saul and the Saulides, and in the interests of David's reputation and dynasty. It is understandable that the idea of the sacral booty should eventually become little more than a metaphor in parenthetic texts such Deuteronomy 2:24, 3:6, 7:2, and 20:17, and in apocalyptic texts such as Isaiah 43:28, Malachi 4:5 (Eng. 3:24), and, Zechariah 14:11.

Authority

The Old Testament or Tanach is like other ancient books in the way it addresses the realities of existence within a violent and imperfect world. It is not right to pick and choose what one wishes to take from it. When violence becomes a habit and a policy, or when it is a luxury to be exercised and enjoyed only by the rich and powerful, or when there are no effective rules to regulate and moderate it, it becomes thoroughly demonic. To some extent, that became a trend among the ancient Israelite kingdoms. Old Testament passages that glorify violence, cruelty, and the misuse of power will always be dangerous when they are applied uncritically in contemporary rhetoric.

Conclusion

I have written what I consider to be a critical yet sympathetic analysis of a number of difficult and sometimes terrible passages from the Bible. I hope that I have shown the truth of these most vital texts and their urgent issues. I earnestly hope that the main benefit that will emerge from this study will be a keen awareness of the Bible's relevance for all serious discussions of the demonic factor in religion. Let us start with the Bible and with other ancient religious books, tracing in them improvements over time, deploring their degradations, acknowledging conflicts, and puzzling out their frequently awful conundrums.

Note

Unless otherwise noted, all translations are my own from the original Hebrew.

CHAPTER 7

THE DISARMAMENT OF GOD

Jack Miles

Homo sapiens is a self-domesticating species whose aptitude for domestication is as innate as any other genetic given. Religion, historically, has been a major form of human self-domestication or acculturation, and myth has been universally a key part of religion. To say even this much is to suggest that change in a major human myth may legitimately be considered under the heading of evolutionary adaptation in the part of the human species that is affected by the myth. As David Sloan Wilson writes in *Darwin's Cathedral: Evolution, Religion, and the Nature of Society:*

> people who stand outside of religion often regard its seemingly irrational nature as more interesting and important to explain than its communal nature. Rational thought is treated as the gold standard against which religious belief is found so wanting that it becomes well-nigh inexplicable. Evolution causes us to think about the subject in a completely different way. Adaptation becomes the gold standard against which rational thought must be measured alongside other modes of thought. In a single stroke, rational thought becomes necessary but not sufficient to explain the length and breadth of human mentality, and the so-called irrational features of religion can be studied respectfully as potential adaptations in their own right rather than as idiot relatives of rational thought.[1]

When the Christian revision of Jewish myth is regarded in this way, when it is regarded, namely, as part of "the length and breadth of human mentality" in the process of endless evolution, the revision is problematized in a new way. Rather than ask "Is it true?" or, much less, "Did it happen?" a questioner working within Sloan Wilson's problematic would ask of this revision "How, if at all, was it more adaptive than what preceded it?" or, more loosely, "What was or still is its point?"

The Bible—comprising both Christianity's edition of received Jewish scripture (the Tanakh as edited into the Old Testament) and Christianity's epilogue to scripture (the New Testament as appended to the Old)—has as its point that God has saved mankind from its sins and bestowed upon it the boon of eternal life. To use Milton's never-surpassed summary of the Christian myth, paradise lost has become paradise regained. Did such an event ever occur? Is it true? Rather than ask these questions, we may prefer to ask in what way it might ever be or have been adaptive to tell such a story week after week, year after year, and to assimilate it to the point that it could influence everyday behavior. The terms of the claim, death as punishment and life as reward, are sufficiently close to evolution's extinction and survival to suggest that the underlying concern is identical or at least related. Assuming that much, we find that the questions that come to the fore are: From just what sins does this alleged salvation save? What is the behavior that the myth intends to proscribe and thereby eradicate or repress? What is the (presumptively adaptive) behavior it intends to impose?

The Self-Disarmament of God as Evolutionary Preadaptation

Torah, the opening five books of the Bible, imposes the death penalty for a long list of offenses, but all of these offenses—even those that seem to refer only to relations among human beings—are religious as well as ethical in character. They are understood to constitute infidelity to God if only because God himself has given them this meaning. In imposing his covenant on Israel, God presents the choice between obedience and disobedience to his commandments as, in the most personal way possible, a choice between fidelity and infidelity to himself. To be sure, apostasy, the actual worship of another god is the supreme offense and the one most frequently mentioned, but all other offenses are understood to imply apostasy and therefore to be not just unethical but also irreligious. Every sin is simultaneously the sin in itself and the sin of disloyalty to or betrayal of God.

Putting theological betrayal into anthropological terms, we find that the meaning of the covenant is that any unlawful act is a seditious act to the extent that it undermines national solidarity. When God warns that he will punish the disobedient with death, his threat extends, significantly, not just to sinful individual Israelites but also and even preeminently to Israel as a whole. He has made Israel into a nation, God warns, and he can unmake it at will. Empirically, his statement may be understood to mean that without a tribal law commanding the widest and deepest assent, Israel will not survive attacks by its many enemies.

The context, in other words, is endless war. Although famine, pestilence, and plague are all mentioned, war is clearly the preeminent peril. It is from war, above all, that God saves whomever he saves and through war that he punishes his enemies, domestic or foreign. "Natural" disasters do occur at his behest, but the context is almost always military. One need only recall the "ten plagues" of the Book of Exodus. Enmity between Israel and its neighbors is expressed mythologically as God's bitter resentment of his divine rivals. Accordingly, if peace between God and his rival gods is simply not an option, if he cannot live and let live in the heavenly realm, then Israel must not be more tolerant than he. The alternatives are victory and defeat. Peaceful accommodation short of either extreme is envisioned only rarely and then not as mutual tolerance but only as the voluntary acknowledgment by Israel's neighbors of the supremacy and benevolence of Israel's God—the joyous eschatological vision of Isaiah 56 and kindred passages.

Now, in the conscienceless terms of evolution, war has often been a highly adaptive behavior. Nations that win their wars tend to survive, and those that lose theirs tend to die out. In the wars that European immigrants to the Americas waged with the natives, the natives lost, and many of the native nations are now extinct. The Europeans won, and their proportion of the overall world population through their New World descendants has greatly increased as a result. In the early portions of the Old Testament, the wars of Yahweh are seen as wars of this adaptive sort—wars whose real results are survival and national success in the form of spectacularly successful reproduction.

Yet war is not always an adaptive behavior. There are Pyrrhic victories. There are stalemates that leave both sides ravaged and exhausted. There are wars in which everyone loses. There are military uprisings doomed from the start. How does *Homo sapiens*, the self-domesticating animal, respond to the threat of imminent but lethally maladaptive war? One way may be by creating religious myths—myths to which existential rather than merely aesthetic assent is given—in which God or the gods eschew violence as the proper resolution of rivalry or as the uniquely adequate response to oppression or the threat of oppression.

In the New Testament, the dissident Jews who founded Christianity at a time of extreme peril for their nation created such a myth. They did not found a wholly new religion with a new central myth and a new God. Instead, they took the God-story they had inherited and gave its plot a revisionist conclusion by turning its divine protagonist from a warrior into a pacifist. The Lamb of God, executed by the empire he was expected to overthrow, the empire that by the terms of the received myth he surely would have overthrown, is a defeat in historical terms. God wins a cosmic victory, to be sure, but the substitution of cosmic for historic victory makes for a decidedly revisionist tale. Two examples of contrasting texts from the Old Testament and the New Testament must suffice to suggest the character of the revision.

In 2 Kings 1, Ahaziah, King of Samaria, suffers an accident and sends to inquire of the god Baalzebub whether he will recover. Yahweh, God of Israel, is offended by this act of homage to a rival god and sends his prophet Elijah to rebuke the king. A confrontation ensues between Elijah and a captain in the king's army.

> But Elijah answered the captain of fifty: "If I am a man of God, let fire come down from heaven and consume you and your fifty." Then the fire of God came down from heaven and consumed him and his fifty. (2 Kings 1:12)

This is ordinarily how Yahweh wins when challenged. In Luke 9:54–55, however, this strategy undergoes the mentioned revision. Jesus' disciples James and John, facing religious opponents (in Samaria, just to make the contrast harder to miss) ask their master:

> "Lord, do you want us to bid fire come down from heaven and consume them as Elijah did?" But he turned and rebuked them, and he said, "You do not know what manner of Spirit you are of; for the Son of Man came not to destroy men's lives but to save them."

To save them from what, exactly? Perhaps to save them from a mistake. This highly self-conscious and highly literary juxtaposition of two instances of religious rivalry and two different responses to it suggests a comparably self-conscious determination to proclaim that

A Nicolas Poussin painting of Emperor Titus destroying the temple in Jerusalem. Erich Lessing/Art Resource, New York.

violence—perhaps particularly in the name of religion—can be lethally maladaptive. Do thus, Jesus says, and men's lives will not be saved but destroyed.

A second, more striking example of the same revision involves a famous line from St. Paul: "O Death, where is thy sting? O Grave, where is thy victory?" A fuller citation, in the King James Version familiar to many from Handel's *Messiah* would be:

Behold, I tell you a mystery;
We shall not all sleep,
But we shall all be changed
In a moment,
In the twinkling of an eye,
At the last trumpet.
The trumpet shall sound,
And the dead shall be raised incorruptible,
And we shall be changed.
For this corruptible
Must put on incorruption

And this mortal must put on immortality.
Then shall be brought to pass
The saying that is written:
Death is swallowed up in victory.
O Death, where is thy sting?
O Grave, where is thy victory?
The sting of death is sin,
And the strength of sin is in the law.
But thanks be to God,
Who giveth us the victory
Through our Lord Jesus Christ. (1 Cor. 15:51–57)

If the entire Bible, Old Testament and New together, were to be reduced to just one word, the word, in my opinion, would be *victory*. But the nature of the victory in the Old Testament and in the New Testament differs crucially. In Paul's vision of resurrection to immortality, the victory will not be won until time—that is, history—has ended. When the trumpet sounds to end history, Christians who have bound themselves to Christ sacramentally in his death will find themselves bound to him as well in his glorious resurrection. Their victory and God's will be over death itself rather than over any one death-dealing human enemy. God will have achieved this victory for them not by defeating his human enemies but by allowing himself to be defeated by them and then triumphing impersonally over the defeat itself rather than personally over the enemies who inflicted the defeat. Were it not so, then Christ's resurrection would be nothing more than a triumph over Pontius Pilate.

The one personal element that does remain in this victory is also cosmic rather than historic. The restoration of human immortality—a gift that God took back when he cursed Adam and Eve—is God's final, definitive victory over and recovery from Satan, whose deception led to that curse and to the blighting of God's creation through all of human history.

Lost in all the excitement of Paul's language is the plain fact that until Christ came, God had endlessly promised imminent victory over human enemies rather than ultimate victory over Satan as the original merchant of death. The paired apostrophes at the climax of Paul's prose poem—"O death, where is thy sting? O grave, where is thy victory?"—are lines from the prophet Hosea that boil to the surface of Paul's Jewish memory at just this peak moment. Paul doesn't have them verbatim. What Hosea actually said was, at least in the text that has come down to us: "O Death, where are thy plagues? O

Grave, where is thy scourge?" (Hos. 13:14; my translation). But as
God spoke these lines to Hosea, they are not a promise but a threat.
We might better catch their sense if we translated "O Death, bring on
thy plagues! O Grave, lay on thy scourge!"

The lines come near the end of a poem in which God is seething
with fury and prepared to tear Israel limb from limb for sinning
against him. "I will destroy you, O Israel," he says, "Who can help
you? Where now is your king, to save you?" (13:9). The Children of
Israel are doomed to a ghastly death:

> I will fall upon them like a bear robbed of her cubs,
> I will tear open their breast,
> And there I will devour them like a lion,
> as a wild beast would rend them. (13:8)
> Because she has rebelled against her God,
> they shall fall by the sword,
> Their little ones shall be dashed in pieces
> and their pregnant women ripped open. (13:16)

That God can speak this way of his own people Israel is not the
point. The point is that his response to their offense, as on other occasions to their enemies' offenses, is mass execution. Death itself, note
well, is not God's enemy but God's weapon. Thus, Paul does not just
quote Hosea out of context when he makes "O Death ... O
Grave ... " part of a vision of immortality; he quotes Hosea in a dia-
metrically reversed context. But the reversal makes Paul's moment of
ecstatic exegesis, so to call it, a fine microcosm for the larger change
I speak of, by which death itself does indeed become God's enemy and
does indeed cease to be his weapon. God has laid down the death
weapon. He has disarmed himself.

Did fire actually come down from heaven and consume the soldiers
confronting Elijah? I assume not. Did the historical Jesus actually
voice the disdain that Luke attributes to him for such religiously
motivated violence? Perhaps, but perhaps not. Luke or whoever wrote
the Gospel According to Luke may have invented the episode or
recorded an oral tradition that was beyond checking at the point
when he received it. As for the blood-curdling tirade that Hosea
places in the mouth of God or the towering vision of immortality that
Paul evokes, the question "Did it happen?" cannot coherently be asked
of either one.

The only thing that matters in either contrasting pair is that the
sanction once given to violence by the violent character of God has

been withdrawn. There are no New Testament Psalms calling on God to rise up and smite Rome. There are, instead, Pauline exhortations to endure under Roman persecution and even Roman martyrdom in the confident hope of resurrection and immortality. Yet if the expression of this change as exhortation is fascinating, more fascinating still is its expression as divine self-characterization. Jesus, according to the Gospel, is the Word of God made flesh. If the character of Jesus-the-Word changes, then God's message changes. It is indeed that simple. At its deepest level, the Gospel is legislation by characterization.

Jesus' warrant for withdrawing divine sanction from religious violence, in other words, is his claim that he is God and therefore has the right to say what God wants or no longer wants. Although in the Elijah example Jesus says that God's character has been misunderstood rather than that it has changed, the effect is the same. A new kind of story is told about God, and in it he wants something new of his creatures. Jesus' disciples, Jesus tells them, do not know "what manner of Spirit [they] are of," which is to say what manner of God has created them. But Jesus claims to know what they do not. Referring to himself as Son of Man, a title he reserves for his most pregnant comments about himself, Jesus associates his mysterious self with the mystery of God, and then reveals that, in effect, God's spectacular career as a warrior is over, the consequence being that they must not be warriors either.

In the Torah God is a mythic figure who acts in history. In the Gospel, Jesus is a historical figure who acts in myth. The kind of victory he promises is to be won not over any historical figure—not, most particularly, over Rome on the eve of Rome's six-decade Jewish War—but, mythically, over death itself and over the Satan who bested God in Eden but will not best him again. As of old, this victory calls for human fidelity and obedience to God; but as God now eschews violence toward his enemies, so fidelity and obedience to him now require that his people eschew it as well. They must do toward their enemies as he does toward his. When Rome comes to crucify him, Jesus—God Incarnate on the terms of the fully developed Christian myth—does not resist. Even after he rises from death to life, turning apparent defeat into redemptive victory, Rome is still Rome, and Caesar still Caesar. And so it was to be when Rome came for his first followers. Unlike God's signature victory over Pharaoh, God Incarnate's mythic, pacific victory over Satan entails neither defeat nor mortal danger for any historical adversary.

We may speculate that the historical matrix for this mythological re-vision was a contemporary intuition on the part of some Jews that resistance to Rome would prove futile—as, in the event, it did. Jerusalem did not fall until forty years after the death of Jesus, but serious bloodshed had begun much earlier. At the death of Herod the Great in 4 B.C.E., quite possibly the year of Jesus' birth, there occurred a violent Jewish uprising and then a mass Roman crucifixion of captured Jewish rebels. During his lifetime and the decades immediately following, Palestine teetered on the verge of war, with recurrent outbreaks of actual warfare, until a climactic mass uprising brought in Vespasian, Titus, and the Roman legions with near-genocidal results. A few decades later, a second, equally desperate uprising under Hadrian brought a second, equally crushing defeat.

Through the onset, duration, and aftermath of this protracted and catastrophic military confrontation, God's identity as a warrior-judge of ruthlessly violent proclivities seems to have come into question in various Jewish circles, not just in the one that produced Christianity. Was God really like that? Or was he *still* like that? The Testament of Abraham, a Jewish text contemporary with the rise of Christianity, first portrays Abraham and God dealing death to sinners as ruthlessly as Moses and God do in Numbers 16, where the Earth opens up and swallows the rebel Korah and his followers, or as Elijah and God do in 2 Kings 1, the passage cited above. But then comes a surprise: God steps in and stops Abraham, suggesting that their joint violence has really been more Abraham's wish than his own and inevitably planting the suspicion in readers' minds that the violence of Numbers 16 and 2 Kings 1 were more Moses' and Elijah's wish than God's. Addressing himself to Michael, the commander of his angelic army, God says:

> Michael, Commander-in-chief, command the chariot to stand still, and turn Abraham back, lest he see all the inhabited world. For if he were to see all those living in sin, he would destroy all the creation. For behold, Abraham has not sinned, and he does not have mercy upon sinners. But I made the world, and I do not wish to destroy any of them. Rather I delay the death of a sinner until he turns and lives.[2]

God's concluding words paraphrase a line from Ezekiel 18:32: "I have no pleasure in the death of anyone, says the Lord God. Turn, then, and live." But there was a great deal of scripture, as the Testament of Abraham clearly recognizes, against which that line could be quoted, most notably Genesis 18, in which God destroys Sodom despite

Abraham's intercession. The Testament of Abraham, as Dale C. Allison Jr., has recently observed:

> turn[s] Gen 18 upside down. In the Bible it is not Abraham but God who determines to destroy the wicked; the patriarch, on the contrary, prays for their deliverance and God's indulgence. So in the *Testament* God and his human "friend" exchange roles.[3]

But if God is prepared to exchange roles with Abraham, then, for the *Testament* author no less than for Luke, God has changed.

In scripture, when God changes, he always seems to do so in an oblique movement, claiming to have always been what he has just become or rejecting as defective and human various behaviors and attitudes he once embraced as divine. Thus Ezekiel 18 begins:

> The word of the Lord came to me: What do you mean by repeating this proverb concerning the land of Israel, "The parents have eaten sour grapes, and the children's teeth are set on edge"? As I live, says the Lord God, this proverb shall no more be used by you in Israel. Know that all lives are mine; the life of the parent as well as the life of the child is mine: it is only the person who sins that shall die. (18:1–4)

But collective punishment has been virtually a signature divine behavior. At Exodus 34:7, in a theophany of maximum solemnity, God boasted of punishing "the parents' fault in the children and in the grandchildren to the third and fourth generation." Jeremiah 31:29–30 quotes the same teeth-on-edge proverb but acknowledges, as Ezekiel does not, that God's conduct had made the proverb applicable—until God changed and decided that "Everyone who eats unripe grapes will have his own teeth set on edge."

The retreat from collective punishment in these texts is scarcely more than an opening, but it is an opening that could be and apparently was seized and exploited when circumstances were favorable. The Wisdom of Solomon, another pseudepigraphical text, written perhaps a century earlier in Jewish Alexandria and eventually included in the Old Testament (although not in the Tanakh), foreshadowed the New Testament use of God's rare conciliatory and peaceable moments to gainsay his many violent ones. In this text, Solomon says to God:

> in your sight the entire cosmos is as a turn of the scale, and as a dewdrop in the dawn alighting on the earth. But you have compassion over all, because you can do all, and you overlook the sins of human beings with a view to their repentance. For you love all that exists, and loathe

nothing which you have created; for if you had hated anything you would never have fashioned it.[4]

Allison speculates about "an oral tradition or . . . a text no longer extant, a tradition or text that raised a critical question mark over biblical tales in which prophets bring down violent judgment upon human beings and cut short their earthly lives."[5] What matters from the evolutionary perspective, however, is less the details of the historical matrix than the fact that the myth that emerged by means of it has acquired a wider applicability with each advance in military technology. With each advance, the madness of "militant" pacifism has moved a step closer to sanity and, beyond sanity, to the commonest of common sense.

So it is that the revision of an ancient myth may come to seem an evolutionary preadaptation, two millennia early, to conditions that may lie nearer in the future than we think. Preadaptation, in evolutionary biology, is the development of traits in one environment that subsequently turn out to be advantageous in quite another environment. An environment may change around an organism as, for example, through climate change, or an organism may migrate into a new, physically different area where a trait that had made little or no difference begins to make a big one. Thus, when bacteria are cultured in the presence of an antibiotic, their surviving descendants commonly have a resistance to that antibiotic. The resistance is adaptation to that initial environment. Adaptation turns out to be preadaptation if and when the bacteria prove resistant to other, quite different antibiotics. It is as if they were preparing for something they did not know was coming.

The Christian myth of a God who no longer tries to defeat his human enemies may well be described as a defeatist myth. This is, famously, just how Nietzsche described it. Given a weak nation confronting an invincible empire, this defeatist myth may well have been locally and briefly adaptive, but it would not necessarily be—and for many centuries clearly was not—universally or durably adaptive. However, as the manmade environment for human conflict has changed, what was true for a single weak nation at a single passing moment may become true for all nations all the time.

Writing about "bio-Armageddon" in the *Los Angeles Times* (October 10, 2002), epidemiologist Scott P. Layne and political scientist Michael H. Sommer wrote as follows:

It costs about $1 million to kill one person with a nuclear weapon, about $1,000 to kill one person with a chemical weapon and about $1 to kill one person with a biological weapon. Low cost alone may dictate that current and future terrorists will opt for the $1 biological killers.

Last year a bombshell of a scientific paper, published in the *Journal of Virology*, revealed that a bioengineered form of mousepox—a close cousin of smallpox—was vaccine-resistant and 100% lethal. It showed that simply inserting one immune-inhibiting gene into mousepox was all it took. . . .

It's no longer hypothetical to bioengineer such an agent. And less than $1 million would be required to create deadly and contagious agents.

In the wrong hands, a bioengineered virus could be bottled and used as an insurance policy against invasion and overthrow. And, if unleashed, it could change the very fabric of remaining modern civilization.

As $1 million shrinks to $1, the means for Armageddon are miniaturized and democratized. At these prices, everyman becomes his own military superpower, at which point peace by way of military victory, even the special case of victory by military deterrence, would seem to become impossible. Only universal disarmament would seem to stand a chance of forestalling the self-extinction of the human species, and universal disarmament, in turn, would seem possible, if at all, only by cultural change.

Let me attempt an analogy. Little boys around the world tend to settle their arguments by fistfights, but little boys have little fists that do little harm. Fistfights among older boys and younger men are another matter. In a barroom brawl, the man who takes the punch may end up with a broken jaw, and the man who throws it with a broken hand. As they move from the culture of boyhood to the culture of manhood, males around the world resort less and less to the fistfight as a way to resolve arguments.

Analogously, then, when the United States had the atomic bomb and Japan did not, the United States used the bomb on Japan. The United States, in that moment, was like a man in its power, and Japan like a boy. When the United States and Russia both had the atomic bomb, neither used it on the other. They were now the adults, and the rest of the world—where hot wars still took place—was like a pack of unruly boys. As the nuclear club has grown larger, wars among its members have so far not occurred. Does it follow that the path to world peace is rampant nuclear proliferation? This is clearly a path that the world—at least the major world powers—would never choose. But if it comes about anyway, then *either* the erstwhile nuclear children—those nations that, lacking weapons of mass destruction,

were at the mercy of those that had them—will become adults and
refrain from their use like grown men declining to settle arguments
with their fists *or* the most unthinkable kind of all-against-all war
will ensue. And to recur to the point earlier made, proliferation is no
longer to be construed as just proliferation to recognized nations but
also to diffuse movements and militant individuals: Everyman his
own military superpower.

Under such circumstances as these, the defeatist Christian myth as
a counterintuitive cultural artifact, bizarre and unworkable as it has
been under hitherto normal human conditions, may begin to seem an
unintended spiritual preadaptation to the maximally hazardous environment into which we are all now moving.

Obviously, this environment was not in place for the entire human
race and the entire human planet at the time when, by the terms of the
myth, God Incarnate chose to die without a fight. For this reason,
when Christianity became the state religion of the Roman Empire, its
pacifist revision of the epic of God the Warrior could be remilitarized
with a vengeance, yet the texts that express the original revision survive and, taken at full strength, can still intrigue and give pause, just
as they have done, at least intermittently, from the very start.

Early in the second century C.E., before Christians and Jews had
defined each other dialectically into two distinct religions to be
known thenceforth by different names, before either the Mishnah or
the New Testament had taken clear shape, and before the notion of an
authoritative and exclusionary canon of scripture had taken hold, a
Christian bishop, Marcion of Sinope, pursued just the sort of disparity that I write of above in a now lost, reportedly voluminous work of
comparative exegesis called *Antitheses*. In it, he concluded that the
God of whom Jesus spoke and the God who had created the world
had to be two antithetical gods, so different were their respective
characters. Marcion's ditheism, like his rejection of the Hebrew
Scriptures, was rejected by the more Judaic Christianity that lived on
to become orthodoxy. But the fact that Marcion's answer was rejected
does not mean that Marcion's problem was entirely resolved. For if
there are not two gods, then—for anyone who accepts the premise
that the Old and the New Testaments speak of one and the same
God—God must have undergone a radical change. The charactero-
logical differences between God and God Incarnate, divine father and
divine son, are simply too salient to ignore.

Two gods or a changed God? *Tertium non datur.* For much of
Christian theology, the notion of change in God has been unaccept-

able, and those parts of scripture that suggest change have been a
scandal to be accommodated rather than an advance to be celebrated.
In my own opinion, it is because the scandal of change is unavoidable
and yet finally manageable within the canonical text that the greater
scandal of ditheism could be rejected as heresy. Allison comments:

> In some Christian circles, the implied critique of 2 Kgs 1:9–12 in Luke
> 9:51–56 made it, at least by Marcion's time, part of a case for distin-
> guishing between the God of the Jews and the God of the Christians.
> But the problem of conflicting theologies was not born with
> Christianity. That predicament was already internal to Judaism. The
> indiscriminately compassionate God of Ezek 33 and Wis 11 is not eas-
> ily thought of as heeding a pitiless prayer for fire, and some Jews saw
> this plainly enough.[6]

Allison is right that the problem of conflicting theologies was not
born with Christianity, but the matter can be stated even more
sharply: Christianity itself was born of the problem of conflicting
Jewish theologies. Rabbinic Judaism sought to resolve this conflict by
midrash, expanding scripture in the middle in a way that muted and
minimized the violence of God. In Lamentations Rabbah, for example, God expresses dismay and regret and even laments his own condition after seeing what he has done to Jerusalem through the
Romans. Christianity, founded by Jews and reading a New Testament
written by Jews, sought to resolve the conflict by expanding scripture at the end, continuing God's story through an epilogue in which
he becomes a human being who goes as a lamb to his own slaughter.
The result, in either case, is a revision—relatively radical or relatively
conservative—of the identity of God and, of greatest eventual consequence, a relative disarmament of God.

   Or so I would contend. Theologians, whether Christian or Jewish,
may disagree; but when change in myth is understood as adaptation
in the interest of survival and when, furthermore, God's repudiation
of violence in a given myth is viewed as a move toward the same
repudiation in a species with a unique capacity to exterminate itself,
then anthropology may embrace what theology resists.

   The story of how the Lion of Judah became the Lamb of God
remains compelling as literature even if it is not relevant or "salvific"
as protopacifist myth, but surely the one possibility need not pre-
clude the other. Both, in any case, were among my motivations for
writing the exploratory *Christ: A Crisis in the Life of God*,[7] a work that
takes its modest place among a number of other "Marcionite" works

produced in the twentieth century by writers of a sociological turn of mind as well as by social scientists working within a literary no less than a societal frame of reference. Particularly in the German *Kultgurgebiet* and under the impact of Adolf Harnack's *Marcion: Das Evangelium vom fremden Gott* (1921), the allusion to Marcion could be quite explicit. It is so, for example, in Ernst Bloch's *Geist der Utopie* (1923). Similarly, in Thomas Mann's post–World War II novel *Doktor Faustus*, Simon Magus, the ancient gnostic sometimes seen as archetype for Faust, becomes the occasion for a meditation on mingled national and civilizational, human and divine failure—as Karen Grimstad has demonstrated in her noteworthy *The Modern Revival of Gnosticism and Thomas Mann's* Doktor Faustus.[8]

In the wake of the mid-century Nazi *Shoah*, Thomas Mann was not alone in raising the question of the goodness of God—a question that often seemed to take priority over the questions of the existence of God. This question was raised with new insistence in many quarters, and with it the question of the goodness or the life-worthiness of the human species. Does this species *deserve* to survive? Can the man or woman who has survived Auschwitz and learned from it the true character of *Homo sapiens* be expected to resume normal life thereafter? In this form, the question of the goodness of God was raised with great poignancy by the apparent suicide of Primo Levi.

The same question appears again in Oscar Hijuelos's recent novel *A Simple Habana Melody (From When the World Was Good).*[9] In this paradoxically enchanting work, an émigré Cuban composer, a bisexual voluptuary who is also a devout Catholic, is interned at Buchenwald because of the accident of his Jewish-sounding name. Israel Levis survives the war and makes his way back to Cuba, but until the last pages of the novel he is sunk in a deep and bitter depression. Not only has he lost his faith in the goodness of God, he has also lost his appetite for music. Why bother with it? The piano in his house sits silent. His former captors' cruel indifference to human life survives, by a final cruelty, as his own indifference to everything, including even music, that once made his life so richly humane and rewarding.

It is no insult to Hijuelos to say that his is one of many post-*Shoah* attempts to engage the goodness of God and the viability of the human life-project as related questions. Only a minority of those many efforts has engaged this question by way of a rereading of the Bible; few, for that matter, have drawn evolutionary biology into the argument. Of the few that have turned to the Bible, most have gravitated not to the Gospel but to the Book of Job as the biblical text that seems most radically to problematize God himself. But in all of these few, it is easy to hear the ghost of Marcion walking.

"If God is good, he is not God," Archibald MacLeish wrote in his *J.B.*; "If God is God, he is not good." Marcion would have had an answer for MacLeish. Marcion lives on as well, acknowledged or not, in critic George Steiner's discussion of Job in *Grammars of Creation:*

> If the Maker is such as his motiveless torment of his loving servant suggests, then creation itself is in question. *Then God is guilty of having created.* (Emphasis added.)[10]

Marcion had no difficulty at all in conceding that God had created the world. God and God's world were both terrible, and terrifyingly inconsistent, in just the same way. Literary figures have been drawn to Marcion and to Gnosticism more generally because the fact that God is lifelike in this larger sense—wonderful and terrible in the way that life itself is wonderful and terrible—constitutes the very core of his appeal on the literary page.

But there are times when an appealing page is not enough. There are historic moments when the survival of a nation or of the human species itself seems to hang in the balance. Such are the moments that yield speculations about a god beyond God and daring stories about unthinkable change in God. Carl Jung, personally and professionally interested in Gnosticism as he was, pursued this question in his *Answer to Job.* The following two excerpts from my book *Christ: A Crisis in the Life of God* present a different but related answer to Job and, in effect, to Marcion as well. No, there are not two gods, I maintain, but the one God has repented and changed.

Or, as we may now choose to put it, God has adapted.

God Repudiates His Warrior Past

The scene: Because of Jesus' fame as a healer, a great crowd has gathered "to hear him and to be cured of their afflictions.[11] People tortured by unclean spirits were cured as well, and everyone in the crowd was trying to touch him since a power came out of him that healed them all" (Luke 6:18–19). They have come from as far south as Jerusalem and as far north as Phoenicia. In all their distress, these people have been on the road for days. A great crowd of such sufferers not patiently waiting their turn but all trying to touch Jesus at once makes for a panorama of extreme emotional and physical agitation.

Mingling with these suffering pilgrims is the growing number of Jesus' local disciples. Just before addressing the throng, he has spent a night praying in the hills and then selected from among them twelve whom he calls "apostles," or emissaries, recalling—inevitably in this Jewish context—the twelve sons of Jacob for whom the twelve tribes of Israel are named and thereby endowing his personal vocation and this already charged moment with national significance.

Earlier, in a Nazareth synagogue, the prophecy of Isaiah that Jesus said was being fulfilled even as he spoke was:

> The spirit of the Lord is upon me,
> for he has anointed me
> to bring good news to the afflicted.

Since the base meaning of the word *messiah* is "anointed," a defensible translation of Isaiah 61:1 is "He has made me Messiah to bring good news to the afflicted." Very well, the afflicted have gathered in unprecedented numbers: What good news does this messiah have for them in the public address that Christian tradition regards as the most important statement of his ethical teaching?

The news he has for them, whether it can be called good or not, is little short of astonishing, for it is a virtual repudiation of what on innumerable previous occasions God has taught his people to expect of him. Addressing his disciples directly but surrounded by the diseased and insane, Jesus says:

> Blessed are you who are poor, for yours is the kingdom of God.
> Blessed are you who now hunger, for you shall have your fill.
> Blessed are you who now weep, for you shall laugh.
> Blessed are you when people hate you, shun you, insult you, and slander your name for the sake of the Son of Man. Rejoice when that day comes, and dance for joy, for, lo, your reward shall be great in heaven. This is the way their forebears treated the prophets.
> But woe to you who are rich, for you have had your consolation.
> Woe to you who are sated, for you shall hunger.
> Woe to you who now laugh, for you shall mourn and weep.
> Woe to you when all speak well of you, for thus did their forebears treat the false prophets. (Luke 6:20–26)

In Deuteronomy 27–28, speaking through Moses, God served notice on Israel that if it were obedient, it would be blessed, and if disobedient, cursed. The nature of the blessings and curses, however, could not be more unlike the blessings and "woes" listed above. Obedient Israelites were not to be blessed in the two stages that Jesus speaks of.

They were not to be, first, poor, hungry, weeping, hated, shunned, and slandered; then, later, sated, laughing, and joyful. On the contrary, God guaranteed them prosperity and hegemony from the start:

> The Lord shall make you abound in possessions: in the fruit of your womb, in the fertility of your herd and in the yield of your soil, in the land that he swore to your forebears that he would give to you. For you the Lord will open heaven, his treasure house of rain, to give your land rainfall in due season, and to bless all your labors. You shall lend to many nations, yet borrow from none. The Lord shall put you at the head, not at the tail; you will always be on the top and never on the bottom, if you heed the commandments of the Lord. (Deut. 28:11–13)

As for the curses on the other side of the ledger, God swore to inflict a blood-curdling assortment of horrors if Israel transgressed against him, and he listed the transgressions he had in mind. To name just a few:

> Accursed be anyone who moves a neighbor's boundary marker. . . .
> Accursed be anyone who leads a blind man astray on the road. . . .
> Accursed be anyone who violates the rights of the alien, the orphan, or the widow. . . .
> Accursed be anyone who has sexual relations with his father's wife. (27:17–20)

The list of possible transgressions was long and detailed, but wealth, satiety, joviality, and good repute—the "woes" of Jesus' list—were not on it.

Speaking through various prophets, God has decried the abuse of wealth, but he has never denounced wealth itself. Through Amos, for example, God said:

> For three transgressions of Israel, and for four,
>   I will not revoke the punishment;
> Because they sell the righteous for silver,
>   and the needy for a pair of shoes,
> They trample the face of the poor into the dust of the earth,
>   and force the afflicted off the road. (Amos 2:6–7)

But one may search in vain among all God's earlier utterances for a statement like "Blessed are you who are poor" without the promise that God will someday make these poor rich. And as for the poor, so, analogously, for the hungry, the mournful, and the scorned. Although smug self-satisfaction and a self-righteous sense that one is beyond the reach of judgment are condemned, usually because they accompany other, more serious offenses, satiety, happiness, and good repute are consistently regarded as blessings.

It may be objected that Jesus does not really invert the traditional values, he simply expands the time frame in which God may deliver good and ill to all according to their merit. Punishment will still be punishment, on this reading, and reward will still be reward; the delivery of each will simply come in heaven rather than on earth. Yet if even this much is true, Jesus must be seen to have sharply revised the emerging meaning of his miraculous cures. The diseased and disturbed have gathered in such numbers because they expect *immediate* relief. The claim that Jesus has made for himself is that, more than an ordinary healer, he is the fulfillment of the grandest promises that God has made to his people rather than yet another postponement of it. Those already suffering so grievously have surely not come so far simply to be told that their misery is their blessing inasmuch as, further along, their reward will be so great. Can this redefinition of weal and woe really be the fulfillment of the promise that the Lord made through Isaiah?

Jesus, preaching frankly against the promise, does not hesitate to say that it can be and indeed it is. His words serve notice, in effect, that he has not come to perform mass healings or mass exorcisms. With a few exceptions, those who are racked with illness or tormented by demons should not look to him for miraculous healing; rather, they should embrace their affliction as analogous to the mistreatment that his own disciples will encounter for their devotion to the Son of Man. Whatever his miracles portend, it is not simple, direct, or, least of all, universal relief from pain.

What follows on this surprise, however, is a far greater surprise:

> But to you who are listening I say this: Love your enemies, do good to those who hate you, bless those who curse you, pray for those who scorn you. If someone slaps you on one cheek, turn the other cheek as well. If someone takes your outer garment from you, let him have your undergarment as well. Give to anyone who asks of you. If someone takes your property, do not ask for it back. Treat others as you would like them to treat you. If you love those who love you, what credit is that to you? Why, even sinners love those who love them! And if you do good to those who do good to you, what credit is that to you? Again, even sinners do that much. . . . Instead, love your enemies, and do good to them, and lend without any hope of return. Then you shall have a great reward, and you shall be children of the Most High, for he himself is kind to the ungrateful and the wicked.

> Be merciful as your Father is merciful. Do not judge, and you will not
> be judged; do not condemn, and you will not be condemned; forgive,
> and you will be forgiven. Give, and it will be given to you . . . because
> by the measure that you use will you be measured. (Luke 6:27–38)

In this sermon, Jesus preaches what he will later practice when his
enemies come for him and he does not resist them. "Turn the other
cheek" has rightly been taken to be his signature teaching. The
phrase is used by millions who might not be able to quote anything
else that Jesus said and by millions more who do not know that it was
he who first said it. It defines him didactically as the Crucifixion
defines him dramatically. Yet the popular reception of this sermon,
for all the fame it has conferred upon Jesus, has been such as to
obscure his deeper originality and his more radical revision of the
tradition he inherited.

This has been so because discussion of his ethic of nonresistance to
evil has so consistently focused on the application of this ethic rather
than on its premise—namely that human beings must do thus *because
God does thus*. But does God in fact do thus? This is a question that
interpretation of this passage generally does not ask. Jesus assumes a
positive answer to that question without ever asking it, but his
assumption elides a drastic revision of the divine identity. When we
recall how God has in fact conducted himself in the face of opposition
or insult from past enemies, it becomes clear that although Jesus
speaks as if God is now as he always has been, he is in fact revealing
(or enacting) an enormous change in God.

God, to repeat, is the model whom Jesus would have us believe that
we imitate when we love our enemies, do good to those who hate us,
and so forth. If we do all this, he says, we "shall be children of the
Most High, for he himself is kind to the ungrateful and the wicked."
When urging mercy, Jesus does not say, "Be merciful because mercy
is better than vengeance." What he says is "Be merciful as your
Father is merciful." But how merciful has the Father shown himself
to be in his previous career? How kind has the Most High typically
been when confronted with the ungrateful or the wicked?

God's classic early characterization of himself comes at Exodus
34:5–7:

> The Lord passed before [Moses] in the cloud and stood with him
> there, and proclaimed the name of the Lord. The Lord passed before
> him, and proclaimed, "*Yahweh! Yahweh!* A god merciful and gracious,
> slow to wrath, and abounding in steadfast love and faithfulness, keep-

ing steadfast love unto the thousandth generation, forgiving iniquity, transgression, and sin, but letting nothing pass and visiting the sins of the parents upon the children and children's children unto the third and the fourth generation."

In this statement, inasmuch as God's love abides "unto the thousandth generation," an unimaginably long time, while his punishment reaches only unto the third and fourth, he may seem to be more loving than wrathful. Even here, however, it is clear that, for him, forgiveness by no means precludes punishment. Sinners may be forgiven, yet their children and their children's children must pay the price. Punishment is never commuted. God lets nothing pass.

It is not principally, however, what God says but what he does that makes him seem a being other than the one whose benignity and neutrality Jesus invokes. The Lord's actions speak much louder than his deeds. Between the Israelites' Exodus from Pharaoh's Egypt and their entry into the promised land of Canaan, to consider only Israelite sinners and only that forty-year period, the Lord executes at least thirty thousand of them. He sees to it that three thousand of his people are put to the sword after the episode of the golden calf in Exodus 32. Later, in Numbers 16, he buries alive some 250 rebellious Levites and Reubenites, along with their wives, their children, and the other members of their households. At a conservative twelve per household, counting concubines and slaves, the total put to death comes to another three thousand. Later still, the Lord fatally poisons an unstated but evidently large number of Israelites when, angry over their complaints of hunger and thirst, he sends "fiery serpents" against them (Num. 21). Finally, after Israelite men consort sexually with the priestesses of a Canaanite god, he slaughters twenty-four thousand (Num. 25). At no point during Israel's desert wanderings does the Lord seem slow to wrath. At one point, much to the contrary, he contemplates exterminating ungrateful Israel altogether and beginning a new nation from the loins of Moses (Num. 14:12). Moses shames him out of this by warning him that he will ruin his reputation back in Egypt and by quoting to his face the "slow to wrath" language of Exodus 34:6.

So much for the Lord's conduct toward his friends. What of his conduct toward his enemies? How does Jesus' characterization of him square with, for example, his characterization of himself to the prophet Habakkuk? In the timber-rattling battle poem found at Habakkuk 3, the Lord portrays himself as a colossus of war who has turned his powers of creation into weapons of destruction, shaking the mountains, gouging riverbeds into the earth, trampling the sea, and terrorizing the very sky. The prophet who receives this vision of cosmic rampage trembles with fear as he alternately describes and prays to the divine warrior who is allegedly coming to his rescue:

> You stave in the sinner's roof beams,
>   you raze his house to the ground.
> You split his skull with your bludgeon,
>   His warriors you blast away,
> They whose joy it was to take us,
>   like some poor wretch, to devour in their lair.
> With your horses you trample the sea,
>   you stir the mighty waters.
> When I heard, I was shaken to the core,
>   my lips quivered at the sound;
> My bones were wrenched loose,
>   my legs gave way beneath me.
> Numb, I await the day of anguish
>   Which will dawn on the people now attacking us. (Hab. 3:13–16)

Although Habakkuk's is a uniquely vivid evocation of the divine warrior in action, the Lord offers essentially identical self-characterizations in dozens of speeches to other prophets. And Israel did not fail to take the point but learned to pray to the Lord as just the fearsome warrior he claimed to be. Thus, to choose a typical passage from the Book of Psalms:

> God is for us a god of deliverance;
>   Lord Yahweh opens an escape from death.
> God smashes the heads of his enemies,
>   the hairy head of him who walks in guilt.
> My Lord said, "I will bring you back from [the mountains of] Bashan,
>   will retrieve you from the bottom of the sea;
> That your feet may wade through blood;
>   that the tongue of your dogs may have its portion of your enemies."
>   (Ps. 68:20–23)

If what Jesus is saying is correct, then such prayers can no longer be offered. The Lord can no longer be praised for smashing the heads of his enemies, for he is no longer a head-smashing kind of god. If the distinction between friend and foe were to be abolished to such an extent that God could no longer be said to have enemies and his worshipers could no longer ask him for help in defeating their own enemies, then the Book of Psalms would have to be retired almost in its entirety, for there are very few Psalms that do not, at some point, allude to a fight in progress and ask God's assistance in winning it. This is true even of the most poetic and meditative of the Psalms. Psalm 139, for example, contains these beautiful quatrains

Whither shall I go from thy Spirit?
  Or whither shall I flee from thy presence?
If I ascend to heaven, thou art there!
  If I make my bed in Sheol, thou art there!
If I take the wings of morning
  and dwell in the uttermost parts of the sea,
even there thy hand shall lead me,
  and thy right hand shall hold me.
If I say, "Let only darkness cover me,
  and the light about me become night,"
even the darkness is not dark to thee,
  the night is bright as the day,
  for darkness to thee is as light. (Ps. 139:7–12)

But the same Psalm, before it concludes, presents the Psalmist urging that God become the enemy of his enemies because he himself has so assiduously been the enemy of God's enemies:

Do I not hate them that hate thee, O Lord?
  And do I not loathe them that rise up against thee?
I hate them with perfect hatred;
  I count them my enemies.
Search me, O God, and know my heart!
  Try me and know my thoughts!
And see if there be any wicked way in me,
  and lead me on the path everlasting! (139:22–24)

To the modern sensibility, hatred and contention come jarringly in after "the wings of morning," but such juxtapositions of delicate sentiment and virulent hatred were familiar and indeed almost conventional when the Psalms were written, or so we must infer from their extreme frequency. That modern readers have the reaction they do is one measure of the historic success of Jesus' radical pacification of the image of God. There are times, of course, when Jesus speaks in a more warlike way, not to mention innumerable times in the course of history when warlike Christians have embraced the bloodiest verses of the Old Testament precisely because they *were* bloody. Nonetheless, the incongruity between Jesus' inaugural sermon and a very long list of earlier biblical texts cannot be gainsaid even after all necessary lexical and anthropological qualifications have been made. There is no denying that the Lord *has been* a head smasher—both by performance and in endlessly repeated aspiration. If he is such no longer, then he must have changed, but what accounts for the change?

One possible answer is that there will be no answer because the Lord intends that there should be none. Although he insisted, when speaking to Moses, on the clarity and transparency of his words and intentions (Deut. 30:11–12), God has grown more remote and more mysterious as the centuries have passed. During Israel's Babylonian Captivity, he began saying for the first time things like "As the heavens are high above the earth, so are my ways above your ways, my thoughts above your thoughts" (Isa. 55:9). Often enough, Jesus talks the same way. And whether or not God Incarnate will choose to make himself humanly comprehensible, God has certainly never acknowledged at any earlier point any slightest *obligation* along those lines. If we grant that Jesus is God Incarnate, then we must grant as well that he has the right to announce a deep change in God—which is to say, in himself—without quite calling the change by that name and without otherwise troubling to explain it. The Lord of All the Earth does as he pleases.

Yet there is no mistaking—particularly in Matthew's version of the sermon quoted above—that Jesus does indeed intend to claim the authority of God for what he is saying, and in his own way he does indeed wish to explain himself. If Jesus were merely a prophet speaking by divine authorization, we would expect to read: "And then the Word of the Lord came to Jesus of Nazareth, saying, 'Say unto the people of Israel, 'Thus says the Lord. . . . '" But both Matthew and Luke read otherwise. On no authority but his own, Jesus boldly characterizes God and proceeds to derive an arresting new morality from his characterization. The crowds are understandably "astonished at his teaching, for he taught them as one in authority, and not as their scribes" (Matt. 7:28).

Jesus emphasizes that his authority is his own by his repeated contrastive use of the phrase "But I say this to you" to underscore the fact that what he is announcing is an unabashed revision. He says, for example:

> You have heard how it was said, "You will love your neighbor and hate your enemy." *But I say this to you:* Love your enemies, and pray for those

who persecute you; so that you may be children of your Father in heaven, for he causes his sun to rise on the wicked as well as on the good, and he sends down rain on the just and the unjust alike. (Matt. 5:43–45, emphasis added)

In Leviticus 19:18, part of which Jesus cites in the passage just quoted, God does not in fact say, "you will hate your enemy," but neither does he say, "you will *not* hate your enemy." What he says, to quote the verse in full, is "You shall not take vengeance on or bear any grudge *against your countrymen.* Love your neighbor as yourself. I am the Lord." The context is clarifying. Directly contradicting what Jesus implies about him, the Lord most certainly did take vengeance and bear grudges against his enemies, his enemies being in every case Israel's; and he both expected and, on various occasions, directly commanded Israel to do the same, imposing obligations upon them that were consistent with his vengeful and grudge-bearing character.

The point may be illustrated from the story of the Lord's long-running grudge and ruthless vengeance against Amalek. When Moses led the Israelites from Egypt to Canaan, Amalek was the first of several nations to attack Israel en route. After the attack was repulsed, the Lord swore to Moses: "Record this in writing, and recite it in Joshua's hearing, that I will utterly wipe out the memory of Amalek from under heaven" (Exod. 17:14). Moses built an altar to witness the oath, saying: "The Lord will be at war with Amalek from generation to generation" (17:16). What the Lord swore and Moses solemnly witnessed were, in more modern language, an oath of genocide. The Lord swore that he would exterminate the Amalekites, however long it took. Over the ensuing two centuries, far longer than the four generations of Exodus 34, the Amalekites and the Israelites were, as predicted, repeatedly at war with each other, but Israel gradually grew stronger. Finally, the Lord decided to fulfill his ancient vow to the letter. He summoned King Saul: "I intend to avenge what Amalek did to Israel—laying a trap for him on the way as he came up from Egypt. Now, go and crush Amalek. Put him under a curse of total destruction, him and all that he possesses. Do not spare him, but slay man and woman, child and babe, ox and sheep, camel and ass" (1 Sam. 15:2–3). Saul carried out the order without hesitation, sparing only— for later demonstrative execution and ritual sacrifice in the Israelite shrine city of Gilgal—Agag, king of Amalek, and the prize livestock of the slaughtered tribe. The Lord, however, was indignant that anything Amalekite had been left breathing. He wanted his vengeance enacted exactly as ordered. In his wrath, the Lord stripped Saul of his kingship, leaving the prophet Samuel to complete the genocide:

> Samuel then said, "Bring me Agag, king of Amalek!" Agag came forward on unsteady feet, saying, "And now, the bitter taste of death!" Samuel replied: "As your sword has left mothers bereaved, so shall your mother be left bereaved among women." Samuel then butchered [that is, dismembered] Agag before the Lord at Gilgal. (1 Sam. 15:32–33)

The Lord did to the last Amalekite (the mother who would have been left bereaved is already dead) only what Amalek would presumably have done to the last Israelite, given the chance. The point to be made is that when the Lord said, through Moses, "Love your neighbor as yourself," he was not saying anything that Moses or he thought incompatible with the Lord's earlier vow "I will utterly wipe out the memory of Amalek from under heaven." The story of Amalek from first attack to last defeat can quite coherently be read as a gloss on Leviticus 19:18, demonstrating, among other things, that the reference group for the word *neighbor* in that verse is Israel alone. Leviticus 19:34 graciously widens the circle to include aliens peacefully resident in the Land of Israel, but enemies are another matter.

The story of Amalek need not necessarily mean, of course, that Israel is allowed, much less that it is commanded, to hate its enemies to quite the violent extreme that God hates his. The Lord concludes his "love your neighbor" commandment, as typically in the Book of Leviticus, by saying, "[you will] love your neighbor as yourself. I am the Lord." He does not say, "you will love your neighbor as yourself because I, the Lord, love my neighbors as myself, and you must be like me." Conceivably, Israel could be held to a stricter standard of forbearance than the Lord intends to impose on himself. The more natural assumption, however, given the fact that Israel's friends and enemies are essentially indistinguishable from the Lord's, has to be that the Amalekite principle is no less valid for Israel than it is for the Lord.

This would seem to be the point of a revealing episode in 1 Kings 20. The Lord has promised Ahab, the king of Israel, victory over Ben-Hadad, the king of Aram. The battle goes just as promised, but aides to Ben-Hadad advise him: "We have heard that Israelite kings are merciful. Let us dress in sackcloth with cords around our heads [the traditional garb of penitence] and go out to meet the king of Israel; maybe he will spare your life" (1 Kings 20:31). Ahab shows himself merciful indeed, making a generous peace settlement and sparing Ben-Hadad's life. The Lord, however, is furious at this conduct. "You will pay with your life," he tells Ahab, "for having set free a man who was under my curse of destruction. It will be your life for his life, and your people for his" (1 Kings 20:42).

From this, it would seem to follow that God wants his people to be no more merciful (or no less vindictive) than he is. In the Books of Samuel and Kings, no less than in the Gospels, God is the model. And it would seem further to follow that Jesus captures the spirit of the ancient commandment accurately enough when he says: "You have heard how it was said: 'You will love your neighbor and hate your enemy.'"

What Jesus would substitute for this conduct, which at its root is no more than the spontaneous and natural discrimination that everyone past early childhood learns to make between friend and foe, is an unspontaneous and unnatural refusal to discriminate. His followers are called on to treat everyone alike, taking the sun as their model, which God makes to shine without discrimination "on the wicked as well as on the good." If this noble refusal to discriminate would be problematic anywhere in the world, it is doubly so in Israel, for Israel was brought into existence as a nation by an act of undisguised and, in fact, proudly proclaimed discrimination on the part of God. What Moses held up as the pinnacle of divine greatness could not be more remote than it is from the indifferent shining of the sun:

> Did ever a people hear the voice of a god speaking from the heart of fire, as you have heard it, and yet live? Has it ever been known before that a god intervened to bring one nation out of another by such trials, signs, and wonders—war waged with mighty hand and outstretched arm, horrendous terrorism—as the Lord your God has done for you in Egypt before your very eyes? . . . But he loved your forebears and, after them, chose their descendants, and for their sake he personally conducted you out of Egypt, showing forth his mighty power, dispossessing for you nations who were larger and stronger than you, to make room for you and to give you their country as your inheritance. (Deut. 4:33–34, 37–38)

God's covenant with Israel *is* this act of discrimination, and he never equates Israel with other nations except when afire with rage.

Yes, rarely, as through Amos, he may snarl in his fury something like:

"Are not you and the Ethiopians all the same to me, children of
  Israel?
"I brought Israel up from Egypt, oh yes,
  and the Philistines from Caphtor,
  and the Aramaeans from Kir.
"Beware! Lord Yahweh's eyes are on the sinful kingdom.
  I shall wipe it off the face of the earth!
(although I will not destroy the House of Jacob completely)," declares
  the Lord. (Amos 9:7–8)

When he talks this way, the Lord aggressively and insultingly secu-
larizes what Moses has declared sacred. He normalizes what Moses
has declared exceptional. Did God bring Israel out of Egypt? Yes, but
so what? God is always bringing somebody out of somewhere, is he
not? Are the Israelites so vain as to think that they are his special
favorites because of a mere population transfer?

But when the Lord talks this way, he taunts Israel only to make
a point. The idea that the Exodus was just another population
transfer is not one that he entertains for long. As the half-retrac-
tion of the closing parenthesis shows, the idea that Israel might be
for him just one among the peoples of the world is finally not one
he is prepared to act upon. Even on this occasion, even pushed—as
he imagines himself—to this extreme, he cannot bring himself to
present perfect neutrality as his own behavior in its ideal form.
And on innumerable other occasions, he boasts of himself as by no
means neutral but, on the contrary, openly and passionately dis-
criminatory.

So, then, what has come over him, now incarnate as Jesus of Nazareth,
that he presents himself so differently? As God Incarnate, Jesus surely
remembers quite well what he once did to the Amalekites. Surely he
remembers as well that he promised no less to Israel's later oppressors.
What has driven him to forswear those oaths and assume so utterly different an attitude? The root of the change, as we have seen, is something
more radical than an intensified commitment to the mercy, patience, and
steadfast love of Exodus 34:6–7, something more than a mere muting of
transgenerational revenge. No, Jesus exhorts his hearers to a profoundly counterintuitive, cost-what-it-may disregard for the most basic
of human differences, the difference between amity and hostility. What
makes this ideal inherently and massively disruptive for God no less
than for Israel is the fact that at the time when Jesus preaches it, he
has behind him a two-thousand-year career based on acknowledging
and exalting one difference above all others—namely the difference

between Israel, the people with whom he has established his covenant, and all other peoples. Israel has been everything to the Lord. Since the time when he first narrowed his focus from mankind in general ("Be fruitful, and multiply") to Abraham ("I will make your offspring like the stars of the sky"), his every word, his every action has revolved around his chosen people. What could possibly induce him to level to nothing a distinction upon which he has based so defining a personal commitment?

The answer is, in two words, extreme duress. In the greatest crisis of his life, God makes heroic virtue of dire necessity. To appreciate what he faces and how he responds to it, we may consider first how he conducted himself during a similar if somewhat less life-defining time—namely, the time leading up to the destruction of Jerusalem by Babylonia and the abduction of much of his people to their infamous Babylonian Captivity. This was an event that, in principle, could have left Israel without a god, and God without a people. The covenant between them, having been established by God's victory over Pharaoh, was predicated on God's guarantee that no other king or god-king would do as Pharaoh had done: subjugate Israel. By rights, then, once Babylonia did just that, the covenant should have become moot.

It did not become moot because God had made his protection conditional. It was guaranteed only if Israel would "listen to the commandments of the Lord your God, which I lay down for you today, and then keep them and put them into practice, not deviating to the right or the left from any of the commandments that I impose upon you today, by following other gods and serving them" (Deut. 28:13–14). If Israel was guilty of any deviation, then "the Lord will raise against you from the far ends of the earth a nation like a raptor in flight, a distant nation strange of speech, grim of face, ruthless toward the old, and pitiless toward the young" (Deut. 28:49–50). By the time of the alien eagle's final victory, the besieged towns of Israel, God warned, would be so desperate for food that "the most dainty and fastidious of your women" would be reduced, after giving birth, to eating their own afterbirth (Deut. 28:56–57).

Israel did indeed deviate from fidelity to the Lord. According to the sixth-century prophets and the Books of Kings, most Israelites were worshiping other gods at the time of the Babylonian Conquest. The fall of Israel, then, did not reflect negatively on the power of God. This was what he had said would happen. God did not simply withdraw his protection and allow Israel's enemies to have at her. The

Babylonian victory, like the earlier Assyrian victory, was not something that had simply befallen Israel, and therefore him. No, it was something that he had actively and purposefully *inflicted* on Israel using these seeming conquerors as means to his end.

The Babylonian Captivity was a calamity, then, for which theoretical provision had been made; yet it still felt like something new, unprecedented, and terrible when it finally came about, scarcely less so for the Lord than for Israel. Speaking to the prophet Habakkuk, God said in wonderment at his own employment of Israel's enemies:

> Cast your eyes over the nations,
> 　gape and be amazed to stupefaction.
> For I am doing something in your own days
> 　Which you would not believe if told of it.
> Behold, I am stirring up the Chaldeans [Babylonians],
> 　That fierce and fiery nation
> Who march across miles of countryside to seize the homes of others.
> 　(Hab. 1:5–6)

Later in that brief but scathingly eloquent book of prophecy, the Lord sends Habakkuk a second vision, in which, as we have seen, the divine warrior marches back into Canaan to wreak vengeance on these very marching and pillaging Chaldeans. The Lord's intent was to establish beyond any shadow of a doubt that both ends of this transaction—both Israel's initial, crushing humiliation and her ultimate, glorious vindication—were his doing and no one else's. But in taking this means to his end, he had to wonder at himself.

Did he achieve his goal? Not necessarily, or entirely, or permanently. True, it may be more painful to imagine that there is no god or that, if there is, you are beneath his notice than to imagine that your god is ruthlessly punitive. After all, a god who punishes may later reward. A god who is in control of the world order, whatever it is, may someday improve it. If this is comfort, however, it is cold comfort, and there were clearly some in ancient Israel who were not willing to wait for it indefinitely. To say this is to recall that the second half of God's punishment-and-rehabilitation promise was never kept. He never delivered the reward that he said would follow on punishment. Yes, some of the Babylonian exiles returned to Israel, but many did not. Yes, a very limited kind of national sovereignty was reestablished, but it did not even include all of traditional Judea, much less all of Israel. In due course, a modest new temple was built, but the divine giant never came striding forth from the mountains of the south, shaking the

earth and terrifying the sky as he had said he would. Despite an inter-
lude of relative independence, Israel seemed to be on a road leading
downward toward permanent subjugation, worsening, at the whim of
its rulers, into outright and brutal oppression.

The psychological cost of this state of affairs, as decades length-
ened into centuries, is set forth with grim and grieving clarity in
Psalm 44:

> You are my king, my God,
> who decreed Jacob's victories;
> through you we conquered our opponents,
> in your name we trampled down those who rose up against us. . . .
> Our boast was always of God,
> we praised your name without ceasing.
> Yet now you have abandoned and humiliated us,
> you no longer take the field with our armies,
> you leave us to fall back before the enemy,
> those who hate us plunder us at will.
> You hand us over like sheep for slaughter,
> you scatter us among the nations,
> you sell your people for a trifle
> and make no profit on the sale.
> You make us the butt of our neighbors,
> the mockery and scorn of those around us,
> you make us a by-word among nations,
> other peoples shake their heads over us.
> All day long I brood on my disgrace,
> the shame written clear on my face,
> from the sound of insult and abuse,
> from the sight of hatred and vengefulness.
> All this has befallen us though we had not forgotten you,
> nor been disloyal to your covenant,
> our hearts never turning away,
> our feet never straying from your path.
> Yet you have crushed us in the place where jackals live,
> and thrown over us shadow dark as death.
> Had we forgotten the name of our God
> and stretched out our hands to a foreign god,
> would not God have found this out,
> for he knows the secrets of the heart?
> For your sake we are being massacred all day long,
> treated as sheep to be slaughtered.
> Wake, Lord! Why are you asleep?
> Awake! Do not abandon us for good.

Why do you turn your face away,
forgetting that we are poor and harassed?
    For we are bowed down to the dust,
and lie prone on the ground.
Arise! Come to our help!
Ransom us, as your faithful love demands. (New Jerusalem Bible; Ps.
    44:4–5, 8–26)

The remnant that reestablished a national life in Israel was a genuinely faithful remnant; and the greater its fidelity, the less plausible the interpretation of continuing foreign oppression as divine punishment. If the congregations that recited or perhaps sang the poignant words of Psalm 44 knew this, then did God not know it as well? And as he heard it, did it not remind him of his own broken promise, made through so many different prophets, that he would restore Israel to its former glory?

How could it not? But if we imagine that God was not, as Psalm 44 imagines, asleep but simply too weak or that he was for some other, still more mysterious reason no longer willing to impose his will on history, then we have in hand a motive for Jesus' revolutionary sermon. The prospect facing God is that if, on the one hand, he cannot defeat Israel's enemies and, on the other, he can no longer claim that when they slaughter his sheep they are doing his bidding, then he must admit defeat. He must admit that, because of his failure rather than Israel's, the covenant between him and his people has definitively lapsed. His failure will be only the more ignominious for his many boasts that Israel's enemies are nothing more than a pack of dogs he has whistled up for his hunt (Isa. 5:26). If those boasts are now exposed as vain, then God may, at most, be honored for his past services. He can no longer be respected for his present power.

God does have, however, one alternative to simply bringing his storied career to an ignominious close. Instead of baldly declaring that he is unable to defeat his enemies, God may declare that *he has no enemies*, that he now refuses to recognize any distinction between friend and foe. He may announce that he now loves all people indiscriminately, as the sun shines equally everywhere, and then urge—as the law of a new, broadened covenant—that his creatures extend to one another the same infinite tolerance of wrongdoing that henceforth he will extend, individually and collectively, to all of them.

Gentiles may imagine that their own goodness, their own attractiveness, was a sufficient motive for God's decision to bring them into the covenant that he had once reserved for the Jews. But if we approach this change from God's side, taking seriously a Bible that presents his covenant with Israel as dwarfing all else in its importance to him, then we must seek the reason for the eventual expansion of the covenant in the troubled state of his role within it. The covenant had to be changed because God could not keep its terms and because, on the eve of a new national catastrophe for Israel, he chose to stop pretending that he could.

The objection may be raised—indeed, must be raised—that it is one thing for God, safe in heaven, to resolve his dilemma by declaring that his erstwhile enemies are now friends, and quite another for human beings, imperiled on earth, to be required to do the same. Clever though it may be for God to excuse himself from the chore of defeating his enemies by declaring that he has none, this is cleverness on the cheap, or so the objection must insist, for it costs him nothing while imposing an unbearable burden on his creatures.

This objection is beyond logical refutation. The radical rejection of human difference, including the difference between friend and foe, does come on the cheap for God—unless and until God becomes a human being and suffers the consequences of his own confession. But in the story we are reading God has become a human being, and we may now begin to see why he has done so. Israel will be slaughtered like sheep, but God has become a lamb. He has made virtue of necessity, yes, but the virtue is real virtue. It is the heroic ideal of universal love.

The Roman *Shoah* and the Disarmament of God

Why did God become a Jew and subject himself to public execution by the enemy of his chosen people? He did so in order to confess that, by choice or of necessity, he was a god disarmed. He knew that genocide against his chosen people was imminent and that he would do nothing to prevent it. The one thing he could choose to do, as the Jew he became, was to break his silence about his own scandalous inaction.

God revealed to the seer Daniel at the court of the king of Babylon that when Babylon fell, the kingdom of God would not come immediately. Instead, there would come—in a succession symbolized by a series of beasts in Daniel's vision (Dan. 7)—the kingdoms of the Babylonians, the Medes, the Persians, and the Greeks of Alexander the Great. Only then would God's kingdom come, symbolized in the vision by "one like a son of man." But as the Gospel opens, instead of

God's kingdom, there has come the kingdom of the Romans, and the iron fist of this new Babylon is tightening around Judea in the last decades before a catastrophic rebellion. If, as the Book of Daniel makes clear, God foresees the historical future in detail, then he knows that he will not rescue his people from the defeat that lies ahead. Rome, enraged by Jewish rebelliousness, will perpetrate genocide, and God will do nothing. The one thing he can do—and does do as Jesus of Nazareth, God the Son—is break his silence about his own inaction.

The word *genocide* above refers to the ferocious escalation of violence that took place in the generation immediately after the execution of Jesus, an escalation that came to its first climax with a Jewish revolt against Rome in 66–70 C.E. The Jews were a formidable opponent for imperial Rome. They were, more than is sometimes remembered, populous, well organized, well financed, and passionately motivated. Rome did not finally defeat them and suppress their revolt until after it peaked for a second time, in 132–35 C.E. After this final Jewish revolt, an uprising led by another Messiah, Simon Bar Kokhba, Rome changed the name of Jerusalem to Aelia Capitolina and made it a capital offense for any Jew to set foot in the erstwhile City of David. Jewish sovereignty in the Land of Israel then came to an end for fully eighteen centuries.

Rome's imperial agenda did not extend to the extermination of all the Jews of the empire. In that one regard, the Roman suppression of world Jewry's bid for freedom differed from the Nazi "final solution" of 1941–45. In two other regards, however, Rome's victory in its sixty years' war with the Jews may plausibly bear the grim designation *genocide*. First, the Roman intent in destroying the Jewish Temple was to end the distinctive national life that the Jewish people had led as an empire within the empire. Second, the portion of the world Jewish population that perished in the first of the Jewish Wars alone is comparable to the portion that perished in the Nazi *Shoah*.[12]

Contemporary estimates of the world Jewish population in the first century[13] range from a low of 5.5 million to a high of more than 8 million. Of these, 1 million to 2.5 million lived in Palestine; 4.5 million to 6 million lived in the diaspora. In the years before the doomed uprisings, the Jews of the Roman Empire, notwithstanding worsening oppression within their homeland, were more numerous, more powerful, and better organized within the greater multinational social order of their day than were the Jews of Europe before the outbreak of World War II. Their remarkable unity—all Jews looking to

Jerusalem as their spiritual capital and all supporting the Temple by
the payment of a Temple tax—mimicked the organization of the
Roman empire itself. This political coherence was admired by the
other, less autonomous peoples of the empire, but it was understandably suspect in the eyes of the imperial authorities themselves.

Perhaps because of latent Roman resentment of Jewish success
within the empire, not to mention various officially conceded Jewish
legal exemptions and privileges, the Jewish revolts were put down
with exceptional violence. The first-century historian Josephus, a
Romanized Jew, reports[14] that 1.1 million died in Titus's siege of
Jerusalem in 70 C.E. The Roman historian Tacitus estimates six hundred thousand dead. Although many modern historians have
regarded these numbers as exaggerations, Josephus in reporting his
figure recognizes that it will seem incredible and explains that
Passover pilgrims from the diaspora had swollen the resident population of Jerusalem to a degree that, although not out of the ordinary
for this pilgrimage city, might well seem unbelievable to outsiders.
He then engages in a surprisingly modern back-calculation from the
number of animals slain for the feast—256,500—to a Passover population of 2,700,200 at the time the siege began.

Jerusalem in that era, it must be remembered, was like Mecca in our
own: the site of an astounding annual concentration of pilgrims, over-
whelmingly male, for whose ritual purposes an equally astounding
number of animals were slaughtered. When the Roman siege began,
the temporary population of Jerusalem was further swollen by
refugees from parts of Palestine where Roman forces had already, and
with great force, been putting down the Jewish rebellion for three full
years. In view of all this, the large casualty figures quoted by Josephus
and Tacitus are not as implausible as they might otherwise seem.[15]

Even if we adjust those figures downward, however, it seems clear
that the first-century slaughter of the Jews of Palestine was large
enough to be comparable in its impact to the twentieth-century
slaughter of the Jews of Europe. The destruction of the Temple in
and of itself would have had a major psychological impact, but this
loss came coupled with staggering casualties; mass enslavements and
ensuing depopulation in the promised land; and, not least, the memory of hideous atrocities. Generally faulted for obsequiousness
toward Rome, Josephus does not flinch from reporting terror-
crucifixions outside the walls of Jerusalem—mass crucifixions aimed
at driving the defenders of the city to despair and panic—or from
reporting that when some of the defenders did flee, Roman merce-

Elijah's Chariot of Fire, folio 200 of the 1526–1529 Latin Bible from the Abbey of St. Amand, France. The Art Archive/ Bibliothèque Municipale Valenciennes/Dagli Orti.

naries took to disemboweling them in search of swallowed gold coins until stopped by the Roman commander himself.

Tales like these bear comparison with the grisliest from the Nazi concentration camps. The memory of them, combined with so devastating a loss of life in the promised land and with major pogroms against the Jews in a number of Roman Empire cities, can scarcely fail to have raised many of the radical or desperate questions about God that, to some, seem to have arisen for the first time in the twentieth century. As for radical or desperate answers to those questions, one seems to have been the Christian vision of the divine warrior self-disarmed.

Historically, there is little doubt that the Jews who rose against Rome expected that their God would come to their assistance, as he had in the historic victories whose celebration remains central to Judaism. There can be equally little doubt that these rebels, as they imagined the God who would assist them, imagined him as knowing the future in detail. This is the image of God expressed so vividly in the Book of Daniel. Literary criticism attending to the character of God within the Old Testament and the New is free to accept this understanding of God (as well as the time and place of the Book of Daniel as given in the text) and then to stipulate about God, as we have done earlier in this book, that, from the Babylonian exile onward, his character is such that he knows the future in the detailed way that human beings know the past.

Yet to imagine a first-century Jew imagining God in this way, even before the disastrous Jewish Wars, is to imagine a Jew in distress. Instead of the predicted kingdom of God, there has come the kingdom of the Romans, and its oppressiveness dwarfs that of all previous oppressors. What was a devout first-century Jew reading the Book of Daniel in a trusting, straightforward, precritical way to think as he or she noted its disconfirmation by events? Had God been mistaken? Had he failed to foresee the rise of Rome? Some such crisis of faith could easily have occurred. What the radical reversal in the divine identity implied by the pacifist preaching of Jesus suggests is that a Jewish writer of powerful imagination projected this crisis of faith into the mind of God, transforming it into a crisis of conscience. God had broken his own covenant, and the fact that he had broken it had to matter to him. He knew he should have stopped Rome. He knew he had not done so. From that simple notion, a composition of enormous complexity could be derived.

A good many historical critics, it should be noted, have based their reading of the Gospels on speculation about the historical consciousness of Jesus. Beginning with Albert Schweitzer in 1901, many have believed that Jesus—living under Roman rule, intensely aware of Jewish tradition, and experiencing what we would now call cognitive dissonance between the two—inserted himself into the received mythology of his day by personifying the Son of Man image of Daniel 7 and then identifying himself as the personage in question. Jesus believed, Schweitzer concluded, that by his own agency and, finally, his own death, Rome would fall, history would end, and God's Kingdom would be established for all time.

More recent scholarship tends to believe that this and related, more or less learned scriptural identifications were made not by Jesus during his lifetime but only about Jesus after his death. So it may well have been, yet the protagonist of the Gospels as we encounter him on the page acts *as if* he has made these identifications himself; and on this literary datum may be grounded an interpretation in which historical speculation about the remembered mind of Jesus yields to literary speculation about the imagined mind of God at that historical juncture. For literary purposes, in other words, it does not matter whether the historical Jesus referred to himself as Son of Man or not, so long as the literary character Jesus Christ does so on the page. Nor need it matter that the effect this character produces on the page, as the page is read today by some contemporary interpreter, may not have been intended by all or even by any of the writers who produced the Gospels. It is proper to a literary classic that it touch readers generation after generation, century after century, in ways that transcend the intentions of the originating author or authors.

But having gone thus far in claiming proprietary space for a literary reading of the Gospels, let me immediately concede that nonhistorical readings vary in the degree to which they are informed by history. A fantastical or mystical or morally didactic reading, for example, might prescind almost entirely from historical information. The reading offered here admits history roughly to the extent that it is admitted in the interpretation of a historical novel. Moreover, although one does not read a historical novel in order to extract history from it, a general awareness of historical time and geographic place colors and contributes to the aesthetic effect, which, as interpreted, may be historically suggestive without entailing any outright historical claim.

Against the usual Christian spiritualization of the Old Testament, the interpretation offered here is a relative materialization of the New Testament, in which God's land-and-wealth-and-offspring promises to the Jews are expected to remain on his mind—which is to say, on Jesus' mind—and in which they are allowed, without shame, to remain on his hearers' minds as well. What such an interpretation of the Gospels suggests about the historical situation behind them is that a theodicy—a moral justification of the behavior of God—whose plausibility had survived several centuries of fluctuating foreign oppression finally came into crisis under the steadily worsening Roman oppression of the first century.

According to the received theodicy, first formulated after Israel was conquered by Assyria and Babylon, that double defeat did not mean what it seemed to mean. The Lord's victory over Egypt had been a real victory, but his apparent defeat by Assyria and Babylonia was not a real defeat. No, Assyria and Babylonia were actually tools in the hands of the Lord, who, far from defeated, was in perfect control of events and merely punishing Israel for its sins. Painful as it might seem to accept the claim that a national god who had once been so favorable had now turned hostile, the alternative was the loss of that god as a potential future support and protection. Since Israel's sense of itself as a people had become inseparable from its sense of covenant with the Lord, life with him even in an angry and punitive mood was preferable to life altogether without him.

By the expedient of attributing its enemies' victories to the action of its own god, Israel saved that god from suffering the same kind of defeat that Israel itself had suffered. But the price of this expedient was high. It required a massive inculpation of the people of Israel— a blaming of the victim, if you will—and an uncomfortable emphasis on anger and vindictiveness in the characterization of the god. Even at the start, these features of the theodicy were felt to be so costly that it was necessary to add, when presenting it, that God would not always conduct himself thus. Israel's national good fortune would be restored before long, and with it a much happier relationship between the god and his people.

But for how many centuries of continuing oppression, especially as different oppressors succeeded one another, could this revision of the covenant remain adequate? The historical suggestion implied by the literary reading of the Gospels offered here is that for a significant segment of the Jewish population, a further revision came to seem necessary. It became necessary to concede the obvious and to redefine the Lord as a god whose return to action as a warrior was not just delayed but altogether canceled, and then to adjust his warlike character accordingly. Not the least part of this adjustment was a revision of his relationship to the other nations of the world, for if the Lord could no longer function effectively as anybody's enemy, then he was necessarily everybody's friend. And if his covenant love was now indiscriminate and universal, then so also must be the love of his covenant partner.

Israel, as God's partner in the original covenant, was expected to demonstrate its status as such by its exclusive devotion *to the Lord*. As the new covenant is proclaimed, Israel's sin, its infidelity and failure to be exclusive in its devotion, is more forgotten than forgiven. The God who will no longer reward or punish his covenant partners as he once did can no longer require of them what he once required. Henceforth, it is not their devotion to him but their devotion to one another and, even more remarkably, to strangers that will signal their status as his. To the extent that they keep this one commandment, to that extent the divine warrior will be excused from ever again taking up arms. Israel will have no enemy because no one will have an enemy other than Satan, the enemy of all.

God Incarnate does indeed understand himself to be, as to his human identity, the "Son of Man" of Daniel 7. But in this capacity, rather than establish the Kingdom of God by military force, he preaches military renunciation: he urges his followers to turn the other cheek. Going dramatically beyond even that, he reveals what he will *not* do—what no one must any longer expect him to do—by going without protest to his own execution on the gallows of the oppressor. The covenant revision is communicated, in sum, not only by prophetic preaching but also by a traumatic, cathartic, climactic, and, not least, ironic sacred drama in which the central role is played by God himself.

Did the historical Jesus actually foresee the worst for his nation, despair of anything like divine rescue, and then—by a bold but conceivable modification of Israelite prophecy—infer that, rather than the prophet of God, he was God himself become incarnate to turn the bad news into an ironic kind of good news? As noted, the all-but-universal assumption on the part of contemporary historical critics is that others turned Jesus into Christ and then into God after his death.

I myself, rather than suppose that Jesus was a simple preacher drafted, as it were, against his will into a larger role, find it historically more plausible to suppose that he was complicitous in his own mythologization, a messenger who intended somehow to become the message, a provocateur who stimulated others to further provocation. Israel Knohl in *The Messiah Before Jesus: The Suffering Servant of the Dead Sea Scrolls*[16] and Michael O. Wise in *The First Messiah: Investigating the Savior Before Christ*[17] claim, on evidence from the Dead Sea Scrolls, to have identified historical figures who, before Jesus, believed themselves or were believed by their followers to be divine, suffering messiahs. One need not accept the exact identifications they propose to recognize that, on the evidence they adduce, the idea of combining these elements—divinity, suffering, and messianism—had grown religiously plausible in Palestinian Jewry well before its Christian enactment.

The new research has attracted as much attention as it has because a chasm separates the claim that the Messiah must suffer from the far bolder claim that the suffering messiah is God Incarnate. And, to be sure, even though Jesus makes this claim in the Gospel of John and notwithstanding the new historical evidence, it remains possible that the idea behind this claim may not in fact have emerged until decades after his death—that is, until closer to the time when the Gospel of John was written. A careful and conservative scholar, the late Raymond E. Brown, asked forty years ago in his great commentary on John whether there is any likelihood that Jesus made such a public claim to divinity as that represented in John 8:58, "Before Abraham was, I AM", or are we dealing here exclusively with the profession of faith of the later Church? As a general principle it is certainly true that through their faith the evangelists were able to clarify a picture of Jesus that was obscure during his ministry. However, it is difficult to avoid the impression created by all the Gospels that the Jewish authorities saw something blasphemous in Jesus' understanding of himself and his role. There is no convincing proof that the only real reason why Jesus was put to death was because he was a social, or ethical, reformer, or because he was politically dangerous. But how can we determine scientifically what the blasphemous element was in Jesus' stated or implied claims about himself? In the clarity with which John presents the divine "I AM" statement of Jesus, is he making explicit what was in some way implicit? No definitive answer seems possible on purely scientific grounds.[18]

There, as it seems to me, the matter still rests. I am content, however, to leave further discussion of this point to the historians, for the myth of God's turning material defeat into spiritual victory is no less remarkable as the creation of Jesus' Jewish contemporaries after his death than as his own creation. The spectacle of the Lord of Hosts put to death by the enemy ought, in principle, to have ended forever a covenant predicated on the Lord's ability to protect his friends and defeat their foes. In practice, for those who made the commemoration of that awful spectacle a covenant ritual, its meaning was that a new covenant between God and mankind had taken effect that was immune to defeat, a covenant that could withstand the worst that Satan, standing (as in the Book of Revelation) for all historical enemies past or future, could inflict. Whatever provoked this adjustment of the idea of covenant (and scholars, significantly, are unanimous that the Gospels were written after the destruction of Jerusalem in 70 C.E.), it is a theodicy conceptually analogous to the adjustment made when the victories of Assyria and Babylonia were defined as the punitive actions of God. What the revision creates, in the end, is a new theodicy, a new way of maintaining that there is still a god and that he still matters in the face of historical experience to the contrary.

While I was at work on this chapter, Rabbi Ovadia Yosef, the spiritual leader of Israel's right-wing Shas party, created a scandal by suggesting in a sermon that the Jews who suffered and died in the Nazi *Shoah* may have died because of Jewish sin.[19] When this statement came up in conversation in Los Angeles, a friend of mine recalled with anger and sadness that, as a boy in the 1940s, he had heard the rabbi in his orthodox *shul* preach this interpretation of the *Shoah* not just once but repeatedly. Reactions against such statements—my friend's sorrow and the scandal that erupted in Israel over Ovadia Yosef—are, of course, as much a part of contemporary Jewish thought as are the statements themselves, but the sorrow and the scandal are instructive for anyone attempting to make sense of Jesus.

How did the divine warrior end up preaching pacifism? Christian theology has tended to speak of this change as spiritual growth in God, although rarely using a phrase like *spiritual growth*. The answer suggested here is that God made a new human virtue of his divine necessity. God was under spiritual duress. He found a way to turn his defeat into a victory, but the defeat came first. For some, to be sure, no divine defeat is so devastating as to extinguish forever the hope of victory. But for others, considering the number and magnitude of the defeats, a different conclusion has seemed inevitable: If God must be defined as a historical-time, physical-world warrior whose victory has simply been postponed indefinitely, then there might as well be no such god. Indefinite postponement is tantamount to cancellation. Effectively, after such a conclusion, the only choices left are atheism or some otherwise unthinkably radical revision in the understanding of God.

This is a question that is called with devastating starkness in Elie Wiesel's *Night*:

> The SS hanged two Jewish men and a youth in front of the whole camp.
> The men died quickly, but the death throes of the youth lasted for half
> an hour. "Where is God? Where is he?" someone asked behind me. As
> the youth still hung in torment in the noose after a long time, I heard
> the man call again, "Where is God now?" And I heard a voice in myself

answer: "Where is he? He is here. He is hanging there on the gallows."[20]

If God will not rescue us, then is there a god? If there is and he still will not rescue us, then is he a weakling or a fiend? It should go without saying that Wiesel did not write this scene as an apology for Christianity. But the scene cannot fail to evoke the Crucifixion for Christian readers, and Wiesel cannot have failed to notice and intend this.

In sum, the disarmament of the divine warrior in the first century mirrors, although with different consequences, his disarmament in the twentieth century. The epigraph to *The Prophets,*[21] the most widely read of the books of the late Abraham Joshua Heschel, the most influential Jewish theologian of the twentieth century, is

To the Martyrs of 1940–45
All this has come upon us,
Though we have not forgotten Thee,
Or been false to Thy covenant.
Our heart has not turned back,
Nor have our steps departed from Thy way . . .
. . . for Thy sake we are slain . . .
Why dost Thou hide Thy face? (from Psalm 44)

Heschel had every reason to think of these lines—from the earlier quoted Psalm 44—when thinking of the martyrs of 1940–45, but other Jews nineteen centuries before him, thinking of other martyrs, had no less reason to turn to the same Psalm; and what one of them, whether or not the one in question was Jesus himself, may have gone on to imagine was a scene like the gallows scene in *Night,* a scene in which the Jew on the gallows, this time, was truly God himself.

Notes

1. University of Chicago Press, 2002, 122–123.
2. Dale C. Allison Jr., "Rejecting Violent Judgment: Luke 9:52–56 and Its Relatives," *Journal of Biblical Literature* 121, no. 3 (2002): 468.
3. Ibid., 474.
4. Ibid., 471.
5. Ibid., 468.
6. Ibid., 478.
7. Alfred A. Knopf, 2001.
8. Camden House, 2002.
9. HarperCollins, 2002.

10. Yale University Press, 2001, 44.

11. This section is an excerpt from *Christ: A Crisis in the Life of God*, (New York: Knopf, 2001) edited and adapted for this current volume. It is taken from Part Two of that former work, "A Prophet against the Promise."

12. I use this Hebrew noun, which means simply "catastrophe," by preference to the more usual *Holocaust*, a word that some find offensive because its original setting is in the Jewish religion itself. *Shoah* is the noun most commonly used in Israel to refer to the slaughter of the Jews of Europe during World War II.

13. Estimates have been lowered somewhat in the past generation, but not in a way that would affect the claim that the Roman and the Nazi *shoahs* bear comparison. Writing in 1971, Salo W. Baron estimated the Jewish population within the borders of the Roman empire at just under 7 million, with slightly more than a million others living outside its borders, mostly to the east; the Jewish population of Palestine he placed at not higher than 2.5 million. *Encyclopaedia Judaica* (New York: Macmillan, 1972), 13:871. Paul Johnson writes, "Though it is impossible to present accurate figures, it is clear that by the time of Christ the diaspora Jews greatly outnumbered the settled Jews of Palestine: perhaps by as many as 4.5 million to 1." *A History of Christianity* (New York: Athenaeum, 1976), 12. Subsequent estimates generally fall between these extremes. Thus, Wayne Meeks in *The First Urban Christians* (New Haven: Yale University Press, 1983) estimates 1 million Jews in Palestine, 5 million to 6 million in the diaspora.

14. F. Josephus, *The Wars of the Jews*, book 6, chapter 9, section 3, in *The Works of Josephus, New Updated Version*, trans. W. Walker (Peabody: Hendrickson, 1987).

15. Compare Salo W. Baron's comment in *Encyclopaedia Judaica:*

> The figures transmitted by such distinguished historians as Josephus and Tacitus ranging between 600,000 fatalities and 1,197,000 dead and captured are not quite so out of line as they appear at first glance. Jerusalem's population had been swelled by countless numbers of pilgrims from all over the Dispersion and refugees from the provinces previously occupied by the Roman legions.

16. Berkeley: University of California Press, 2000.

17. San Francisco: HarperSanFrancisco, 1999.

18. Raymond E. Brown, *The Gospel According to John I–XII*, Anchor Bible Series (New York: Doubleday, 1966), 29:367–368.

19. John F. Burns, "Israeli Rabbi Sets Off a Political Firestorm Over the Holocaust," *New York Times*, August 8, 2000, sec. A., p. 100.

20. Elie Wiesel, *Night* (New York: Bantam Doubleday Dell, 1982), 79; originally published in 1958.

21. Abraham J. Heschel, *The Prophets*, vol. 2 (1962; New York: Harper Torchbooks, 1975). A more recent, psychologically shaped Jewish theology is found in David R. Blumenthal, *Facing the Abusing God: A Theology of Protest* (Louisville: Westminster John Knox Press, 1993). Theological reflection on these passages seems almost inevitably, in our day, to yield a theology of protest. Literary reflection on them in the first century may have yielded at least a protest in pantomime.

CHAPTER 8

ABRAHAM AND ISAAC: THE SACRIFICIAL IMPULSE

Donald Capps

Throughout human history, children have been used, against their will, in adults' attempts to satisfy or placate their gods. Children have been sacrificed to deities because adults believed this was what the deities required of them. In most instances, the adults have been motivated to comply with these demands out of fear, the same fear that children themselves exhibit when they are the object of parental abuse. Adults are afraid not to comply with the demand that they sacrifice their children to the gods because they are afraid of the consequences, not only to themselves personally but also, and more important, to the community in which they live. Children have been offered up to various deities in order to protect the community against war, disease, pestilence, and drought. They have been offered to the gods as an expression of the community's repentance for acting against the deities' will.

The people of Israel were critical of the Canaanites' sacrifice of children to Molech, as was Augustine of Carthaginians' child sacrifices to Saturn. Although Christianity has dissociated itself from actual rites of child sacrifice, it has not denounced the theory of sacrifice. In fact, because there are no periodic reminders of its consequences via rites of child sacrifice, there has been little social pressure to rethink the idea of a religion of sacrifice. As a result, Christianity has legitimated the physical and psychic deaths of hundreds of thousands of children throughout the centuries.

As Lloyd deMause (1988) shows in *The History of Childhood: The Untold Story of Child Abuse*, Jesus' attitude toward children—"Do not despise one of these little ones"—did not inaugurate a new era in which children were no longer endangered. He writes: "The history of infanticide in the West has yet to be written, and I shall not attempt it here. But enough is already known to establish that, contrary to the usual assumption that it is an Eastern rather than a Western problem, infanticide of both legitimate and illegitimate children was a regular practice of antiquity, that the killing of legitimate children was only slowly reduced during the Middle Ages, and that illegitimate children continued regularly to be killed right up into the nineteenth century" (25).

During the first few centuries of the Christian era, infanticide was still an accepted, everyday occurrence. Children were thrown into rivers, flung into dung heaps and trenches, "potted" in jars to starve to death, and exposed on hills and roadsides, a prey for birds and wild beasts. Girls were valued far less than boys, and it was very rare for a family to raise more than one daughter. The others were exposed to die. Households consisted of one or two children, rarely three or more. Deformed children were almost always exposed to die. The theme of exposure loomed large in myth, tragedy, and even comedy, which was built around the subject of the misadventures involved in trying to chop up and roast a baby. The killing of legitimate children even by wealthy parents was so common that Polybius blamed it for the depopulation of Greece, and in the two centuries after Augustus, some attempts were made to pay parents to keep children alive in order to replenish the dwindling Roman population. Yet it was not until 374 C.E. that killing an infant was declared to be murder (25–27).

DeMause claims that a high incidence of infanticide continued throughout the eighteenth and nineteenth centuries in Europe:

Even though Thomas Coram opened his Foundling Hospital because he couldn't bear to see the dying babies lying in the gutters and rotting on the dung-heaps of London, by the 1890s dead babies were still a common sight in London streets. Late in the nineteenth century Louis Adamic described being brought up in an Eastern European village of "killing nurses," where mothers sent their infants to be done away with "by exposing them to cold air after a hot bath; feeding them something that caused convulsions in their stomachs and intestines; mixing gypsum in their milk, which literally plastered up their insides; suddenly stuffing them with food after not giving them anything to eat for two

days. . . ." Adamic was to have been killed as well, but for some reason
his nurse spared him. (29)

The history of childhood in Christian nations is a disturbing chronicle of systematic and deliberate abuse and neglect.

Why were Jesus' words of compassion for "the little ones" so casually disregarded? Why have Christians been so cavalier regarding the
physical and emotional fate of their own offspring? A possible clue is in
the frequent charge by non-Christians that Christians were engaged in
the killing of babies in secret rites. As deMause points out, when so
accused, Christians were quick to point out that their accusers were
guilty of putting their own offspring to death in public rituals. Yet,
while these accusations against Christians were self-serving, what is
striking about them is that they accused Christians of doing in secrecy
what they themselves were doing publicly.

I am not here concerned with the literal truth of these accusations,
but rather with the perception that Christianity was no less a sacrificial religion than the religions it sought to replace. That this perception was extant could only be due to the fact that, while it renounced
the ritual of child sacrifice, its theology was deeply informed by the
sacrificial idea itself. In his writings on infanticide, David Bakan
(1966) has suggested that the Christian Eucharist takes the place of
the ritual of child sacrifice in other religions, making Christ, rather
than a child, the holy victim. By emphasizing that Christ is "truly
present" in the sacrament, the sacrifice is repeated Sunday after
Sunday, and participation in this real sacrifice is substituted for the
law as a way of restraining infanticide (229). Thus, in his view, one
purpose of the Eucharist was to forestall actual acts of infanticide by
reenacting the sacrificial death of Christ instead.

Yet, if this was the intention behind the Eucharist, the high incidence of infanticide in Christian nations indicates that the ritual has
had little success in this regard. It replaces one ritual with another,
but does not address the more fundamental problem that Christianity
has not been able to shed the sacrificial idea itself. In fact, while we
might have expected Christianity to have defined itself over against
the religion of sacrifice, it has, instead, allowed itself to be defined as
a religion of sacrifice. And this means that it has become a religion
that requires an innocent victim who pays for the sins of the community. This self-definition of Christianity needs itself to be exposed, for
its construal of the relationship of God to believers is reminiscent of
the abusive relationship of parent to child.

Giambattista Tiepolo's *Sacrifice of Isaac.* The Art Archive/Palazzo dell'Arcivescovado Udine/Dagli Orti.

The Aborted Sacrifice of Isaac

For Christians, the initial source of the sacrificial idea is the story of Abraham's aborted sacrifice of Isaac. This powerfully disturbing story has made a deep impression on the psyches of readers of the Bible. It is surely the best known of biblical "texts of terror" (Trible, 1984; Culbertson, 1992). We may well deplore the great notoriety of the Abraham and Isaac story, especially the fact that it so eclipses the story of the actual sacrifice of Jephthah's daughter, but the basic fact that this story is among the best-known stories in the Bible cannot be ignored. It is also a story that Christians, through the ages, have applied to their own lives. In *The Bible in Pastoral Care,* Wayne Oates (1953) tells about a woman who, on hearing a sermon on this story, returned home and assaulted her daughter with a knife, believing that this is what God had commanded her to do. The fact that Abraham was a father and Isaac was a son was unimportant to her. Nor did the fact that the story ends with Isaac being spared seem to affect her understanding of it. All that mattered is that the story was about a parent being commanded by God to kill the child whom he loved.

We should not be surprised that Alice Miller has written about the Abraham and Isaac story since it is central to her theme of parental abuse of children. In a chapter in *The Untouched Key* (1990) titled "When Isaac Arises from the Sacrificial Altar" (137–145), she tells about her search for an illustration for the jacket of the British edition of her earlier book, *Thou Shalt Not Be Aware*. Two Rembrandt depictions of the sacrifice of Isaac came to mind. In both, the father's hand completely covers the son's face, obstructing his sight, his speech, and even his breathing. As Abraham's use of his hands to control forcibly Isaac's powers of sight, speech, and even breath fit the themes of her book, Miller recommended this detail of Rembrandt's paintings to her publisher for the cover. But recollections of these paintings also prompted her to go to an archive to look at other portrayals of Abraham and Isaac. She found thirty in all, painted by very dissimilar artists, and with growing astonishment she discovered that all of them depicted Abraham with eyes turned upward, "as though he is asking God if he is carrying out His will correctly. . . . In all the portrayals of this scene that I found, Abraham's face or entire torso is turned away from his son and directed upward. Only his hands are occupied with the sacrifice" (138).

Also, as she looked at depictions of Isaac, she was struck by the fact that he was invariably portrayed as an adult at the peak of his manhood, and that he was simply lying there, quietly waiting to be murdered by his father. In some of the versions he was calm and obedient; in only one was he in tears, but in none was he rebellious or even questioning. He does not ask: "Father, why do you want to kill me, why is my life worth nothing to you? Why won't you look at me, why won't you explain what is happening? How can you do this to me? What crime have I committed? What have I done to deserve this?" (138).

Miller suggests that such questions cannot even be formulated in Isaac's mind because they can only be entertained by someone who feels himself to be on an equal footing with the person being questioned, and only if he can look the other in the eye: "How can a person lying on a sacrificial altar with hands bound, about to be slaughtered, ask questions when his father's hand keeps him from seeing or speaking and hinders his breathing? Such a person has been turned into an *object*. He has been dehumanized by being made a sacrifice; he no longer has a right to ask questions and will scarcely even be able to articulate them for himself, for there is no room in him for anything besides fear" (139).

Nor does the father ask any questions. He submits to the divine command as a matter of course, the same way his son submits to him: "He must—and wants to—prove that his obedience is stronger than what he calls his love for his child. . . . If the angel didn't intervene at the last moment, Abraham would become the murderer of his son simply because God's voice demanded it of him" (140).

As she continued to review these depictions of the scene, Miller was also struck by the fact that none of the artists gave this dramatic scene an individual, personal stamp. While the dress, colors, surroundings, and positions of the bodies varied, the psychological content was remarkably uniform. An obvious explanation for this is that the artists were attempting to be faithful to the biblical text, but this does not satisfy Miller, for one would expect that artists—of all persons—would allow their imaginations to range freely, and to question the validity of the biblical story: "Why did all of these artists accept the story as valid? The only answer I can think of is that the situation involves a fundamental fact of our existence, with which many of us became familiar during the first years of life and which is so painful that knowledge of it can survive only in the depths of the unconscious. Our awareness of the child's victimization is so deeply rooted in us that we scarcely seem to have reacted at all to the monstrousness of the story of Abraham and Isaac" (141).

In her own imaginative revisioning of the story, Miller considers two possible scenarios: One is that an enraged Isaac uses every ounce of his strength to free his hands to wrest the knife from his father's hands, so as to plunge it into his father's heart. The other is that he uses every ounce of his strength to free his hands so that he can remove Abraham's hand from his face. Then, "he would dare to use his eyes and see his father as he really is: uncertain and hesitant yet intent on carrying out a command he does not comprehend. Now Isaac's nose and mouth would be free too, and he could finally draw a deep breath and make use of his voice. He would be able to speak and ask questions, and Abraham, whose left hand could no longer keep his son from seeing and speaking, would have to enter into a dialogue with his son, at the end of which he might possibly encounter the young man he had once been himself, who was never allowed to ask questions" (143–144).

In this second scenario, there would be a confrontation between the two, with the son challenging the assumptions behind the father's actions. If Abraham explains his action as a matter of his desire to obey the will of God, then Isaac will ask him how he can set aside his own feelings in deference to the deity, and he will ask him what kind of God this is who would demand such a thing as the murder of one's own child. In this scenario, the son does not want to be rescued by the angel who rewarded Abraham for his obedience. Instead, the son refuses "to let himself be killed, and thereby not only saves his own life but also saves his father the fate of being the unthinking murderer of his child" (145).

Thus, what Miller envisions is the child's refusal to be a sacrificial victim. He steps outside the sacrificial frame, challenging its validity, exposing it as spurious. If, for the parent, the sacrificial frame is so entrenched that he is unable to extricate himself from it, the child, at least, can refuse to participate in it by frustrating the parent's efforts to carry out what he believes to be his God-given duty.

But Miller's alternative scenario is likely to raise questions of its own: Why does Isaac allow himself to be his father's victim? Surely, one or both of the alternative scenarios that Miller envisions has been considered by Isaac himself. He must have considered using his physical strength either to resist his father's knife or even to turn the knife against him. Yet he does not act upon those revisionings. Is this because he believes that he will eventually be delivered, that his father will come to his senses or that some "angel" (the other parent or a sympathetic sibling) will intervene? Or is it because he identifies with his aggressor, sharing his father's belief that it is his father's God-given duty to attack the child because it is the child's God-given duty to be a sacrificial victim? Miller seems to imply that Isaac has no beliefs of his own, that he accepts his fate unquestioningly simply because "there is no room in him for anything besides fear." But the biblical Isaac believed in the same God that his father believed in. Otherwise, his father's answer to his question about the identity of the sacrificial victim—"God will provide, my son"—would merely have generated additional questions: "What do you mean, God will provide?" "And who is this God you serve anyway."

Thus, believing in the same God that Abraham believes in, and believing that he has been ordained to be the sacrificial victim this God requires him to be, Isaac does not ask questions because he hasn't any. He so much identifies with his aggressor that we might even expect him to assist his father in the murderous act should his father's nerve begin to fail him and his hand begin to tremble. The dilemma here is that the child adopts the parent's perspective as his own, and the fact that he is filled by fear only reinforces this basic fact.

Another concern that Miller's alternative scenario raises is its assumption that Abraham can be reasoned with, that if Isaac questions what his father is doing, the older man may be persuaded to listen to reason. But can we assume this? If Abraham were acting only on his own initiative—if he were, in fact, only acting out of personal anger or vengeance—perhaps, then, he could be talked out of what he was intending to do. But we should not forget that he understands himself to be carrying out the will of God. He is a true believer, and true believers are not disposed to listen to reason. Isaac's questions are likely to strengthen this resolve, for they would only reinforce Abraham's view that what he is doing is in response to divine—not human—will.

A third consideration has to do with the very notion of sacrifice. The idea of sacrifice—that payment is demanded—is so deeply rooted in the human psyche, and in the structure of human society, that we rarely question its validity. Abraham does not challenge the notion that a sacrifice is required, nor does Isaac. Nor do most readers of the story question the storyteller's assurance that Abraham was commanded by God to do this thing, and that it was also by divine agency that Isaac was spared. Why do most readers of the text accept this claim and why do they not entertain the alternative theory that Abraham—like the woman in Wayne Oates's story—was out of his mind? Why we do not dispute the storyteller's assurance that God commanded Abraham to act as he did, thus questioning the whole premise of the story, tells us something about how deeply rooted is the sacrificial view of human life, both personal and societal, and how deeply rooted is the belief that this view has a religious legitimation.

Perhaps the fundamental reason that none of the artists was tempted to give this dramatic scene an individual, personal stamp is that the sacrificial idea is so deeply rooted in the human psyche, and in our understanding of how human society must work, that an alternative scenario is hardly imaginable. The biblical story itself accepts the sacrificial frame as a fact of human existence, so that it envisions only a variation within this frame—an alternative victim—and not the abrogating of the sacrificial frame itself. To put their individual, personal stamp on the scene, the artists would also have had to challenge the religious legitimation of the whole sacrificial event, to convey somehow that Abraham was not in fact hearing the voice of God but listening to voices in his own tortured mind. In this sense, the alternative scenario that Miller envisions—of Isaac speaking up to his father and questioning him—does not go nearly far enough, as it does not raise fundamental questions regarding the biblical story's effort to provide a religious legitimation for the sacrificial idea itself: that God requires a victim and if one is not offered there will be hell to pay.

It is true that Miller relates the story of Abraham and Isaac to the contemporary situation in which older men prepare wars that younger men are sent to fight and die in and that she strongly advocates resistance to participation in war by the current generation of Isaacs who are in a position to know precisely what their fathers are doing, that is, sacrificing them on some altar because the older men are listening to the voice of their governments without questioning its validity (139–140). But any vision of massive resistance to the victimization of the younger generation would be as utopian as the vision of life that Miller abhors is apocalyptic. Moreover, it does not seriously challenge the religious claims that are made in behalf of the sacrificial idea itself, the idea that the sacrifice is demanded by God himself. The most that Miller has to say in this regard is her suggestion that Isaac ask Abraham what kind of God this is who would demand such a thing as the murder of one's own child? This is a valid question for Isaac to ask, and the asking of it does take us a significant step beyond the perspective of the biblical storyteller who does not think to ask this question. But to ask this question is not yet to have asked the much more fundamental question, Why should we give the idea of sacrifice—in whatever form—a religious legitimation, invoking the will of God in its support?

The Religious Legitimation of Sacrifice

The issue of the religious legitimation of sacrifice is taken up by Søren Kierkegaard in his well-known interpretation of the Abraham and Isaac story in *Fear and Trembling* (1983). I will not attempt here a thoroughgoing study of this fascinating text, but will focus only on the first section where Kierkegaard does what Miller says the artists ought to have done, namely, imagines the different scenarios that might have substituted for the one presented in the biblical text itself. In envisioning these alternative scenarios, Kierkegaard seeks to penetrate the mind of Abraham, who might have been expected to consider the various ways he might deal with the situation at hand and to evaluate the short- and long-term consequences of these various alternatives.

Before presenting these alternative scenarios, however, Kierke-gaard begins with his own interest in the biblical story, noting that a "man"—presumably himself—had heard the story of Abraham and Isaac as a child and had found it "beautiful": "Once upon a time there was a man who as a child had heard that beautiful story of how God tempted Abraham and of how Abraham withstood the temptation, kept the faith, and, contrary to expectation, got a son a second time" (9). Later, when the man read the story, it impressed him even more: "When he grew older, he read the same story with even greater admi-ration, for life had fractured what had been united in the pious sim-plicity of the child" (9). He kept returning to the story as he grew up: "The older he became, the more often his thoughts turned to that story; his enthusiasm for it became greater and greater, and yet he could understand the story less and less." Finally, "he forgot every-thing else because of it, his soul had but one wish, to see Abraham, but one longing, to have witnessed the event" (9). His craving was not to see the beautiful regions of the East, not the earthly glory of the Promised Land, not the God-fearing couple whose old age God had blessed, not the remarkable figure of the aged patriarch, not the vig-orous adolescence God bestowed on Isaac. No, "his craving was to go along on the three-day journey when Abraham rode with sorrow before him and Isaac beside him. His wish was to be present in that hour when Abraham raised his eyes and saw Mount Moriah in the distance, the hour when he left the ass behind and went up the moun-tain alone with Isaac—for what occupied him was not the beautiful tapestry of imagination but the shudder of the idea" (9). The idea that Isaac must be sacrificed because God commanded it.

Kierkegaard then proposes four possible scenarios that the man who accompanied Abraham and Isaac up Mount Moriah may have witnessed. In the first, Abraham's party travels for three days until, on the morning of the fourth day, Abraham sees Mount Moriah looming in the distance. He leaves the young servants behind and takes Isaac's hand, and they walk up the mountain together. Suddenly, Abraham stands still and lays his hand on Isaac's head to bless him, and Isaac kneels to receive the blessing. Abraham's face epitomizes fatherliness, his gaze is gentle. But Isaac does not understand his father's action, and his soul is not uplifted. He begins to beg for his life, suspecting that something strange is going on, and for his beau-tiful hopes. But Abraham is reassuring as he lifts Isaac up and they continue walking, although Isaac still does not understand what is going on. Then Abraham turns away from his son, for a moment, and when Isaac sees Abraham's face again, it has changed. His gaze is wild, his whole being is sheer terror. He seizes Isaac by the chest, throws him down on the ground, and says, "Stupid boy, do you think I am your father? I am an idolater. Do you think it is God's command? No, it is my desire." Then Isaac trembles and cries out in his anguish: "God in heaven, have mercy on me, God of Abraham, have mercy on me; if I have no father on earth, then you be my father!" Whereupon Abraham says quietly to himself, "Lord God in heaven, I thank you; it is better that he believes me a monster than that he should lose faith in you!" Kierkegaard concludes this scenario with an allusion to the mother who blackens her breast so that it is no longer inviting to the child who needs to be weaned: "So the child believes that the breast has changed, but the mother—she is still the same, her gaze is tender and loving as ever. How fortunate the one who did not need more terrible means to wean the child!" (11). Thus, in scenario one, Abraham falsely attributes the divine command to his own murderous desires so that Isaac would have faith in God instead.

In scenario two, Abraham and Isaac ride along the road in silence for three days, and Abraham stares continuously and fixedly at the ground. On the fourth day, he methodologically arranges the firewood, binds Isaac, and silently draws the knife. Then he sees the ram that God provides, sacrifices it, and goes home: "From that day henceforth, Abraham was old; he could not forget that God had ordered him to do this. Isaac flourished as before, but Abraham's eyes were darkened, and he saw joy no more" (12). Kierkegaard concludes this second scenario with another reference to the weaning of a child, this time noting that a mother will conceal her breast and then the child has no mother: "How fortunate the child who has not lost his mother in some other way." Thus, here, Abraham performs as commanded, the outcome is precisely as the biblical story tells it, but Abraham has lost faith in God because of what God commanded him to do.

In the third scenario, Abraham rides thoughtfully down the road, and he thinks of Hagar and his son—Ishmael—whom he drove out into the desert. When he reaches Mount Moriah, he throws himself down on his face and prays God to forgive him his sin, that he has been willing to sacrifice Isaac, having forgotten his duty to his son. From that time forth, he often rides this lonesome road, finding no peace: Was it a sin that he had been willing to sacrifice to God the best that he had? And if it was a sin, how could it ever be forgiven, for what more terrible sin is there than a father's willingness to sacrifice his own son? Kierkegaard concludes this scenario with still another reference to the weaning of a child, and focuses on the mother's sorrow, because in the weaning process "she and the child are more and more to be separated," and they will never again be so close: "How fortunate the one who kept the child so close and did not need to grieve anymore!" (13). Here, Abraham discerns that it was wrong for him to have been willing to give up his son, and he is left to struggle with the moral and spiritual implications of having forgotten his duty to his son. Hadn't he already abandoned Ishmael to an uncertain fate in the desert? Isn't it a father's duty to value his son's life and protect it as even more precious than his own? And hasn't his willingness to give up his son—even if he subsequently thought better of it—cast a permanent shadow on their relationship together? In this scenario, it is the father who is left with all the questions, and who is unable to find any peace.

In the fourth scenario, Abraham and Isaac arrive at Mount Moriah, and Abraham, calmly and gently, makes everything ready for the sacrifice. But when he draws the knife, Isaac sees that Abraham's left hand is clenched in despair and that a shudder is running through his whole body. When they return home, Sarah comes out to meet them, but Isaac has lost his faith: "Not a word is even said of this in the world, and Isaac never talked to anyone about what he had seen, and Abraham did not suspect that anyone had seen it" (14). Kierkegaard again alludes to the weaning of a child, and notes that, when the child needs to be weaned, the good mother has stronger sustenance at hand so that the child does not perish: "How fortunate is the one who has this stronger sustenance at hand" (14). Thus, in this scenario, Abraham believes that he has carried out his role as required of him, but Isaac has seen his father's own despair, his own fear and trembling, and this makes such an impression on Isaac that he can no longer believe in Abraham's God. Unlike the first scenario, where Abraham ensures that Isaac will believe in Abraham's God by representing the sacrifice as his own malevolent idea, here Abraham unwittingly undermines Isaac's belief because his left hand—the one that does not hold the knife—betrays him.

Kierkegaard notes that these four scenarios plus many others occurred to the "man" as he pondered the story, but all left him as uncomprehending of Abraham as was the Isaac of scenario one. Following these scenarios, he offers a brief eulogy on Abraham, in which he considers what it was that made Abraham the greatest of all men, for, unlike men whose greatness was in their power, wisdom, hope, or love, Abraham was "great by the power whose strength is powerlessness, great by that wisdom whose secret is foolishness, great by that hope whose form is madness, great by that love that is hatred to oneself" (16–17). As the very meaning of Abraham's life involved his son Isaac, the test to which God put him challenged his life's very meaning, "for what meaning would it have if Isaac should be sacrificed!" (19).

What impresses Kierkegaard about Abraham's decision to go through with the sacrifice of Isaac is that by doing so he was a man of absolute faith. Had he doubted, he would have placed himself on the altar—"for what is an old man compared with a child of promise"—and plunged the knife into his own heart. Instead, he arose early in the morning, hurrying "as if to a celebration," and prepared the sacrifice without a shred of hesitation or doubt:

> And there he stood, the old man with his solitary hope. But he did not doubt, he did not look in anguish to the left and to the right. . . . He did not challenge heaven with his prayers. He knew it was God the Almighty who was testing him; he knew it was the hardest sacrifice that could be demanded of him; but he knew also that no sacrifice is too severe when God demands it—and he drew the knife. (22)

As if he had studied the same paintings of the scene that Miller reviewed, Kierkegaard goes on to note that "anyone who looks upon this scene is paralyzed. Who strengthened Abraham's soul lest everything go black for him and he see neither Isaac nor the ram! Anyone who looks upon this scene is blinded" (22). But Abraham was neither paralyzed nor blinded. He never doubted, and this made the difference:

> If Abraham had doubted as he stood there on Mount Moriah, if irresolute he had looked around, if he had happened to spot the ram before drawing the knife, if God had allowed him to sacrifice it instead of Isaac—then he would have gone home, everything would have been the same, he would have had Sarah, he would have kept Isaac, and yet how changed! For his return would have been a flight, his deliverance an accident, his reward disgrace, his future perhaps perdition. Then he would have witnessed neither to his faith nor to God's grace but would have witnessed to how appalling it is to go to Mount Moriah. (22)

Kierkegaard concludes his eulogy to Abraham with the observation that, of all remarkable fathers, Abraham does not need a eulogy, for eulogies are for fathers who need someone to snatch their memories from the power of oblivion. This is not the case with Abraham, "for every language calls you to mind." The man who heard the story of Abraham as a child, who struggled with it throughout his early youth and manhood, will never forget the Venerable Father Abraham who in his one hundred thirty years of life "got no further than faith" (23).

The reader of Kierkegaard's eulogy on Abraham cannot but be inspired by his stirring endorsement of Abraham's witness to his faith. What makes Abraham's faith so powerful is precisely that he does not even consider the alternative scenarios that entered the mind of the man who pondered this event. What is so truly startling and incomprehensible about Abraham is that he did *not* think of alternative scenarios such as pretending to be the one who contrived the sacrifice so that Isaac would not lose his faith in God, or going through the motions of sacrificing Isaac and relinquishing his faith in the process, or asking God to forgive him for even considering the sacrifice of his beloved son, or going through with the sacrifice but with such despair that Isaac cannot but notice and lose his own faith in God because of his father's own fear and trembling. No, Abraham's faith is incomparable precisely because he does not ponder these alternative scenarios but instead hurries up the mountain, "as if to a celebration," and prepares to sacrifice his child without a shred of hesitation or doubt.

Kierkegaard's Idealization of Abraham

The question we have to ask is, Why does Kierkegaard himself, once having envisioned the alternative scenarios, which take account of the moral and religious ambiguities of the sacrificial idea, proceed to extol Abraham for his own utter disregard of these moral and religious ambiguities? If readers of the biblical story have difficulty comprehending Abraham, is this because Abraham is a man of such great faith that he allows nothing—even his beloved son—to come between himself and his God, or is it because he is so certain of himself, so sure that he is acting in response to the command of God, that we necessarily wonder—precisely because he *is* so certain of himself—whether he is not deluding himself? Why should he not consider the alternative scenarios that Kierkegaard has put forward? Why are they not even worth his consideration? And why is Kierkegaard so willing to reject these scenarios in favor of the one in which Abraham proceeds with the sacrifice as though it were a celebration? Why should Abraham not ask God to forgive him for even considering the sacrifice of his son? Why should Abraham not exhibit such despair that Isaac cannot but conclude that the God his father is trying to serve is unworthy of him?

I think that Kierkegaard is willing to reject these scenarios as the mere "ponderings" of a "man" who has been gripped by the story since childhood because he is unable or unwilling to face the initially disturbing but ultimately liberating truth that human sacrifice, whatever form it may take, has absolutely no religious legitimation— which is to say that, if Abraham thought he was acting in response to a command from God, he was deluding himself. Moreover, if the biblical storyteller thinks that Abraham was hearing a voice from God and not merely hearing voices—in the same way that paranoid and dissociative personalities hear voices—then he is also self-deluded, and his "alternative scenario" that God accepts alternative victims is based on the fallacious idea that God, and not humans, is the author of victimization.

I believe that Kierkegaard was unable to accept this conclusion because, like Isaac, he identified with the aggressor, adopting the perspective of the abusing father as his own, which included the abusing Father's religious legitimation for the abuse. But why was he unable to accept this conclusion? I believe it was because of his intense desire to be a son to a man like Abraham. Note that he says that, as a child, he heard "that beautiful story of how God tempted Abraham and of how Abraham withstood the temptation." Since Kierkegaard's own father was a man who was known to have given in to various temptations (Kierkegaard's own mother had been his father's sexual partner before his first wife's death), the child Søren was introduced through the beautiful story of Abraham to a father who was above temptation, and who was therefore reliable, a father on whom a son could always depend. Conversely, consider what it would be like to be a son of such a father! Would he not be able to bask in his father's glory, to take great personal pride in the fact that he was the son of such a man as this?

This desire to be the son of Abraham is reflected in the fact that Kierkegaard chose to eulogize Abraham, as if to imply that he, Kierkegaard, is among those who grieve the death of Abraham, experiencing it as a deep, personal loss. Toward the end of the eulogy, he refers to himself as "a late lover" of whom Abraham had no need, as his memory will survive without Kierkegaard's celebratory words, but whom Abraham continues richly to reward: "You reward your lover more gloriously than anyone else. In the life to come you make him eternally happy in your bosom; here in this life you captivate his eyes and his heart with the wonder of your act" (23). He then goes on to ask Father Abraham to "forgive the one who aspired to speak your praise if he has not done it properly" (23).

All of this is spoken like a son for whom Father Abraham is a powerful ideal, a father figure who fully satisfies his son's desire for a father who is inwardly secure and, because he is secure, is able to secure his son's own self. As psychoanalyst Heinz Kohut points out, parents who are inwardly secure, who have a healthy narcissistic self, will not be put off by their child's idealization of them, but will accept it, recognizing that it serves a vital role in enabling the child to feel secure and protected. Conversely, parents who are bored, embarrassed, or rejecting of such idealizations will withdraw, leaving the child confused, despairing, and inwardly empty. Such parents fail to realize how much the children's own sense of self depends on their idealization of parents being mirrored back to them (Kohut, 1971, ch. 5, 1977, 171ff.). In their paper on the disorders of the self, Kohut and his colleague Ernest Wolf (1986) offer the following illustration:

> A little boy is eager to idealize his father, he wants his father to tell him about his life, the battles he engaged in and won. But instead of joyfully acting in accordance with his son's need, the father is embarrassed by the request. He feels tired and bored and, leaving the house, finds a temporary source of vitality for his enfeebled self in the tavern, through drink and mutually supportive friends. (184; see also Kohut, 1971, 139–140)

Kierkegaard's own father made him feel self-conscious, aware of his insecurity and self-depletion. In his *Journals* (Kierkegaard, 1958), he recalls the impression it made on him some years earlier when, "filled with a youthful and romantic enthusiasm for a *master-thief*, I went so far as to say that it was only the misuse of powers, and thus such a man might still be converted," to which his father replied very solemnly, "There are offences which one can only fight against with God's continual help." Whereupon, the young Kierkegaard "hurried down to my room and looked at myself in the glass" (54). Instead of mirroring his son's idealization of a resourceful criminal, his father used the occasion to teach a lesson about how continual must be the struggle against sin, leading Kierkegaard to view himself in the mirror as a guilty, despicable culprit. In contrast, Kierkegaard saw in Abraham a father who represented the romantic, exciting, and risky attitude toward life with which the child Søren identified the master thief, but that his own father dismissed with a routine truism about the struggle against sin, a struggle that his father often lost. Given the contrast between Abraham and his own father, one can easily imagine that Kierkegaard envied Isaac, who had a father who could be idealized because he was a man of absolute faith.

If this is what Abraham means to Kierkegaard, it is not surprising that Kierkegaard does not question Abraham's treatment of Isaac, or suggest (with Miller) that Isaac engage in the questioning of Abraham. But Kierkegaard's own desire to be Abraham's beloved son need not deter others of us from challenging Abraham and from raising questions about the biblical story's effort to provide religious legitimation for the idea of sacrifice. In fact, if we take exception to Kierkegaard's own embracement of Abraham for the personal reasons we have just adduced, we are then free to consider the alternative scenarios that he himself imagines, and others besides. What is striking about his alternative scenarios is that each concludes with a reference to a mother weaning her child. In the context, these maternal images seem out of place as the story is clearly focused on what is occurring between father and son, not on the mother who has been left at home. And yet, the weaning theme offers an alternative way of understanding the disunity between parents and children, and the roles that both play in the working out of this disunity.

Isaac: Son of Sarah

If the father and son view the disunity in terms of sacrifice—and therefore assume that the son is destined to be a victim—the mother and son take a more measured view, seeing their disunity as the inevitable consequence of the separation of mother and child, as an experience over which both must grieve. If weaning and not sacrifice becomes the key metaphor for the deep fissures that exist at the core of human society, then this experience has its own legitimation, and there is no need to put forward a religious legitimation for what is an entirely natural, if profoundly sad and sorrowful event. Weaning has its costs too, but, as Kierkegaard puts it, "How fortunate the child who has not lost his mother in some other way"—which is also to say that fortunate is the child whose fate is not taken over by the fathers, who will demand sacrifice, but whose fate instead remains in the hands of the mothers (or the fathers with a mother's heart), who see to it that as the weaning occurs, strong sustenance is at hand so that their children do not perish without them.

If it seems strange to speak of weaning in the case of Isaac, who, as Miller shows, is on the verge of adulthood, these words by Bert Kaplan (1977) are apropos:

> While many children, sadly, do meet great severity, privation, and harshness early in life, I believe the full seriousness of weaning is ordinarily encountered . . . by the young adult who has recently left his or her family, that most womb-like of human institutions and has "come into the world." Students report that the sense of being weaned from family care develops slowly over a period of years and that it is experienced partly as a function of their own desire for independence and freedom. Nevertheless, the full force of the fact of being alone in an indifferent world is a good deal more than they have bargained for. (392)

Thus, while the story of Abraham and Isaac directs our attention to the threatened killing of Isaac by his father, the event that goes unnoticed is the fact that father, son, and servants set off on their journey to Mount Moriah—where presumably important things happen—leaving the mother, Sarah, at home to grieve and to fear for her son's fate in the world that men have made for him. In each of Kierkegaard's alternative scenarios, Sarah is briefly mentioned: In one version she watches them from the window as they go down the valley until she can see them no longer. In another she kisses Isaac, the one who "took away her disgrace, Isaac her pride, her hope for all the generations to come." In still another she kisses Isaac, "her delight, her joy forever." In the fourth scenario, the one in which Abraham's despair is seen by Isaac, she is again mentioned, but this time as running out joyfully to meet them as they return, only to discover that her son "had lost the faith."

The critical event in this story is not, as the storyteller claims, what happens between Abraham and Isaac, but what is happening between Sarah and her son. The weaning of a son from his mother is a sad event, made the sadder because it happens almost without notice, as though it is a mere detail in an otherwise momentous tale about fathers and sons. It goes unremarked in the biblical setting because it *is* such a natural event, and the Bible intends to be a religious book, a book about our struggles with our thoughts and feelings toward God. Yet if weaning is a mere natural event, having none of the power and glory of the sacrificial event on Mount Moriah, it does have its religious consequences, as, in the weaning process, the son is sent into an indifferent world that is a good deal more than he bargained for, and, as one of Kierkegaard's scenarios suggests, it is possible that a son will lose his father and will return home to his mother's arms, disillusioned and demoralized. The question this scenario raises, a profoundly religious question, is whether she will have even stronger sustenance at hand so that his spirit does not perish, so that he is fortified to go out again, believing in himself when he can no longer believe in his father and his father's God.

If there is no religious legitimation for what Abraham proposed to do to his son Isaac, how do we explain his behavior? Why would a father do such a thing? While Kierkegaard eulogizes Abraham as a man of "absolute faith," in David Bakan's view (1966), the "paradigmatic sacrifice tale" reveals a profound ambivalence on the part of Abraham. For Bakan, Abraham has "the wish to kill Isaac," but projects this wish onto God, so that it appears as God's command to Abraham: "When a human being inflicts pain upon another human being, he characteristically believes that he does so out of necessity. In the case of Abraham, it is out of obedience to God" (117). But, Bakan points out, we can reasonably ask about the locus of the necessity: "A common psychodynamic mechanism is to convert desire so that it appears as external necessity. It is thus an open question in each instance whether what appears to be external necessity really is that, or is simply a facade concealing some internal pressure" (117).

Bakan suggests that the internal pressure may have to do with questions in Abraham's own mind, questions concerning who was in fact the father of Isaac. In Bakan's view, the biblical story of Sarah's conception of Isaac "allows for an interpretation of dubious paternity of Isaac." He hastens to add that he is not making an effort to find out what "really happened," as this would be rather odd when one has to do with a mythic figure, but that he is "seeking to understand the nature of the bibilical text as a document which renders a state of mind for our understanding" (212). He notes that on two occasions Abraham conceals the fact that Sarah is his wife, allowing her to appear to be married to someone else, indicating that their marriage had its share of opportunism and deceit. The story of the visit of angels to Sarah's tent can be interpreted to mean that she conceived Isaac while Abraham was outside the tent, and that her expression of fear on hearing the prediction that she would give birth to a child, together with her explicit denial that the prediction had caused her to laugh, was because she anticipated Abraham's anger at her and possible revenge against the child.

Bakan notes that the allegation that Isaac was not Abraham's but Abimelech's son was known to the rabbis, and suggests that such doubt may even have been on Saint Paul's mind in Romans 9:6–8 (NRSV): "For not all who are descended from Israel belong to Israel, and not all are children of Abraham because they are his descendants; but 'Through Isaac shall your descendants be named.' This means that it is not the children of the flesh who are the children of God, but the children of the promise are reckoned as descendants." Thus, in Bakan's view, the point of the Abraham and Isaac story is that Abraham had "some internal pressure" to attack Isaac, but that he does not in the end act on this pressure but instead exercises restraint. Isaac is spared, and, as Kierkegaard puts it, Abraham "got a son a second time"—that is, Isaac now becomes Abraham's son because Abraham had the power to kill him but he did not. Rather, he adopted Isaac as his own.

In emphasizing Abraham's resentment owing to the particular circumstances of Isaac's birth, however, Bakan does not give sufficient attention to the jealousy of *any* father who is aware that his son is his wife's true delight, and who cannot bear the thought that he, the son of another woman, perhaps one whom his wife fears or despises, is not himself her true delight. It is the child in him that finds this situation frustrating and demeaning, and it is the child in him that seeks to do something about it. In this sense, Venerable Father Abraham is a child with murderous impulses against another child, as it is also only a child who would believe that killing a small animal instead will solve the problem of his murderous jealousy.

Whether Bakan's explanation for Abraham's inner provocation to harm Isaac is convincing is not the critical point. What *is* critical is his point that "a common psychodynamic mechanism is to convert desire so that it appears as external necessity." The sacrificial impulse is an instance of this psychodynamic mechanism. A very human desire is attributed to God and represented as a divine command. To persuade the reader that Abraham was acting on the command of God, the storyteller has the angel of the Lord call to Abraham at the critical moment when he is about to plunge the knife into Isaac's heart, telling him not to lay a hand on the child. This divine intervention seems to establish the validity of the storyteller's claim that it was God—external necessity—who commanded Abraham to do this thing, thereby dissuading the reader from exercising a healthy skepticism regarding the very idea that the sacrificial impulse has any other source than the heart and mind of Abraham himself.

If Abraham is finally worthy of being remembered, it is not, as Kierkegaard supposes, because he was a man of unquestioning faith, but because he finally came to his senses and repented of what he had intended to do to Isaac. This does not mean that Isaac was not traumatized and terrorized by the episode, and it does not mean that no harm was done to him. Yet, we can say that it was the staying of Abraham's hand that is the sole basis for viewing him as a man of faith, for it is an expression of faith when a man is able to see the error of his ways and to repent of the evil he has planned in his heart.

References

Bakan, D. (1966). *The duality of human existence.* Chicago: Rand McNally & Company.

Culbertson, P. (1992). *New Adam: The future of male spirituality.* Minneapolis: Fortress.

deMause, L. (1988). The evolution of childhood. In L. deMause (Ed.), *The history of childhood: The untold story of child abuse* (1–73). New York: Peter Bedrick Books.

Kaplan, B. (1977). The decline of desire as the ultimate life crisis. In D. Capps, W. H. Capps, & M. G. Bradford (Eds.), *Encounter with Erikson: Historical interpretation and religious biography* (389–400). Missoula: Scholars Press.

Kierkegaard, S. (1958). *The journals of Kierkegaard* (A. Dru, Trans.). New York: Harper & Brothers.

Kierkegaard, S. (1983). *Fear and trembling* (H. V. & E. H. Hong, Trans.). Princeton: Princeton University Press.

Kohut, H. (1971). *The analysis of the self.* New York: International Universities Press.

Kohut, H. (1977). *The restoration of the self.* New York: International Universities Press.

Kohut, H., & Wolf, E. S. (1986). The disorders of the self and their treatment: An outline. In A. P. Morrison (Ed.), *Essential papers on narcissism* (175–196). New York: New York University Press.

Miller, A. (1990). *The untouched key* (H. & H. Hunter, Trans.). New York: Doubleday.

Oates, W. (1953). *The Bible in pastoral care.* Philadelphia: Westminster.

Trible, P. (1984). *Texts of terror: Literary-feminist readings of biblical narratives.* Philadelphia: Fortress.

CHAPTER 9

THE EVOLUTION OF A PAULINE TOXIC TEXT

Charles T. Davis III

Introduction

The earliest followers of Jesus authored their identity narrative within the metanarrative of Jewish faith thereby creating a new Jewish-Jesus sect. The Christian identity narrative arose as a new story and could not call upon either a Jewish or a Pagan metanarrative for its justification. It was a new creation inspired by the Spirit and authored by Paul. With his guidance, the Pagan followers of Jesus, Christians, articulated their personal and communal experiences of empowerment by the Spirit in a new identity narrative that would in time establish itself as the dominant metanarrative for Western civilization. Members of the Jewish-Jesus community in Jerusalem immediately denied the validity of the Christian narratives. They sought to subjugate the new story to their official and dominant story that one had to be Jewish in order to follow Jesus. Paul urges the Christians to remain faithful to their personal stories of empowerment by the Spirit. Unfortunately, he also resorts to the use of toxic texts to disenfranchise his Jewish opponents.

Paul is deeply enmeshed in a religious family feud. He insists upon maintaining connections with his Jewish heritage, he is dependent upon the Jewish-Jesus leadership in Jerusalem for approval, and he never loses hope that he will bring the Jewish community into his new faith as a natural evolution of the Jewish story. He uses toxic texts within this context of a passionate family fight. Unfortunately, these caustic texts, like a rotten apple in a barrel, tend to corrupt other aspects of the Pauline proclamation. First, we will consider a methodology of assessing toxic texts from the perspective of narrative therapy. Second, we will explore the social situation that forms the context of the Pauline use both of personal stories of empowerment and of toxic texts. Finally, we will examine the Pauline interpretation of Genesis 16 and 21 given in Galatians 4:21–31, a toxic text with a multiplicity of implications for Paul's message as a whole.

Defining a Toxic Text

Narrative therapy emerges at the intersection of a multiplicity of domains including literary theory, psychoanalysis, anthropology, family sociology, and narrative theology. In their pioneering work *Narrative Means to Therapeutic Ends*, Michael White and David Epston (1990) build upon the work of anthropologist Gregory Bateson and the literary psychologist Jerome Bruner as they propose a narrative model for understanding the function of the family. White and Epston argue that as family members organize their lives around specific meanings that constitute a narrative, "they inadvertently contribute to the 'survival' of, as well as the 'career' of the problem" (3). Following Michel Foucault, White and Epston argue that one narrative may emerge as the dominant story claiming a universal validity with the result that it subjugates all other stories to itself (20). Persons who come for therapy may be understood as persons whose full experience of their own reality is being truncated by a subjugating story. Therapy seeks to challenge the dominant narrative by leading the client to externalize the story so that it may be examined with greater objectivity. Concurrently, attempts are made to uncover moments of unique outcome—moments when one did not enact the dominant story but acted positively in a novel manner (15–16). These previously unstoried moments are thereby made available for a process of reauthoring one's life story.

From White and Epston's perspective, toxic stories are subjugating stories. The subjugating process is clearly at work within the family-oriented Jewish milieu of the first century where Jewish factions were engaged in a fierce struggle to re-vision Jewish identity in the Hellenistic world. Luke T. Johnson (1986) argues in *The Writings of the New Testament* that the Jewish symbolic world was being redefined by interpretative acts among Sadducees, Pharisees, Zealots, the Coveneters of Qumran, and the apocalyptic sects like that of John the Baptist even before the appearance of the Jewish-Jesus sect founded by Peter in Jerusalem. Symbols such as the "People of God," "the Temple," "the martyr," and the "resurrection" were being redefined in a variety of contexts (47).

There is, however, another dimension of the problem of identifying toxic texts. Alan Parry and Robert E. Doan (1994) in *Story Revisions: Narrative Therapy in the Postmodern World* call attention to the collapse of the major metanarratives of the West: the Bible (5ff.), Science as the Hope of a Better Future (9), Progress (9), and Democracy and the Triumph of the People (9). They argue that "each person's stories become self-legitimizing" in the postmodern world (26). Toxic stories emerge as dominant individuals attempt to question the validity of another's personal narrative in the name of an external story having normative value. Parry and Doan argue that in the postmodern context such attempts are nothing less than a form of interpretive terrorism perpetrated against an Other. Such attempts are

coercive, and to the extent that such methods are used to silence or discredit a person's stories, they represent a form of terrorism. We use such a strong word advisedly, for when one person tries to silence the legitimate voice of another, this is done invariably by throwing into question that person's only resource for discerning reality, her/his own judgment. All those who are thrown into that position of self-doubt are being thrown out of their own stories and robbed of their own voices. (27)

Building upon the insights of Parry and Doan, we can classify stories as revelatory tales or as toxic texts. Revelatory tales, as defined by Belden C. Lane (1981) in *Story Telling: The Enchantment of Theology*, heal through their power to facilitate the discovery of one's authentic story. Toxic texts subjugate one's authentic voice to a dominant story by inappropriately claiming the privilege of superior validity.

Parry and Doan incorporate the ethical insights of the French philosopher Emmanuel Levinas into their understanding of narrative therapy. Levinas argues that Western thought in its quest for universal truth has privileged the Same over the Other (Davis, 1996, 34). Unerringly, the West has destroyed the Other by incorporating it into the Same or by excluding it altogether (Davis, 1996, 3). We may say, according to Levinas, that Westerners, both Christian theologians and philosophers, have a cultural bias toward the creation of subjugating interpretations that masquerades under the prestigious emblem of the search for universal truth. Levinas also argues that the ethical demand of the Other is prior to both knowledge and consciousness of self and activates them. Accordingly, the ethical is prior to myth and storytelling, and it calls them into being (Cohen, 1986, 1–9). Parry and Doan (1994) conclude that in the postmodern world

> A personal metanarrative would play the role metanarratives have always played: calling forth responsibility toward the Other, or, in other words, addressing the ethical domain. (30)

Parry and Doan stress against relativism that the collapse of metanarratives is not an invitation to self-indulgence. As we live in an increasingly multicultural world, "difference rather than sameness becomes the order of things and the other becomes the ethical challenge of the present" (31).

Are the insights of Parry and Doan potentially applicable to the New Testament? I am convinced on historical grounds that they are. The Hellenistic Age was, in many respects, like the postmodern era. Alexander's religious reforms sought to impose a single official, Greek religious story upon the Empire. This led to the collapse of the city-state and other local corporate religions. A new quest for a personal religious story began that brought into existence the Mystery Religions, including Christianity (Godwin, 1981; Johnson, 1986). Given this state of affairs, it is appropriate to look for subjugating texts in the New Testament of the type that seeks to suppress the voice of the individual in the name of an older but effectively defunct national religion. The tension between Jewish religious identity and Jewish national identity reached the breaking point when the Temple was destroyed in 70. Jewish religious identity survived this epoch-making event. Two new world religions emerged at the end of the century: Orthodox Judaism founded by Rabbi Johanan ben Zakkai and Christianity.

Richard Q. Ford (1997), in *The Parables of Jesus: Recovering the Art of Listening*, identifies an additional toxic tendency by means of which the Other is excluded. The gospel editors denigrate the subordinate characters in their stories on the assumption that "the economically superior figure represents some aspect of divine intent" (3). This assumption sets up a "black and white" pattern of exclusion and inclusion in which the superior figure is the source of all resolution while the subordinate figure is the source of all difficulty (4). This process of projection by means of which one person is viewed as the source of the solution is evoked by the rubric of the idealizing of the superior character (3). Ford urges his readers to approach the parables in anticipation of "a balanced and complex tension between two persons, with each contributing to the evident pain of their compromised interdependence" (5). In the drama that develops in a parable, neither figure should be regarded solely as constructive or as destructive.

Ford's observations apply equally to the editors of the Gospels as authors and to the modern reader. There is a tendency on both sides to idealize the superior figure and to exclude the subordinate characters as in some sense other and thereby unworthy of positive attention. Readers should resist the tendency to subjugate the stories of the biblical characters to an official, theological story or cultural metanarrative. For example, both the Apostle and the Pharisee should be viewed with a regard for their positive and negative aspects. The quest for theological unity and historical continuity easily leads to the idealization of the perceived superior characters.

The Pauline Situation

Acts narrates a story of communal conflict over the root story (Fackenheim, 1972, 8–14), the foundational story, of the religious experiences associated with the resurrection/transfiguration. Peter and the community in Jerusalem, which was solidly rooted in Judaism (Capon, 2000, 50; Küng, 1998, 71), argue that the resurrection experiences are to be understood within the context of the Pharisee story of the End of Time (Acts 3:11–26; 2:14–21). Jesus will return a second time, after the devout of the Jewish community have recognized that he is appointed as the Christ by God. He will then fulfill the prophetic promises associated with the End of Time. This leads to a situation in which Peter is attacked by the Sadducees for the proclamation of the resurrection (Acts 4:1–3; 5:17–18) but is defended by Pharisees (Acts 5:33–39). From this perspective, the good news of the End is only for Jews. Pagans will either be subjugated or destroyed. Consistent with the interpretation of the resurrection in the context of the Pharisee story, we discover in Acts 15:1 that

> certain individuals came down from Judea [to Antioch] and were teaching the brothers, "Unless you are circumcised according to the custom of Moses, you cannot be saved." (New Revised Standard Version [NRSV])

Their identity is revealed in Acts 15:5:

> some believers who belonged to the sect of the Pharisees stood up and
> said, "It is necessary for them [the pagan followers of Jesus in Antioch]
> to be circumcised and ordered to keep the law of Moses." (NRSV)

It is most likely that this Jewish (Pharisee) Jesus party gives rise to
the so-called Judaizers who attack Paul's mission to the Pagans.

Stephen, and later Paul, places the resurrection experiences within
the context of a different root story and undermines "the exclusive
saving function of the comprehensive halakhic system" (Küng, 1998,
113). Stephen articulates a new interpretation of the resurrection
through the story of his personal mystical vision (Acts 7:55–56). He
sees Jesus enthroned as the Son of Man promised by Daniel (Dan.
7:13–14): a heavenly King whose subjects are persons from all races,
nations, and languages. Stephen's interpretation of the resurrection
abolishes the boundary between Jew and Pagan. This incorporation
of the Pagan Other into the Divine plan of salvation is immediately
and brutally suppressed. Stephen is stoned to death under Paul's
direction. Ironically, it is Paul who takes Stephen's place following his
vision of God taking the form of Jesus on the cross, the so-called
Damascus Road experience.

For Paul, the Story of the Cross is the context within which the
resurrection experiences are to be understood (1 Cor. 1:17–18; Gal.
2:14–16). Paul now comprehends under the Greek term *nomos* the
Pharisee halakhic system that includes the written Torah as well as
the oral Torah and soundly rejects it in favor of the Story of the Cross
(Küng, 1998, 46). He challenges his Jewish contemporaries to recognize the failure of the older Jewish root story:

> We ourselves are Jews by birth and not Gentile sinners; yet we know
> that a person is justified not by the works of the law [Torah] but
> through faith in Jesus Christ. And we have come to believe in Christ
> Jesus, so that we might be justified by faith in Christ, and not by doing
> the works of the law [Torah], because no one will be justified by the
> works of the law [Torah].
>
> For through the law [Torah] I died to the law [Torah], so that I might
> live to God. I have been crucified with Christ; and it is no longer I who
> live, but it is Christ who lives in me. And the life I now live in the flesh
> I live by faith in the Son of God, who loved me and gave himself for me.
> (Gal. 2:15–20, NRSV)

Mount Sinai is replaced by the Cross on Calvary as the locus of God's
saving activity.

The prophecy of Saint Paul at Ephesus, by Eustache Lesueur.
Reunion des Museoes Nationaux/Art Resource, New York.

Paul is aware that the Story of the Cross is offensive in terms of the
metanarratives of both the educated Jew and the educated Pagan (1
Cor. 1:18–25). Both regard the Story of the Cross as foolishness—
unjustified personal stories. Nevertheless, for Paul, it is the root story
of the cross that gives meaning to the resurrection as a sign of the
universal possibility of redemption. The writer of Ephesians understood the import of the new root story of the cross as the source of
the Pauline proclamation:

He has abolished the law with its commandments and ordinances, that
he might create in himself one new humanity in place of the two, thus
making peace, and might reconcile both groups to God in one body

through the cross, thus putting to death that hostility through it. (Eph. 2:15–16, NRSV)

Athens and Jerusalem can be reconciled through the symbol of the Cross.

The nature of the conflict between Paul and the Pharisee followers of Jesus in Jerusalem is clear. The Jerusalem faction argues for the primacy of the Pharisee root story as the context of the resurrection narratives while Paul argues for the primacy of the Story of the Cross grounded in the personal experience of the individual who is redeemed. This is a conflict in which the Jerusalem representatives of an official, privileged story are attempting to subjugate Paul's Christian, personal story. In their view, Paul's new personal narrative is undermining the Jewish cultural metanarrative of God's revelation of the Torah to Moses in the presence of all the people (Fackenheim, 1972, 10). The problem is stated graphically in Acts 21:18–22:

> The next day Paul went with us to visit James; and all the elders were present . . . Then they said to him, "You see, brother, how many thousands of believers there are among the Jews, and they are all zealous for the law. They have been told about you that you teach all the Jews living among the Gentiles to forsake Moses, and that you tell them not to circumcise their children or observe the customs. What then is to be done?" (NRSV)

The personal, prophetic experience of Paul cannot be allowed to destroy the faith of the community.

Paul stands upon his personal experience and will not relent in the face of community pressure. In Galatians 1–2 where Paul defends his claim to apostleship by invoking the story of his prophetic calling, he is at pains to stress his independence from culture. Paul receives his gospel by revelation. He received no aid or instruction from the Jewish-Jesus tradition or its representatives in Jerusalem. The Christian metanarrative, the Story of the Cross, has replaced the Jewish metanarrative of the Story of Mount Sinai.

Paul as Champion of the Personal Story

In 1 Thessalonians, Paul uses a clever rhetorical device as a means for telling the Thessalonian community its own unique story:

> We always give thanks to God for all of you and mention you in our prayers, constantly remembering before our God and Father your work

of faith and labor of love and steadfastness of hope in our Lord Jesus
Christ. (1 Thess. 1:2–3, NRSV)

To remember in a Jewish context is to tell the story of the acts of God
so that the boundaries between past and present reality collapse as the
past experience becomes a present imaginative reality. Paul is, in effect,
claiming that he constantly tells God the Thessalonians' story as a
means of bringing them into the presence of God. The story themes are:
the imitation of Paul who imitates Christ on the cross, the Pagan
Pentecost experience of receiving the Spirit, and the community's steadfast witness to God in the midst of persecution. The Thessalonians'
story is such an inspiring one that it has spread throughout the region
and has preceded Paul to many locations. Paul urges the Thessalonians
to be true to their own authentic experience. Under no circumstances
should they allow it to be subjugated by an official Jewish-Jesus story
coming out of Jerusalem. To this point in the letter, Paul is the champion of the authentic personal voice that is threatened with extinction
by the culturally dominant story. Unfortunately, Paul turns caustic at
2:14–16 as he seeks to reinforce the Thessalonians' story by casting the
Jews as villains in the Christian story:

> For you, brothers and sisters, became imitators of the churches of God
> in Christ Jesus that are in Judea, for you suffered the same things from
> your own compatriots as they did from the Jews, who killed both the
> Lord Jesus and the prophets, and drove us out; they displease God and
> oppose everyone by hindering us from speaking to the Gentiles so that
> they may be saved. Thus they have constantly been filling up the mea-
> sure of their sins; but God's wrath has overtaken them at last. (NRSV)

Paul's actual opponents in both Galatia and Thessalonica appear to
be the Jewish-Pharisee-Jesus followers of Acts 15. Paul generalizes
their opposition into a story of a persecution of Christians by Jews.
Despite his role in the earliest persecution, Paul shows no sympathy
for the plight of his opponents, unlike Peter in the Acts speeches.
Why would Paul shift the blame from his Jewish-Jesus opponents to
Jews generally? Are we confronting what Parry and Doan (1994,
39–39) describe as the "survival story"?

In inventing survival stories, children shift blame from the real
source of the threat or abuse to another object so as to "avoid at all
costs actions and even fantasies that might offend their parents, and at
the same time . . . develop behaviors and attitudes that invite parental
approval" (Parry and Doan, 1994, 39). Paul depends upon the Jesus
community in Jerusalem. Despite Paul's denials of being in subjection

to Jerusalem in Galatians 1–2, he nevertheless needs, seeks, gains, and boasts of their approval. By making the population of Jerusalem responsible for the death of Jesus, Paul may be seeking to gain the approval of the Jerusalem followers of Jesus who likewise appear to blame the general population for the death of Jesus (Acts 2:23; 3:13–15; 4:10; 10:39–41). The new and extreme element is that Paul scapegoats the religious people of Jerusalem whereas Peter is presented by Luke as attributing their acts to an understandable ignorance (Acts 3:17). Paul urges the Thessalonians to boost their confidence in their own story by denigrating Jews globally. Moreover, they are asked to understand their pagan enemies according to the same caustic narrative. The historical events that are being storied by Paul as a part of the Christian root experience now include the Jews of Jerusalem as prophet killers and persecutors of Christians (1 Thess. 2:15, NRSV). To be sure, the Story of the Cross implies a story of those who demanded Jesus' death, but this need not lead to the accusation that the Jews of Jerusalem are prophet killers. In later theories of atonement, the blame is shifted to the devil, as in the Ransom Theory, or to God, as in Anselm's Satisfaction Theory (Capon, 2000, 114–122). Nevertheless, Paul has introduced a potentially caustic element into the interpretation of Christian identity.

Paul as a Caustic Interpreter of Scripture

Under pressure from Jewish followers of Jesus, the Galatians have come to doubt the validity of Paul's claim to apostleship, and they are giving up their personal story for the sake of some version of the Jewish-Jesus official story. Paul's authority is in question. He is exasperated. How can the community betray its unique personal story for traditional religious practice (Gal. 4:8–11)? Paul challenges the community:

> Tell me, you who desire to be subject to the law [Torah], will you not listen to the law [Torah]? (Gal. 4:21, NRSV)

Paul directs their attention to Genesis, chapters 16 and 21. He will interpret these chapters allegorically. The following equations are established:

> Hagar is the slave wife who is to be rationally glossed as the Mount Sinai Covenant and the historical Jerusalem; (Gal. 4:24–25)
> Sarah is the free wife who is glossed as the New Covenant and the Heavenly Jerusalem. (Gal. 4:26)

Christians are to understand themselves as types of Isaac, the child of promise (Gal. 4:28). Conversely, Jewish persons are to be understood as children of slavery, descendents of Abraham's Egyptian slave wife Hagar through her son Ishmael (Gal. 4:29). Just as the Ishmael of the Genesis narrative is said to have persecuted Isaac, so the Galatians are to understand that the Christians, such as themselves and Paul, are being persecuted by the Jews from Jerusalem who seek to impose Jewish requirements upon them.

Through the allegorical interpretation of the Jewish scripture, Paul has turned the traditional people of God into an Other to be driven out as enemies of God. The Galatian community is to cast out the descendents of the present day Jerusalem as fleshly enemies of the spiritual children who are types of Isaac. Paul concludes with a ringing call for rebellion against Jerusalem:

For freedom Christ has set us free.
Stand firm, therefore, and do not submit again to a yoke of slavery.
    (Gal. 5:1, NRSV)

Paul's allegory robs the Jerusalem community, and Jews generally, of their own story. The racial/historical descendents of Abraham are identified with the Edomites and the Egyptians through Ishmael while the pagan-Christians take on the identity of the children of Abraham. The pagan-Christians are types of Isaac, the spiritual son of the promise through whom the people of God descend. Paul is using literary interpretation to discredit the voice of the Jewish community in the eyes of Christians and is thereby engaged in "a form of terrorism," to use Parry and Doan's phrase (1994, 27).

In Galatians 3:23–29 Paul equates the Jewish scripture and the tradition of its interpretation with the condition of slavery. Life in Christ brings freedom from the Torah as a disciplinarian:

Now before faith came, we were imprisoned and guarded under the law [Torah] until faith would be revealed. Therefore the law [Torah] was our disciplinarian until Christ came, so that we might be justified by faith. But now that faith has come, we are no longer subject to a disciplinarian, for in Christ Jesus you are all children of God through faith. As many of you as were baptized into Christ have clothed yourselves with Christ. There is no longer Jew or Greek, there is no longer slave or free, there is no longer male and female; for all of you are one in Christ Jesus. And if you belong to Christ, then you are Abraham's offspring, heirs according to the promise. (Gal. 3:23–29, NRSV)

Things become more ominous as Paul goes on to identify the condition before Christ as one of servitude under the elemental spirits (Gal. 4:3). Colossians defines this term *slavery* in a properly Pauline manner as a synonym for the flesh (*sarx*):

> See to it that no one takes you captive through philosophy and empty deceit, according to human tradition, according to the elemental spirits of the universe, and not according to Christ. (Col. 2:8, NRSV)

The full power of this Pauline identification of all culture as demonic is made evident by the writer to the Ephesians:

> You were dead through the trespasses and sins in which you once lived, following the course of this world, following the ruler of the power of the air, the spirit that is now at work among those who are disobedient. (Eph. 2:1–2, NRSV)

It is Satan who holds the present-day Jerusalem in subjection, even as he once held the Christians prior to Christ (Eph. 2:3). From this interpretive trajectory, we see the seriousness of Paul's re-visioning of the Jewish story. The identification of "slavery" with the "elemental spirits" casts the inhabitants of Jerusalem as a community dominated by Satan, just as the pagans are. The struggle between Jerusalem and the Christians is a cosmic battle of Christ against Satan. The Gospel of Luke, the Pauline gospel, takes up this theme and interprets the Passion Narrative as a cosmic battle (Luke 22:3; 31; 53).

Paul condemns the Torah Book in 2 Corinthians 3 when he associates it and its interpreters with the image of the "ministry of death, chiseled in letters on stone tablets" (2 Cor. 3:7, NRSV). The book is replaced by an inner experience. Christians are characterized by the image of "a letter of Christ, prepared by us, written not with ink but with the Spirit of the living God, not on tablets of stone but on tablets of human hearts" (2 Cor. 3:2–3, NRSV). If the Jewish community disputes this interpretation, Christians should understand that Jewish people cannot authentically interpret their own scripture because:

> their minds were hardened. Indeed, to this very day, when they hear the reading of the old covenant, that same veil is still there, since only in Christ is it set aside. Indeed, to this very day whenever Moses is read, a veil lies over their minds; but when one turns to the Lord, the veil is removed. (2 Cor. 3:14–16, NRSV)

Only Christians, the people baptized with the Spirit, may properly comprehend the scriptures of Israel through the method of allegory. The authentic Jewish voice is subjugated to the Story of the Cross.

The Gospel of Matthew stands in radical contrast to Paul. The Torah Book stands as a prophetic promise that is fulfilled in and through Jesus. In this Jewish-Christian gospel, the validity of the Torah is unconditionally affirmed (Matt. 5:17–18). It is the tradition of interpretation that is rejected as antiquated by the perfect interpretation given by Jesus as the Christ (chapters 5 and 15). Matthew concludes with the vision of the disciples going forth to incorporate all nations into the New Israel through their obedience to all that Jesus has taught the disciples regarding the true Halakha (Matt. 28:20).

As readers, many of us have an unconscious tendency to take the promise/fulfillment theme found in the Jewish-Christian Gospel of Matthew and inject it into Pauline thought. This allows us to disregard the serious import of Paul's paradoxical stance vis-à-vis the Torah as book. Marcion did not make this mistake. He both perceived and exaggerated the toxic effect of Paul's criticism upon the Torah Book. Marcion eliminated it from his canon as a testimony to an alien god. Gnostics generally tended to develop the Pauline ambivalence to the Torah Book into an increasingly caustic interpretation by means of which Jewish people were demonized as servants of Ialdabaoth, the god of this world.

Christians have a tendency to project responsibility for anti-Semitism. Capon (2000) correctly observes in *The Fingerprints of God* that "images have the power to corrupt as well as to edify—and bad images have the power to corrupt absolutely" (117). Although he absolves Paul and his immediate successors of responsibility, Capon recognizes the importance of corrupting influences upon Christian interpretation and writes:

> anti-Semitism (wildly popular during the Middle Ages and still alive and well in Luther and others) had been plaguing the church's mind since the middle of the second century, if not before. (124)

Hans Küng (1998) is more willing to recognize the problem in the New Testament itself. He writes:

> James [the brother of Jesus] is mentioned only eleven times (in Acts only three times), which according to some present-day exegetes indicates a suppression of Jewish Christianity (and the brothers of Jesus) in the Gentile Christian church. (99)

He acknowledges that "Christian patristics for a long time understood Jewish Christianity uncritically . . . as a single heretical entity"

(99). Küng follows J. Louis Martyn in maintaining that "Jewish Christians even seem still to have been engaged in a mission to the Gentiles requiring observance of the Law in the second century. They may already lie behind *Paul's opponents in Galatia*" (100). Unfortunately, Küng exonerates Paul and his successors by blaming anti-Semitism on the victims: "The *excommunication of Christians* by the now Pharisaic establishment preceded all the persecution of Jews by Christians" (87). Here again we see the phenomenon of idealizing the superior person (movement). A balanced analysis suggests that both parties to this family feud resorted to subjugating the other's story. Unfortunately, Paul's performance was attached to a new tradition of scriptural interpretation that perpetuated it. As members of this tradition, we should heed Wayne Rollins's (1999) injunction in *Soul and Psyche* that interpretation must earmark "the dark biases that enjoy advocacy in certain biblical texts and continue to cause harm in human affairs. . . . It means attending to interpretations of the Bible, as well as to the original texts themselves, for the pathologies they can propagate" (177).

Conclusion

The Jewish-Jesus movement participated in the culturally dominant Pharisee story as an apocalyptic sect. This community asserted the truth of the Pharisee narrative for the End of Time by proclaiming the resurrection of Jesus and an imminent Second Coming predicated upon Jewish repentance of the error of failing to perceive that he was God's Christ (Acts 2:23; 3:13–17). The crucifixion was a mistake rather than a demonic act. The resurrection was the Divine remedy making possible the Second Coming as an immediate possibility (Acts 3:17–21).

The plight of Stephen, Paul, and the Antioch Christians was that they were asserting individual prophetic/mystical experience against the official stories of both the Jewish and the Pagan cultural worlds. Paul, like the Hebrew prophets before him, stood on the story of his calling. Through the Damascus Road experience, the Story of the Cross became the metanarrative for Paul's personal story. On the positive side, Paul urged the Christians to stand courageously on their own personal stories of empowerment by the Spirit and not to trade this for a place in the official Jewish story advocated by the followers of Jesus in Jerusalem. On the negative side, Paul fell victim to the urge to demonize and to destroy his enemies, thus betraying the ethical obligation of love taught by Jesus. In his attempt to ground Christian experience in the authority of Jewish scripture, Paul applied the Hellenistic allegorical method to the biblical narrative in a manner designed to re-vision the pagan-Christians as the true descendents of Abraham. In the process, he dispossessed Jews of their own story and even of their scripture. Only through the Spirit-inspired allegory revealed to the unveiled mind could the true intent of this scripture be divined.

Paul's toxic texts must be understood in the context of a family feud narrative rather than as a theoretical manifesto. He was not expounding a theory of Jewish-Christian relations nor did he realize that his words would become holy writ. Nevertheless, as these texts were elevated to the status of scripture, they became a fountainhead of the toxic story of anti-Semitism that has accompanied the story of the cross for the past 2000 years. We Christians tend to deny this reality by invoking the technique of idealizing the superior character that Ford finds already present in the gospel editing. We act as if Paul, the Apostle to the Gentiles, and his apostolic successors must surely be the source of all correct patterns of behavior while the Jews and the non-Christian pagans are the source of all perversion. We can break this tendency to idealize by viewing Paul and his antagonists in a more balanced manner. Paul may be our guide in learning to give priority to our own authentic experience in the face of subjugating official stories. His example should also serve as a cautionary tale.

References

Capon, R. F. (2000). *The fingerprints of God*. Grand Rapids: Eerdmans.

Cohen R. A. (1986). Introduction. In R. A. Cohen (Ed.), *Face to face with Emmanuel Levinas* (1–9). Albany: SUNY.

Davis, C. (1996). *Levinas: An introduction*. Notre Dame: Notre Dame.

Fackenheim, E. L. (1972). *God's presence in history*. New York: Harper.

Ford, R. Q. (1997). *The parables of Jesus: Recovering the art of listening*. Minneapolis: Fortress.

Godwin, J. (1981). *Mystery religions in the ancient world*. New York: Harper.

Johnson, L. T. (1986). *The writings of the new testament*. Philadelphia: Fortress.

Küng, H. (1998). *Christianity: Essence, history, and future* (J. Bowden, Trans.). New York: Continuum.

Lane, B. C. (1981). *Story telling: The enchantment of theology* [Cassette]. Minneapolis: Bethany.

Parry, A., & Doan, R. E. (1994). *Story re-visions: Narrative therapy in the post-modern world.* New York: Guilford.

Rollins, W. G. (1999). *Soul and psyche.* Minneapolis: Augsburg Fortress.

White, M., & Epston, D. (1990). *Narrative means to therapeutic ends.* New York: W. W. Norton.

CHAPTER 10

Retribution and Agency in the Dead Sea Scrolls and the Teaching of Jesus

Mark Adam Elliott

Introduction

Among other questions raised by these volumes is one that strikes at the heart of every religion that looks to the Bible for guidance. Does the Bible contribute to war, terrorism, or violence? Passages like Deuteronomy 7:1–4 seem to supply an unambiguous affirmative answer:

> When the Lord your God brings you into the land which you are entering to take possession of it, and clears away many nations before you, the Hittites, the Girgashites, the Amorites, the Canaanites, the Perizzites, the Hivites, and the Jebusites, seven nations greater and mightier than yourselves, and when the Lord your God gives them over to you, and you defeat them; then you must utterly destroy them; you shall make no covenant with them and show no mercy to them. You shall not make marriages with them, giving your daughters to their sons or taking their daughters for your son. For they would turn away your sons from following me, to serve other gods; then the anger of the Lord would be kindled against you, and he would destroy you quickly. (Deut. 7:1–4, Revised Standard Version [RSV])

What could be a clearer sanction of violence for faithful readers of the Bible than this? That it is not quite so straightforward, however, is suggested by several other facts all related to the historical contingencies and context of the passage. For example we know from the same parts of the Bible, where it becomes a significant theme in its own right, that Israel did not successfully or effectively carry out the prescribed genocide. We see that God did not endorse many other of Israel's battles, particularly those launched without prior divine endorsement. We note that occasionally war was internecine and quite futile. The Pentateuch also presents God as promoting the cause of the relatively weaker Israel against the stronger nations (Deut. 20:1–4) hardly a sweeping endorsement of aggression, particularly by stronger peoples against weaker ones. Some experiences of conflict were mediated, in the sense of divine intervention (Deut. 20:1–4; Josh. 10:1–27; Judg. 4:14–16), and divine miracle occasionally prevented unnecessary loss of life (cp. Judg. 7; 2 Kings 7; 2 Chron. 14). Even with regard to the text quoted above from Deuteronomy 7 it is not entirely clear what is envisioned in this apparently preemptive strike. Is it a matter of God miraculously, or Israel more conventionally, dispossessing the indigenous peoples first and then annihilating only those who refused to leave or otherwise carried out a counteroffensive (cp. Num. 33:50–53; Deut. 20:10–16)?

More likely the purpose had something to do with eliminating any and all who might represent a residual of counterpropaganda and thus provide a potential temptation to idolatry (Deut. 7:4; 20:15–18). The rabbis repeated the biblical notion that total annihilation was for the purpose of removing the temptation to idolatry. Indeed, many scholars, on the basis of the scholarly belief that the first five books of the Bible were penned centuries after the events they describe, view the Pentateuchal perspective as *retrospective*; that the writer's point was that Israel should have annihilated the idolatrous nations and that subsequent history served to bear this out. In any event the passage seems to presuppose a divide-and-conquer policy where idol-worshiping peoples could be expected to persist in promulgating propaganda against their conquerors. This would make more understandable, although perhaps no less morally questionable, this apparent policy of ethnic cleansing.

Exposition

This type of sociohistorical course of argument has frequently been made and can be summed up in the contention that religion without war was inconceivable in the ancient Near Eastern world. In other words, one should not judge the past by the standards of the present. This, of course, is a highly subjective point of view that depends on the authority ascribed to present standards and that assumes that ancient peoples were incapable, due to circumstances, of avoiding war altogether. It is unquestionable that ancient religious policy was defined by local and state interests; there was no other kind of war than a religious war, since the god was always involved and the god's status was bound up with the success of the war. To put it simply Israel would have been quite unable to promote Yahwism (the religion of its Lord, Yahweh) or any other distinct religion or to have remained socially distinct without anticipating war as a result. For Israel even to exist, as a distinct people with a unique religion, was an invitation to be attacked. The very status of every other god was at stake. It was a matter of attack or be attacked.

None of the preceding arguments are intended to be taken as necessarily representative of the views of the quorum of scholars, or as definitive for what we ought to believe about the biblical examples of holy war. The point of these various rationalizations is that they at least exhibit a concern with the historical contingencies of the scriptures themselves. They engage in a dialogue with the ancient Near Eastern historical context and entertain exegetical considerations. Exegetical, in this and the following context, means relating to the task of interpretation. Even in reading the text, in other words, justifications for *not* going to war can be discerned that counter any tendency to automatically reapply the text indiscriminately, or take it as guidance, in our day, thousands of years after it was originally penned. Biblical passages are context bound. The nature of biblical law and revelation is that it is context specific, or *historically contingent*.

Revelation, even within the pages of the Bible, grows and changes with increased understanding. There is a certain development evident, for instance, between the Pentateuch, on the one end of the spectrum, and the Psalms and Prophets, on the other, when it comes to the rationalization of violence and war. We see a process of disassociation beginning with the kind of miraculous and mediatorial elements we have already noted; further distancing occurs through other processes of spiritualization and adaptation of violent images in the later poetic and prophetic texts (e.g., Isa. 24:21–23; Pss. 34, 37, etc.). To read such passages as Deuteronomy 7 in the light of the entire canon of the Hebrew Scriptures is to better understand in what context such sayings belong, although, admittedly, even that can be a difficult task.

To reduce the issue to a matter of hermeneutics, or interpretation of scripture, is not merely to contradict traditional thought forms

Egyptian soldiers surrender to an Israeli patrol in Sinai during the Six-Day War. Snark/Art Resource, New York.

with modern wishful thinking. The rabbis who codified (300–600 C.E.) Talmudic law had already adopted this methodology.[1] For the good of Judaism, which remained vulnerable following the Jewish Wars when Rome destroyed the temple and much of Jerusalem (70 C.E.), eventually displacing Judaism from its capital, forcibly paganizing the city (135 C.E.), and compromising the social and military status of Judaism, the pragmatically motivated Rabbis wished to steer clear of the notion of Holy War and discourage it among their people. The option of excising war from the Scriptures was not open to them, and so they proceeded to find exegetical means for accomplishing this end. To do this the Rabbis distinguished between discretionary wars, that is, permitted wars, and commanded wars. In the campaign of conquest, described in Deuteronomy 20, there was discerned by some an example of commanded war (cp. Mishnah *Sotah* 8:7). The wars of David, on the other hand, were discretionary (cp. *Sotah* 44b).

The Rabbis also advised Israelites not to return to Zion en masse in a way that could provoke a military response. There was also a diffusion of the motivation of going to war through exegetical means, in the ruling that while God had commanded Israel not to return to

Zion he had also commanded the gentiles to exercise restraint, mitigating any need for action (*Ketuboth* 110b–11a).[2] The Six-Day War reawakened interest in the potential and effectiveness of military options after centuries of avoiding the subject, and success in the two major encounters in Palestine in the last century (1948 and 1967) raised in the mind of some Jews the possibility that the Messiah was soon to come. Modern Zionists subsequently nullified the ancient rabbinic prohibition against resettlement and reawakened the idea of commanded war, considering themselves the avant garde of the Messiah.

But well before the Rabbis attempted to protect from retaliatory warfare the Judaism emerging from the ashes of 70 C.E. groups within Judaism had already confronted the options. The Judaism of the critical period between the second century B.C.E. and the first century C.E. experienced the desecration of the Greek king Antiochus IV, the nationalistic restoration of the Maccabees, the conquest of Jerusalem by Roman Pompey, and the Second Great Destruction of Jerusalem in 70 C.E. Their theology of war was stamped out in the die of hard and cruel experience. How two of these groups, the people of the Dead Sea Scrolls, and Jesus of Nazareth and his followers, reacted to the situations and the options available is instructive for how people of the Bible can think about the option of violence and going to war.

Retribution and Agency in Dispossessed Groups and Movements of the Late Second Temple Period

In various degrees most religions balance the positive need to promote public welfare with concepts like love and tolerance and the vocation to enforce the standards established by the religion and its moral laws.[3] In the interests of the perceived need to enforce standards, there often emerges some notion of retribution, punishment for serious disobedience especially when voluntary compliance seems unlikely. Whether God or the people of God are thought to dispense the judgment reveals that the question of agency, or instrumentality, also plays into the matter of retribution. The options are several, from complete human agency, to various degrees of direct or indirect instrumentality, to total nonagency and complete transference of responsibility for the required action.

It has become a truism of the sociology of religion that the militant option is most readily embraced by dispossessed groups either against the unfaithful in their own society or against the unbelieving in the

world-at-large or against both. These groups are responding to mar-
ginalization and disenfranchisement in order to restore a sense of self-
validation and vindication of their cherished causes. The rhetoric of
divine retribution, which is theologically and scripturally informed
and inspired, assists in this aim and is often stated to be an issue of
obedience in contrast to those who are disobedient or neglectful. Holy
War language is also accompanied by a defining social or ethical dualism, us against the world. Several groups in Second Temple Judaism
fit well the disenfranchisement paradigm, and some even selected the
complete human agency option in dispensing retribution (Zealots)
including to a point the celebrated Maccabees. But as we shall see, not
all chose violence. This proves that biblical obedience even among the
disenfranchised does not automatically result in militancy.

Among these latter groups are those who penned the so-called quietistic or pietistic literature. While such terms are generally no
longer used, they nevertheless validly describe important aspects of
these writings. These writings include books like 1 Enoch, Jubilees,
Psalms of Solomon, Testaments of the Twelve Patriarchs, 4 Ezra, 2
Baruch, and the like, which were all written within the late Second
Temple period, namely, before, or soon after, 70 C.E. During periods
of intense threat the kinds of disenfranchised groups who penned
these writings apparently chose to avoid or escape violent engagement and in the case of two major stormings of Jerusalem: one in 63
B.C.E. by Pompey the Great (but the city was *not* destroyed), and again
in 70 C.E., when some members of this movement apparently chose to
escape Jerusalem rather than to engage in conflict. The attitude of
abandoning the city and escaping appears to have accompanied the
view that the leaders in the capital were already out of line with
God's will and had come out from under the umbrella of divine protection and deserved to be judged along with the city. The purpose of
this escape was therefore to avoid the judgment of God justly coming
upon the city, a judgment the pious protestors had long warned was
going to come.

One document in particular portrays this escape on the part of a
group of Davidide aspirants for the throne, descendants of King
David who were apparently disenfranchised by the leading non-
Davidic Hasmonean ruling dynasty but continued to claim the
throne. The Psalms of Solomon (cp. esp. 17:16–18) record in poetic
style reminiscent of the biblical Psalms the emotions of one (or more)
of the members of this party, brought on by the recent turn of events.
He recalled how one of the illegitimate (in his eyes) Hasmonean con-

tenders for the throne opened the gates of the city to the Roman Pompey. Apparently some time prior to this event, since opening the gates would have decisively alleviated the physical threat to the city and effectively made the escape unnecessary, the members of this threatened minority group, who neither shared the policies nor wished to share the fate of the ruling party that they opposed, packed up and fled the city. The group apparently tried to warn the others of coming doom, but were ignored (2:8). Their subsequent departure from Jerusalem is spoken of by the psalmist as being "saved" from evil and from the midst of the sinners (17:5, 16–18; it was their "salvation," cp. 15:6; 16:4f.; 17:17). God providentially protected the righteous in supplying this deliverance (13:1–4; 16:5; 18:1f.).

This desire to escape from, rather than confront, conflict may well have characterized the group that we will deal with momentarily, the people of the Dead Sea Scrolls (Qumranites). Was it also out of a desire to escape from the compromised political circumstances leading up to 63 B.C.E. that some or all of the community headed out into the wilderness to a certain place called "Damascus" (possibly an enigmatic cipher referring to the Qumran site by the shores of the Dead Sea) to "prepare the way of the Lord" (à la Isa. 61:1; CD 7.14–17)? This question will perhaps never be answered with certainty, but it is worth noting that several of the scrolls evidence the conviction that Jerusalem is an apostate city, and other scrolls or portions thereof can be read to suggest a period in which part of the movement living in Jerusalem left the city in favor of greener pastures. A short allusion in the War Scroll (1QM 1.3) speaks this way of the retreat into the "wilderness of Jerusalem." Then there is that much-discussed letter among the Dead Sea Scrolls known as "4QMMT" written by this group. Apparently penned outside the city and then carried by messenger to the priestly authorities inside the city, it set out in no uncertain terms the position of the nonconformists. After reflecting on the sins committed in the city the authors explain how "we have segregated ourselves from the rest of the people and . . . we avoid mingling in these affairs and associating with them in these things" (4QMMT 92f. = 4QHalakhic Letter^d = 4Q397 7f.). Upon making this statement the authors proceed to reveal that, in their opinion, the things that are coming upon Jerusalem were foretold by Moses, David and the prophets for the "end of days" (ll. 95ff.) during which time Israel is to be afflicted by the "counsel of Belial" (i.e., an evil angel, or devil; l. 115). A similar separation and retreat from Jerusalem appears to be the allusion of a small fragment (4Q183 = 4QHistorical Work) when it refers to the way the author's community "went away from the path [of the people]" (5f.).

It is not totally surprising that this sense of predestination or predetermination of judgment has been a constant feature of Jewish books of protest from 1 Enoch (among the earliest writings)[4] through the Psalms of Solomon and perhaps again witnessed in the "survivor in the land" motif of 4 Ezra, written shortly after the destruction in 70 C.E. Apparently this option of escape was repeated not only by Jews during the days leading up to the sacking of the city in 70 C.E., as suggested by 4 Ezra and noted by Josephus, but also by Jewish Christians. In the days immediately before the siege established tradition tells us that Christians took flight to Pella in Transjordan, and the accuracy of the tradition, although doubted by some, has tended to be confirmed. In any event there is no evidence that any of these groups, Jewish or Christian, chose to bunker down and fight or otherwise thought of themselves as retreating temporarily in the hope of reengaging the enemy at a more opportune time or place. Although members of the Jewish movement of protest had much in common theologically and ideologically with the Zealots, this particular action proved that they did not belong to the militants; they certainly would have been charged as betrayers and renegades by the Zealots.

One might ask why these various groups did not vie for the military option, since this option had proven effective in the highly successful Maccabean campaigns of the then recent historical memory, a memory that was revered by the masses. The reason was apparently not fear or cowardice; it may not even have been the pessimistic attitudes of such groups toward the prospect of successfully defending the city. To answer the question involves detailed sociological considerations that we are unable to attend to here; suffice it to say that the vital difference was apparently the nationalistic element lacking in their make up.[5] While the Maccabees played into nationalistic sentiments the nonconformist groups no longer sought to restore the old national ideals as contained in the image of a golden age of Israel, but had largely abandoned hope for many of their compatriots and saw many of the national institutions as hopelessly perverted, violated and permanently rendered unclean. It is understandable from this rather strict position that they would fail to enjoy the support of the masses enjoyed by the Maccabees. Partly as a result of the fact that they were in the minority and could not therefore hope to fight off the mighty empires on their own, and partly from the fact that they no longer sought to challenge the national structures, to defend the symbolic and ritual center of the nation, or to come to the aid of the political establishment, there was really no question of taking up arms. This did not mean that they did not anticipate divine retribution, only that God was already in the business of carrying out that retribution against the Israelite people through the instrumentality of the Roman army. These groups were not necessarily composed of pacifists, but when it came to attempts to save the present form of Judaism they were noticeably passive. So, contrary to the usual sociological typology, perhaps these disenfranchised groups did *not* opt for violence or militarism.

Retribution in the Dead Sea Scrolls

The people who authored the sectarian documents from the Dead Sea Scrolls tended to express a middle-of-the-road position between militarism and passive noninvolvement when it came to the matter of retribution, and especially so with regard to the matter of agency in that retribution. Scholars of the Scrolls, it should be pointed out, are in disagreement about how confidently we can discern any single attitude about such beliefs since there are so many Scrolls and, potentially at least, many different points of view presented in them. It is also now becoming clearer that the famous Scrolls are not the product of a small monastic community that spent all or even most of its time near the Dead Sea. Statistically speaking, the sheer number of Scrolls, the diversity of copyist hands, the wide spectrum of types and provenances of writings and the lengthy period represented by these writings suggest that the collection originated from a fairly wide movement in Judaism that lived in Palestine over a lengthy period of time.[6] The ideas and historical allusions represented in this selective library tend to sustain the view that this group was part of a fairly large and well-represented Jewish movement with a lengthy history. It was not mainstream Judaism, if such a term can be used to speak of more officially sanctioned schools in Judaism, but it was nevertheless a large and well-coordinated sectarian movement that attracted a substantial minority of Israelites. While the size of the movement suggests diversity, however, other facts point to a fairly cohesive and delimited belief structure. It seems beyond doubt, in this regard, that the Scroll collection as a whole, composed of writings originally hidden in caves for protection from the Roman invasion of Jerusalem, does exhibit a special character. It was a selective library typical of any religious sect that had notions about what should and should not be preserved in a good library and that guarded carefully that standard. It was a collection that tended to promote the views of the group.[7] The fact that the library contained most of the pietistic/quietistic writings mentioned previously tends to confirm that the movement represented by the Scrolls was pretty much identical to, or overlapping with, the movement represented by those groups. The entire movement has been characterized by this author elsewhere as an eclectic and exclusivist movement of protest: in Hebrew parlance, a remnant movement.[8]

The War Scroll

The long-standing conventional view that this group was related in some way to the Essene movement has never been successfully challenged, and contrasts sharply to the significant, if small, minority of scholars who have viewed the Scroll community as in continuity with the Zealot movement. The claim has been made, based on certain texts (1QS 10.19; 11.2), that the Scroll community was decidedly pacifistic[9] but since this opinion is based on so few texts whose meaning and import are not entirely clear, it would probably be hasty to conclude this much from so little. There exists, on the other hand, only one important and unambiguously militaristic document in the entire Scroll collection, and the importance of this particular document may have been overemphasized due to certain accidents of discovery, that is, the fact that it was among one of the larger and more complete Scrolls and among the very first to be located and retrieved by scholars. The document is the so-called War Scroll (1QM), which, while theories to the effect that it originated outside the group have been proffered, nevertheless appears to sustain the same sectarian, eclectic, and exclusivist minority beliefs as the rest of the sectarian Scrolls. I will return to this document in more detail; however, first we might ask what other evidence exists for militaristic tendencies in this group.

Considered one of the sectarian documents, those authored by the sect's members, rather than borrowed from elsewhere, and exhibiting a characteristic interpretive methodology known as *pesher*, the Habakkuk Scroll (1QpHab) presents the elect community as instruments of retribution. Conventionally the passage of interest has been translated, "God will not destroy His people by the hand of the nations; but God will judge all the nations by the hand of His elect ones. And it is by the chastisement which the elect will dispense that all the wicked of His people will atone" (1QpHab 5.3–5).[10] "By the hand" is, of course, a semitism for "through the agency of." The biblical idiom that stands behind the wording of this short passage, together with the theology of "atonement for the land" to which it relates, prompts the view that the *pesher* interpreter was expressing two matters: (1) the elect community would be used by God as instruments in a war first against the apostates among their own people and then also against the rest of the nations, and (2) it is through the death of these same transgressors that God would again be able to bless the people of Israel. This purging would leave only a righteous remnant to resettle the land of Israel and enjoy a period of prosperity and blessing. This materialistic theology is inspired partly by Leviticus 26, which also led to the view that Israelite apostates as well as pagans would need to be purged from the Holy Land indiscriminately if the blessing was ever to come.

Another allusion to this action against other Israelites can be discerned in the second half of the passage, which implies that the death of wicked Israelites would serve as the only effective sacrifice for "atoning for the land," which, in this case, means setting things right.[11] What is nonconformist about the passage is the exception it takes to the notion that the gentile Romans, like the Babylonians in the period of the Exile, are the instruments of God; this time, righteous Israelites will be the instruments of divine retribution on the nations as well as on Israel itself. This instrumental view is continued in the War Scroll, as is the notion that the great approaching assize would target other Israelites as well as Gentiles. The sociological implications of an ostracized group aspiring to bring divine retribution against their Israelite opponents, the immediate society against which the group is in protest, rather than the Roman oppressors themselves are, of course, obvious.

To summarize the subject matter and intention of the War Scroll in a few paragraphs is presumptuous to say the least, but its most important contents for our purposes here can be succinctly delineated. The War Scroll describes a future battle resembling, in a sense, a battle plan of the type that might have been reported by any ancient historian, but with some peculiar features. The battle is, first of all, clearly a future one, being prophetically announced beforehand to a leader of the community, the Instructor. It is a war to be fought by the "sons of light"—righteous Israelites no doubt equated with the author's community—against the "sons of darkness" (also referred to as "the lot of Belial"), which clearly includes not only the heathen "Kittim" (a code name for the enemies of Israel) but also the wicked from within Israel who live in Jerusalem, and quite possibly also their angelic counterparts or colleagues. It is noteworthy that Jerusalem is apparently the first city to be attacked by the exiled sons of light before war against the Romans and other nations can be undertaken. It is as if Jerusalem must first be liberated before war can be made against the rest of the world.

There are other dissimilarities to a conventional report of battle. While some superficial guidelines are given for battle formation and strategy, it is really only important to point out that it is the priests who lead in the battle (2.1–3) and the units regularly fall in behind them. Considerations of formation and strategy obviously carry little real importance in what is a highly providential war. Much more important is it to describe the various biblical and symbolic slogans or catchphrases that are attached to the battle attire of the sons of light (on the trumpets, for example, are written slogans like "Rallied by God" and the names of the chiefs). The description of the construction of the weapons and armor is also idealistic and impractical (e.g., the gold trimming). In other words this is a battle that is not fought by the normal means and recalls the intervention or mediatory acts of God during the period of occupation; thus, for example, the motto "Confusion of God" is written on one of the banners, recalling Joshua 10:10 and 1 Samuel 14:20.

Accordingly debate has raged over whether a real battle is even intended in this document, whether in fact a heavenly war is being described as much as a conventional earthly engagement. Most approaches at the very least see this as an eschatological (future, final) battle and so a kind of ultimate battle fought in some way on both heavenly and earthly stages.[12] In that case the issue is less urgent as to how or even whether the people of God engage in combat during the battle, for an eschatological war will be executed by God and his angels, and the outcome will be final and decisive. However, the concept of such a battle taking place comes across as a very real possibility for a group like this, and eschatological characterizations of this war might mask the very temporal and very material urgency of the battle. The relevance of a battle in which God, through the instrumentality of the sons of light or through divine miraculous intervention or some combination of both, reclaims the Holy City for his righteous people in history and places Israelites back in power, is obvious.

There are other realistic elements. For one thing the intervention is not total and the battle does not proceed without a hitch. The introductory column of the work lays out the see-saw nature of the fighting: "In the war, the sons of light will be the strongest during three lots, in order to strike down wickedness and in three others the army of Belial will gird themselves in order to force the lot of [God] to retreat" (1.13f.). On the other hand it must be remembered that the outcome of the battle is never in doubt. The alternation of triumph and retreat appears to be conventional, and follows the biblical model of war to a point. Noteworthy it is that it is never actually said that the retreat involves an amount of bloodshed on the part of the sons of light corresponding to that of the enemies in the periods of advance; indeed no blood is mentioned in the description of the battle, although notably within the poetic portions it is (cf. 19.3f.), which is also a feature lacking in the other retribution passages in the Scrolls. The language is mostly annihilatory of evil, with the wicked utterly destroyed. Terminology of annihilation may imply that in divine warfare there is no opportunity for human suffering in the normal processes of war, but merely annihilation, or that the real interest of the author lies with dispensing with unrighteousness and vindicating the righteous, and so it is not so much an interest in revenge or bloodshed.

On balance, while the motivations and some aspects of the war in the War Scroll seem to be real enough, the sons of light appear to be little more than passive witnesses to divine warfare mediated on their behalf. Prior to the battle the teacher can envision how God will take the saints to victory, and while many periods of engagements will be required these are all clearly predetermined. The symbolism of the entire war adds to the impression that even before a spear is raised the "battle is the Lord's," a confession repeatedly made in the poetic portions of the work (cp. 11.1, etc.).

The Hymns

All of these aspects raise the question whether biblical warfare has not actually been objectified or distanced through a process of eschatologizing and effectively mythologizing holy war. The Scroll people simply did not want to fight, which may again be a function of their minority status, but may be also a matter of principle. We might recall that the Essenes, to whom the Scroll people appear to be related, are never unambiguously recorded as engaging in historical battles, and consensus has it that the Essenes, like their forerunners the Hasidim, rejected the militaristic preoccupations of the Maccabees. Moreover, concern for purity and especially abhorrence for shedding of blood, and perhaps even the association of war and bloodshed with evil, among these groups (cp. esp. the Book of Jubilees, found in multiple copies in the Qumran library) would seem to have discouraged or even precluded direct engagement in combat.[13]

More evidence for this disassociation from war comes in the hymnic or poetic literature of Qumran, apparently composed in the same immediate circles that composed the other sectarian literature in the Scroll library. The Hymn Scroll offers a kind of corroborating evidence of this inclination from a broadly psychological perspective, for here a selection of military terms is given completely nonmilitary associations. The hymnist-author speaks of himself and his community as a "besieged city" (1QH 11[3].7), employing naval-military terms for the existential situation of persecution and widespread immorality and unfaithfulness in which his community finds itself (11[3].13–15), while the Lord serves as a massive rampart or a sturdy fortification for their protection (11[3].37; 15(7).7–9). The following hymn contains such figurative allusions and sums up these kinds of thoughts and attitudes:

> I am like someone entering a fortified city,
> And looking for shelter in the rampart until salvation.
> My God, I lean on your truth,
> For you place the foundation upon rock
> And the beams to the correct size,
> And the plumb line [lacuna] . . . tested stone
> For a strong building which will not shake.
> All those who enter there will not stagger,
> For a foreigner will not penetrate it;
> Its gates are armoured gates
> Which do not permit entry;
> The locks are massive and cannot be broken.
> No band at all with its weapons of war will enter,
> Even though it is loaded
> [with weapons] of the wicked battle.
> Then the sword of God will pounce
> In the era of judgment,
> And all the sons of his truth will awaken,
> To destroy wickedness,
> And all the sons of blame will no longer exist.
> The hero will bend his bow and break the encirclement

To an endless broad place.
He will open the everlasting gates
To take out weapons of war,
And they will rule from one end to the other.
There will be no salvation for guilty inclination,
It will be trampled to destruction
Without there being a remnant.
There is no hope in the profusion [of their weapons,]
Nor for all the heroes of war will there be shelter.
For to God Most High [the battle belongs . . .] (14[6].25–33)[14]

This hymn seems to move from military metaphors of present suffering to the future (perhaps imminent) hope for the experience of the final battle in which God will pour out retribution on the opponents of the author and bring vindication for the righteous community. One senses from the military-metaphorical coup in the early part of the hymn, in which the author hardly intends literally the military images by which he expresses the experience of evil and persecution, that the language of divine retribution later on in the hymn may not itself be intended literally. Perhaps more to the point, the author does not hope for a literal fulfillment of the death wish so much as for his vindication and that of his community. Indeed, the language is evasive and nonliteral ("the sword of God" is anthropomorphic), a note of disarmament is sounded, and toward the conclusion of the hymn military methods are shown to be ultimately ineffective.

Certainly one does not get the feeling that the author soon intends to proceed to fulfill his intentions militarily in a Zealot-like fashion and to personally exact retribution from his opponents and enemies. It is not that the author is not in a literal war, indeed his panic suggests he knows physical dangers; but rather, he like David the hymnist hides from the violent intentions of his enemies (13[5]11–17; for another persecution hymn with military metaphors, cp. 10[2].11–17, 20–29), for in this war the author and his community are the hunted, not the hunters. Like the War Scroll God is the instrument of judgment and the participation in the war of the righteous themselves seems reluctant at most. Perhaps the minority position of this group has the effect of dissolving any military ambitions, but for whatever reason the hymn writer falls short of expressing serious military threats or advising violent methods. He speaks of an upcoming war as an inevitable part of his traditional expectation, but also distances himself from engagement through spiritualizing the conflict.

Violence and Piety

These various examples suggest a process of the transference of anger to piety. Worship served to dissipate the anger felt by the author and the community. This anger, appropriately reflected in poetic piety, evinces a kind of reinterpretation or even existentialization of the language of divine warfare, thus disarming the violent aspects of the language. It is probably fair to say of the Dead Sea Scrolls that there is a discernible movement toward disassociation from violence, and the poetic literature especially suggests that reflection and existentialization within the context of a minority dualistic sectarianism are on the way to replacing commitment to literal military retribution, at least where the people of God act as chief agents. They believed in retribution and even counted on it, but again it is a matter of agency. God would be the chief cause of the retribution, it would be in his time and at his providential ordering, and while the instruments of that retribution would be the righteous, there is little evidence that this instrumental role preoccupied the minds of the sectarians or led to any concrete planning for their active part in the event. Their attitude toward violent military engagement perhaps owes something to their minority status as well as to their rejection of nationalistic objectives.[15]

With the Dead Sea Scrolls, therefore, we are witness to a disenfranchised group that chose not to adopt a military response, or even apparently to sponsor or encourage violence in the name of their objectives. Thus while there is a tendency among sociologists of religion to link dualism with militancy, it is apparently not the dualism or the sectarianism itself that is sufficient to sustain violent and aggressive attitudes and beliefs.

The conclusion would seem to be that the Dead Sea community, like the author of the hymn above, represented some kind of a halfway point between religious militancy, encouraged by their Scriptures literally interpreted, and religious pacifism, which was no doubt receiving less ambiguous expression among other Jewish groups. The Qumran exegetes were too faithful to the scriptures to ignore the tradition of holy war or divine warfare, but they were also too religiously committed to their spiritual ideals, and too separate from the nationalistic interests of their countrymen, to adopt militaristic goals to attain their ends. Two contradictory exegetical products were vying for their devotion and allegiance. With their heads they embraced retribution, but with their hearts they could not easily sanction bloodshed. The Scrolls accordingly represent a watershed in the process of discerning appropriate responses to the perceived need for retribution.

The Teaching of Jesus

As with the Scrolls, a small but significant minority of scholars have suggested that Jesus was sympathetic with the Zealot option, or even more directly involved with the Zealot party.[16] The reasons given for this view include, among others, the form of Jesus' execution, between two Zealots, and with the incriminating inscription placed over the cross, his action in driving buyers and sellers out of the temple, the presence among his disciples of possible Zealot connections, as well as a few sayings involving swords. This amalgamation of evidence from the life of Jesus has exercised a significant influence on theology, politics, and recent history. Revolutionary approaches to Jesus, as well as political, social, and theological movements of liberation, have sometimes been based on this understanding of his teaching.[17]

This view, however, has been so thoroughly refuted in terms of the whole argument and approach, as well as in details,[18] that it may fairly be said to be disproved with as much force as any historical argument can be said to be disproved.[19] Admittedly there are aspects of Jesus' actions as described by the Gospels that might sublimely suggest, to one already looking for the evidence, that Jesus had nationalistic revolutionary ambitions. There are sayings attributed to him that might be interpreted the same way (Matt. 10:34–36; Luke 22:36–38). We are on better ground, however, to view such texts as representing a biblical fulfillment theme, with very little of their militaristic aspects taken seriously,[20] and to judge instead those few sayings wherein, in their greater context, Jesus expressed an ethic of nonviolence as carrying a high likelihood of authenticity. Included are the famous words of nonviolence taken from the Sermon on the Mount (Matt. 5:9, 38–48; cp. also 26:52; Mark 14:47–48; John 18:10f.), and although the Sermon is clearly a composite of a variety of traditions, scholarship today generally finds little reason to attribute them to any other source than Jesus himself.

That Jesus taught a form of pacifism comparable to the total nonviolence of Gandhi, however, is a conclusion based on an admittedly small number of texts, and it might be noted that words spoken to a handful of disciples and others for their own instruction, regarding the situation of Judaism at a specific period in history, does not amount to a sweeping condemnation of all wars everywhere and at all times. Space precludes taking up the question whether Jesus would have dismissed the possibility of a just war for any cause whatsoever; however, the words from the Sermon on the Mount, and the spirit of his message as it has been discerned throughout the ages, probably justifies the conclusion that there is no such thing in Jesus' mind as holy war.[21] War may be inevitable or necessary, but as the highest form of the expression of God's will or to bring in the Kingdom of God, no![22]

The question that interests us here concerns how it is that Jesus could justify ignoring biblical precedent, if that is what we wish for the sake of argument to call it, and teach an essentially nonviolent form of revolution? Answers that might prove worthy of a hearing include the following:

Jesus' willingness to critique the Scriptures based on his own revelatory authority. The so-called antitheses in the Sermon on the Mount (Matt. 5:21–48) have been cited as evidence that Jesus placed his own teaching above that of the law and advocated values and qualities in ethical decisions that transcended, or even ignored, the commandments. While Jesus did seem to relativize the law, debate rages over virtually every relevant passage as to whether Jesus actually contradicts the meaning of the law or merely sharpens or radicalizes obedience to the law. Since at least some of the sayings in question clearly express an authority independent and even critical, not only of current biblical interpretation, but of the law itself[23] and given that precedent already existed in Judaism for relativizing the biblical revelation,[24] it seems likely that Jesus did see his own ministry as a development over, if not an actual contradiction of, the biblical revelation.

Jesus' independent understanding of God. Much has been made of the fact that Jesus' personal intimacy with God went well beyond that of his contemporary Jews. That the gospels relate Jesus' familiarity with God in terms not conventionally used by Jewish teachers may be a valid claim, but there is little doubt that many pious Jews of the time aspired to a close personal familiarity with God, even if they used different terms to express it. That this relationship, in Jesus' case, led to the rejection of violence in the Scriptures seems to be implied by sayings like, "if anyone strikes you on the right cheek, turn to him the other also . . . Love your enemies and pray for those who persecute you, *so that you may be sons of your Father who is in heaven*" (Matt. 5:39, 45).

Jesus' rejection of nationalistic ideals. While this aspect of Jesus' teaching is debated, it seems reasonably certain that Jesus, following a similar understanding as his colleague John the Baptist, shared in some respects the understanding of groups in protest who controverted nationalistic ideals in favor of more personal and individual expressions of faith. Assuming the authenticity of material such as that found in the Synoptic Apocalypse, Mark 13, and parallels, we can say that Jesus stood among those who warned of Jerusalem's judgment and probably viewed it as divine retribution. The motivations for armed resistance were effectively eliminated through transference of agency to the Romans.

Jesus' understanding of the terms of the restoration. There is beginning to emerge, from the renewed attention to the Jewishness of Jesus and his message, a scholarly consensus that Jesus was a preacher of restoration, namely, that he embraced the prophetic concept of the restoration of Israel.[25] Could Jesus' vision for Israel's restoration have taken account of the Isaianic promise, summed up in the *locus classicus* of a realization of peace in Israel and the world . . .

> They shall beat their swords into plowshares,
> And their spears into pruning hooks;
> Nation shall not lift up sword against nation,
> Neither shall they learn war any more . . . (Isa. 2:4b,c, RSV)?

The Cross and the wrath of God. One other aspect of the teaching of Jesus that may have played a formative role in his pacifistic teaching is his view about the meaning of his death. It has been fashionable in the last century or more to deny to Jesus the belief that his atoning death would function to divert the retributive wrath of God. On the other hand, there are several traditions about Jesus in the gospels that are difficult to explain if he did not, in fact, hold this kind of belief. This includes the authentic-sounding reference made by Jesus to his death as a baptism (Mark 10:38f.; Luke 12:50),[26] the way he apparently compared his fate with that of John the Baptist (Matt. 11:7–19; 17:12f.; Mark 9:13; Luke 7:24–35), the killing-of-the-prophets theme, and perhaps also the Son of Man designation that Jesus gave to himself and by which he described his mission.[27] Debated also is to what extent Jesus held to the pattern of the Suffering Servant presented in the latter chapters of Isaiah, and particularly to the substitutionary portions of that passage:

> Surely he has borne our griefs
> And carried our sorrows

Yet we esteemed him stricken and smitten by God and afflicted.
But he was wounded for our transgressions,
He was bruised for our iniquities;
Upon him was the chastisement that made us whole,
And with his stripes we are healed. . . .
The Lord has laid on him the iniquity of us all. (Isa. 53:4–6; cp. vv.
    10–12, RSV)

On the whole scholars are less skeptical than they once were that there existed in Judaism a Suffering Servant messianology. While it would be impossible to definitively attribute this understanding to Jesus, we do know that the early church made much of the idea, and, given the way suffering themes in the gospels tend to hark back to the life and example of Jesus, the simplest explanation for this may be that they were themes already taught by him. In combination with his prophetic ministry of warnings against Jerusalem and the temple, there would appear to have been in Jesus' original teaching something of the view that the retribution, or wrath of God, would be circumvented by the substitutionary death of the Messiah, probably at least for his followers if not for all of God's people. Either Jesus or the later church accordingly concluded that the ultimate agent of retribution was Jesus, not because he would dispense retribution, but because he would assume the wrath of God.

While, therefore, the symbolism of violence still remains in the Christian tradition, understood properly the gospel also offers the opportunity to deflect anger toward the ultimate symbol of the Cross. The church has, of course, for centuries developed this theology in its incarnational and sacrificial soteriology, and in its teaching about the imitation of Christ, but it ought to be noted that the context of Jesus' ministry would suggest that such sayings originally referred to the coming judgment on Jerusalem and Jesus' atoning ministry for Israel, and were only later applied, again in line with prophetic expectation, to the world as a whole.

What Are the Options Today?

This short survey of beliefs about retribution in the Dead Sea Scrolls and the teaching of Jesus provides a backdrop against which to discuss options for those who hold to the sacred authority of ancient documents. An important observation from our review is that nationalism appears to be more influential, when it comes to opting for violent forms of retribution, than either the factor of disenfranchisement or the biblical precedent of violence. While admittedly the perpetuation of the symbolism of violence by sacred texts may indirectly continue to contribute to acts of violence in society, the complete abandonment of such language was probably not an option for any Jewish group of the time. To rather different degrees our examples show how the language of violence was reinterpreted and how this eventually affected the resultant behavior of two groups. People of the Bible do not need to act violently, or to sanction violence, in order to be biblically faithful.

With the availability of weapons of mass destruction it is becoming critical in these days to win the war for the hearts and minds of people capable of waging the peace. This means offering conservative religious minds options that satisfy their particular presuppositions. What options do religious groups have when their scriptures appear to endorse violence? The first and obvious requirement is that they must sustain a historical-contextual view of revelation, something that is unfortunately lacking in many conservative, particularly Fundamentalistic, commitments to the Bible and to other sacred scriptures in other religious cultures. For Western society this hermeneutical advancement required an intellectual enlightenment, but it is obvious that ancient interpreters were not totally unenlightened in this regard. Superficial readings are not just a matter of intellectual capacity but of religious commitments, psychological predispositions, and bigotry. Where these commitments did not interfere ancient exegesis frequently evidenced quite profound understanding of the historical context of scripture.[28]

So what options exist for interpreting scriptures pacifistically? Some will find it satisfactory to settle for belief in total nonagency, in which anger is delayed and comfort is taken in the confession, "leave room for the judgment of God." Others will prefer a more intellectual rationalization, such as those contained in sociohistorical interpretations, which reason that while war was inevitable in the ancient world, things today have changed. Other approaches will reinterpret, spiritualize, internalize, and adapt revelation. Anger can be transferred and thus dissipated through such means of reflection and rationalization.

Another option that might be urged is to allow for the development or relativization of revelation. While generally thought to be an innovation of the Apostle Paul, in terms of the temporary nature of the ancient Torah; and of the author of the Epistle to the Hebrews, in terms of perfectionism, this view that revelation grows and changes is also surprisingly integral to a certain sector of Jewish belief of the period we have studied.[29] The ambiguous form and temporary nature of revelation are often taken quite seriously by groups otherwise strongly committed to biblical revelation. This option is not limited to a Christian or secessionist position but may be adopted, and has been adopted, to a degree, in all the major biblical religions. Only a dead Bible, one that is decontextualized, can be held to contribute to war or terrorism.

Finally, what could properly be called teleological elements in interpretation make for an effective reinterpretation of scripture. In the Perfect Vision of the future in Judaism, known today as restorationism, peace is a centrally important goal for the future (cp. Isaiah's "swords into plowshares"). Some quarters of Judaism were animated with the hope of the imminent coming of their restoration, and militant options were rejected in favor of peaceful hopes for prophetic fulfillment. Christians generally believe that Jesus brought the restoration in the form of the Kingdom of God, and so it is perplexing that many still hold to the notion of war in Christian causes. Part of the blame for this is the tendency to reeschatologize the message of Jesus, a process that opens the door to new concepts of holy war. All traditions and religions embrace the notion of a peaceful resolution of the course of history in the plan of God. We must begin to encourage this for everyone.

Both sides in every engagement, real or potential, must be committed to these goals. I remain cautiously optimistic that the building blocks for peace already exist in all of the respective traditions and can be exploited for peace.

Notes

1. The rabbinic texts cited below are adopted from a presentation by Prof. Reuven Firestone of Hebrew Union College, Los Angeles, during a public lecture at McMaster University in Hamilton, Ontario, "Divine Authority and Mass Violence: Holy War in Judaism, Christianity, and Islam" (October 17, 2002).

2. Maimonides was representative of the alternative attitude that "holy war" (*milherem mitzvah*) is still binding until the biblical seven idolatrous nations (see Deut. 7:1–4) are totally obliterated, and he pronounced the command to settle the land of Israel "equal to all of the commandments" (*Mishnah Torah*, chapter 5; *Positive Commandment*, 187).

3. Compare Firestone.

4. The Book of Admonitions, one of the major components of 1 Enoch, presents Enoch and Noah praying that God might grant an escape from the coming destruction, which may be yet another allusion to the escape from conflict that we have discerned in the other writings.

5. To say that they were not nationalistic does not necessarily mean that they abandoned their national identity or hopes for the nation per se, but that the primary focus of identity was no longer the nation so much as a group of righteous individuals within the nation. They were not hesitant to critique what they saw to be corrupt national institutions and did not hold that all compatriots were automatically included in the covenant. Compare Mark Adam Elliott, *The Survivors of Israel: A Reconsideration of the Theology of Pre-Christian Judaism* (Grand Rapids: Eerdmans, 2000), especially 33f.

6. Attention to these facts was most effectively brought to the scholarly world by Norman Golb, *Who Wrote the Dead Sea Scrolls? The Search for the Secret of Qumran* (New York: Scribner, 1995), even though few have accepted his own theories about the provenance of the Scrolls. Compare Elliott, *Survivors of Israel*, 17–21.

7. The few possible exceptions to this selective nature, such as works which were considered evil or magical, seem to have been written cryptically (in an inverted cipher, for example) in order to make these dangerous writings less accessible.

8. Elliott, *Survivors of Israel*, 235–243.

9. A. R. C. Leaney, *The Rule of Qumran and Its Meaning* (London: SCM, 1966), 33.

10. The translation is that of A. Dupont-Sommer (translated, in turn, from the French by G. Vermes), *The Essene Writings from Qumran* (Glouster: Peter Smith, 1961), 261, with one minor adjustment.

11. For details and translation, compare Elliott, *Survivors of Israel*, 67–72.

12. It is problematical to view the scroll as composed for use in the imminent war with the Romans leading up to 66 C.E., a position held by the scroll's original translator and analyst Y. Yadin, *The Scroll of the War of the Sons of Light against the Sons of Darkness* (ET Oxford: Oxford University Press, 1962), who is followed by P. R. Davies, *1QM, the War Scroll from Qumran: Its Structure and History* (Rome: Biblical Institute Press, 1977). The work is too impractical to be of much service for this engagement, and the opening column of the scroll rather suggests that it is the exiles who return to do battle on apostates and the nations, not a battle initiated by Rome.

13. The opinion has been expressed by A. R. C. Leaney, *Rule of Qumran*, 33, that the group was pacifistic but that this pacifism would not excuse them from participation in the final eschatological battle. He points to their condemnation of violence (1QS 10.19, 11.2) and to their withdrawn life as evidence that they were not zealots: "Their willingness to fight was confined absolutely to the eschatological war to which in their belief God would summon them."

14. Translation is that of F. García Martínez, *The Dead Sea Scrolls Translated* (Leiden: E. J. Brill, 1994), 341f.

15. In this posture they come close to the view of the Jewish historian Josephus, who condemned the zealot nationalists and returned to the notion that the *Romans* were God's instruments in bringing judgment upon them (cf. *War* 6.251).

16. The presentation of Jesus as zealot nationalist is associated with R. Eisler, *Iesous Basileus ou basileusas*, 2 vols. (Heidelberg: C. Winter, 1929–30); S. G. F. Brandon, *The Fall of Jerusalem and the Christian Church: A Study of the Effects of the Jewish Overthrow of A.D. 70 on Christianity* (London: SPCK, 1951; 2nd ed. 1957); Brandon, *Jesus and the Zealots: A Study of the Political Factor in Primitive Christianity* (Manchester: Manchester University Press, 1967); Brandon, *The Trial of Jesus of Nazareth* (New York: Stein & Day, 1968); and J. Carmichael, *The Death of Jesus* (London: Victor Gollancz; New York: Macmillan, 1963) among others.

17. See the introduction by J. Reumann to M. Hengel, *Was Jesus a Revolutionist?* (ET Philadelphia: Fortress, 1971), xv, and the words of Hengel himself, 27–32.

18. See especially, Hengel, *Was Jesus a Revolutionist?* and E. Bammel and C. F. D. Moule, eds., *Jesus and the Politics of His Day* (Cambridge: Cambridge University Press, 1984).

19. We ought to note only one point, which has been justly called the "litmus test" of militant nationalism and that is the fact that in Gethsemane *neither Jesus nor his disciples* took up arms to resist arrest. Moreover, Jesus would never have eaten with tax-gathers, who were the archenemies of Zealots; but this cannot be explained as an invention of the church.

20. Matthew 10:34–36 is not a program for militancy, but a warning against attack. Luke 22:36–38 is better seen as indicating fulfillment of Scripture, but also a disavowal of the violent associations falsely attributed to Jesus. Hengel, *Was Jesus a Revolutionist?* remarks that "it does not signify the sword which the church of Jesus wields in a crusade against her persecutors but, as Adolf Schlatter has correctly shown, that sword which the persecutors use against the church" (23). As with the Scroll people, the community is the hunted, not the hunters.

21. Indeed there is *much* in the teaching of Jesus to suggest that he was not only not a militant nationalist Jew, but that he discouraged anything but peaceful resistance, and did that by *example;* it is doubtful that even so-called just war would have been considered acceptable to him. His teaching everywhere promoted *faith* or *dependence on God* and the *imitation of God* in spite of all: "the birds of the air . . . neither sow or reap . . . " (Matt. 6:26). For someone to speak this way and then encourage militant rebellion would be a great contradiction to say the least. Compare G. M. Styler, "Argumentum e silentio," in *Jesus and the Politics of His Day*, 101–107, 106f.

22. Jesus' rejection of the zealot option may not be automatically equated with the abandonment of the notion of retribution altogether. There may also be the question again of *agency*. Would Jesus, for example, have agreed with the view of Paul to "leave room for the justice of God" (Rom. 12:20)—which is the ultimate expression of *non-agency* in the matter of retribution?

23. Compare H. Merkel, "The opposition between Jesus and Judaism," in *Jesus and the Politics of His Day*, 129–144, 134–144.

24. Compare Elliott, *Survivors of Israel*, 121–142.

25. As suggested in works representative of the so-called Third Quest or Jewish Quest for the historical Jesus like B. F. Meyer, *The Aims of Jesus* (London: SCM, 1979), and E. P. Sanders, *Jesus and Judaism* (London: SCM, 1985) and followed by a host of other writers on Jesus' ministry.

26. The "baptism" in Mark 10:38 would appear to be inseparably connected with the idea of wrath, since the "cup of wrath" features so widely in the Hebrew Scriptures to speak of God's anger and subsequent judgment (cp. Ps. 75:8; Isa. 51:17–23; Jer. 25:15–28; etc.).

27. For more on this and the following points the reader is asked to consult the forthcoming volume by the present author, *Like a Flood. The Baptismal Foundations of Jesus' Teaching and other Aspects of Early Christian Theology*.

28. Firestone holds that this is relevant in any discussion of contemporary militant forms of Islam in which the militant passages in the Qur'an have not been mitigated by exegesis (or anything comparable to the interpretative traditions of the rabbis) or by modernistic attitudes, since Islam has not experienced an Enlightenment similar to that which came to the West. One could add that these problems also exist in any movements in Judaism or Christianity that refuse to mitigate militant passages by exegetical means.

29. Compare Elliott, *Survivors of Israel*, 121–142.

CHAPTER 11

The Qur'an, Muhammad, and Jihad in Context

Charles T. Davis III

Judaism, Christianity, and Islam often relate as if they were members of a dysfunctional family. Negative archetypal energies, strong emotions, surface from the unconscious to block dialog. Even before 9/11, Christians heard the term *jihad* as having an alien and menacing ring. We are tempted to see a simplistic contrast between a peaceful Christianity and a militant Islam, forgetting that Christians have had a theological rationale for the "just war" since St. Augustine (fifth century) and archetypal images of the Christian as a Warrior-Martyr since the appearance of the St. George Legend at the end of the third century. For Westerners, the mention of a crusade evokes positive images of courageous Christian soldiers. We fail to perceive that the term *crusade* evokes exceptionally strong negative, threatening images of Christian hostility for the Muslim. Such responses on both sides are deeply rooted in both historical events and the unconscious structure of the personality. But there are other barriers to Muslim/Christian dialog that are apt to become exaggerated by recent events. Since Jews, Christians, and Muslims share many common elements, we are easily deceived into thinking that they understand matters like prophethood, holy scripture, law, community, interpretation, and the just war in comparable ways.

As we Westerners consider Muhammad and the Qur'an, we tend to regard our Christian and Western religious and scholarly traditions as if they were absolute Truth. It is true that Judaism, Christianity, and Islam are generally alike in having the twin focal points of a prophetic founder and a book of scripture: Moses and the Torah; Jesus and the Bible, Muhammad and the Qur'an. Christians and Muslims also have doctrines defining the just war and religious militancy. Here the similarity ends. The methods by which one appropriates the founder and the scripture are quite different in the three communities. Our ability to have empathy with other members of the Judeo-Christian-Islamic family can be greatly enhanced as we respect both the similarities and the differences between the Bible and the Qur'an, Jesus and Moses, Jesus and Muhammad, and jihad and the just war.

The Scriptures: Hebrew Bible, New Testament, Qur'an

W. C. Smith (1993) reminds us in *What Is Scripture?* that "people— a given community—make a text into a scripture, or keep it scripture: by treating it in a certain way" (18) appropriate to the life of the community. The books of the Hebrew Bible (also called "the Torah, the Prophets, and the Writings," or TANAK), the Christian Bible, and the Qur'an were not scripture when first written but literary texts. The various books became scripture through their impact upon the life of the community and the process of canonization; consequently, scripture never exists apart from a particular community's interpretation of the texts. Interpretation creates scripture.

Interpretation may be either oral or written. The term *Mikra* is used as a synonym for TANAK by Jewish scholars in *Mikra: Text, Translation, Reading, and Interpretation of the Hebrew Bible in Ancient Judaism and Early Christianity* and suggests both the "correct reading of the sacred words, as they have been handed down . . . [and] the way in which the sacred text has always been and ought to be recited . . . and understood by those who have been closely connected with the texts" (Mulder, 1990, xiii). Contemporary Christianity, in contrast, places the most emphasis upon the intellectual act of reading despite the origins of much of the New Testament as oral proclamation. The Qur'an, like Mikra, places the central emphasis upon the act of recitation as worship. Muhammad wrote, or dictated, the auditory revelations he received. Christians study the Bible; Muslims chant the Qur'an. The written tradition of interpretation is central for Christians rather than the cadences used in worship. There are other major differences affecting how we regard the sacred texts.

Koran, thirteenth-century Seljuk era, from Iran. The Art
Archive/Turkish and Islamic Art Museum Istanbul/Dagli
Orti (A).

The Jewish TANAK (Protestant Christian: Old Testament), like
the New Testament, derives from multiple authors and includes
books collected over time. This allows for the lively historical and literary study of these works by scholars apart from any consideration
of their status as scripture. Since the Qur'an derives from a single
prophet who received revelations between 610 C.E. and 632 C.E., it
does not provide a very bountiful field for the application of the
scholarly methods so fruitful for the study of the Bible. As Smith
(1993) observes, critical biblical scholarship studies biblical books "at
that historical point" when these "texts were not yet scripture" (3).
The most criticism can do with the Qur'an is to classify and describe
the characteristics of the Suras deriving from the early work of
Muhammad in Mecca as opposed to those that derive from Medina
where the Prophet was the leader of the first Muslim community or
ummah. It can also seek to construct the biography of the Prophet
and to identify historically reliable reports about the acts of the
Prophet. Muslim scholars have engaged in such studies for centuries,
but they do little more than prepare a reader for approaching the
Qur'an as scripture, the Word of Allah (God). Critical studies do not
touch the essence of the Qur'an as an oral recitation that has been
preserved in a scripture and a continuous history of worship.

The Bible has a loose narrative structure. As one reads from Genesis to II Chronicles (TANAK) or the Revelation of St. John, events follow a discernible historical progression. In contrast, the Qur'an has an arbitrary arrangement of Suras, or chapters, moving from the longest (Sura 2) to the shortest (Sura 114). It defies the reader looking for a narrative to which familiar reading methodologies might be applied.

The Jewish, Christian, and Muslim scriptures became scripture through very different historical processes. Assumptions that apply to the TANAK and/or the Christian Bible cannot be easily transferred to the reading of the Qur'an, as the following brief summaries of their different histories will make clear.

The TANAK

Stern (1976) observes in *A History of the Jewish People* that "next to monotheism the rule of the Torah, which encompassed all aspects of life, leaving nothing untouched, was one of the most outstanding characteristics of the development of Judaism . . . " (283). How did the books of the Jewish Bible become the Torah, the comprehensive plan of God for Creation?

The Torah Book, that is, Genesis through Deuteronomy, was first a Jewish legal code issued by the prophet Ezra around 400 B.C.E. to be used as the law binding upon Jews in Palestine under the general umbrella of Persian law. In the centuries that followed, the prophetic books and the writings were added as a commentary upon the Torah to be utilized in determining how to apply the Torah's legal provisions to contemporary social problems. This mode of interpretation was radically altered when Antiochus IV revoked the code and imposed Greek law and religion upon Palestine. This action precipitated the Maccabean Revolt (167–164 B.C.E.), a successful military defense of the Torah and its tradition. According to R. T. Beckwith (1990) in *Mikra*, the complete TANAK already existed by 164 B.C.E. when the Maccabees restored the scriptures that had been destroyed during the persecution waged by Antiochus IV (57). The Hasidim, or Pious Ones, who were the backbone of the revolt, would begin to evolve a new approach to Torah through oral interpretation according to which the TANAK would become a scripture interpreted according to the doctrine of God's plan for creation that now informs every aspect of Jewish life (Stern, 1976, 57). It was in the first century B.C.E. with the development of the oral tradition of *halakah*—"the path where Israel walks"—that the TANAK was transformed by the oral tradition's Torah doctrine (Stern, 1976, 57). At this point, we may speak of the Torah Book as scripture with a high degree of certainty. When the Roman conquest of Palestine and the destruction of the Temple (66–72 C.E.) eliminated the option of interpreting the Torah as civil law, it was the rabbinic formulation that survived. How, then, was the Torah understood and interpreted as scripture rather than as civil law?

We know historically from the evidence of the Dead Sea Scrolls that the people of Qumran regarded the scripture as a revelation given in historical stages by God to Moses and then to the prophets and finally to the people of Qumran through their inspired Teacher of Righteousness. M. Fishbane (1990) observes in *Mikra* that "the sectarians viewed the relationship between the Mikra and Interpretation as a continuity of divine revelations, viz. the revelations to Moses and the prophets were succeeded by *exegetical revelations* to the authoritative teachers of the sect" (376). This historical understanding is carried forth in the New Testament, and Islam has this same concept of the succession of prophetic revelations. A trajectory of revelation extends from Adam to Muhammad, culminating in the final revelation of Allah's Qur'an through Muhammad—the final prophet, the Seal of Prophecy. Ironically, this historical element is lost in Rabbinic Judaism as the Bible is transformed through halakic interpretation into an eternal text revealed *in toto* by God to Moses in the presence of the community at Sinai. This leads to the primacy of midrash, or metaphorical interpretation, that "completely ignores both the context and the rules of biblical language" (Kasher, 1990, 560). The text is henceforth regarded as the Word of God, which existed even prior to creation as a blueprint utilized by God in creating the world. Since every word of the TANAK is regarded as if it were dictated to Moses at the same time, all texts may be interpreted in light of each other. The scripture is no longer interpreted in a temporal-historical context. Christianity continued the development of metaphorical interpretation without abandoning the historical interpretation inherited from Qumran. Christians read scripture in terms of the historical "promise of God/fulfillment" pattern even as they search for eternal truths. In Islam, the greatest weight is placed upon historical interpretation with a single major legal school (the Mu'tazilites) developing metaphorical interpretation as its complement.

The shift in Jewish interpretation from the historical chain of prophetic revelation to the image of the Bible as an eternal text resonates with the Muslim claim that the Qur'an is recited by God from a heavenly archetype (Esposito, 1991, 20), but the shift from an historical perspective on revelation to a metaphorical emphasis upon the spiritual nature of revelation creates a tension between Muslim and Rabbinic interpretation. Islam views this shift as a corruption of the prophetic revelation that is being corrected by the Qur'an.

The New Testament

The writings of St. Paul and the four Gospels were collected and circulated very early. We know from the Muratorian Canon that these texts in practice had become scripture by the end of the second century. It was the struggle over the correct interpretation of these texts that primarily led to the creation of the New Testament.

Within a religious tradition, there arises a multiplicity of experiences leading to a wide variety of interpretations. Groups may even differ as to what constitutes the root story—the founding story—of the tradition. At some point, the community has to determine which of its experiences constitute the normative revelation. The various subgroups that make up the larger tradition interact and debate the merits of their experiences. Out of this process of debate and interaction, there arises a canon, a collection of sacred writings that are to be used by later generations as a yardstick for measuring what is "true" experience within the community. This process of debate may split a tradition into factions of "orthodoxy" and "heresy." If the heresy is large and well organized, it may survive, as did the Roman Catholic Church when it split from the Orthodox Church and Protestantism when it split from the Roman Catholic Church. Otherwise, it becomes an historical footnote like the Arians, the Sabellians, the Gnostics, and the Ebionites.

The first group to proclaim Jesus as the Prophet-Teacher, the Judaizers, or Ebionites, was destined to become a heresy and perish. The Ebionites viewed the man Jesus as the bearer of the final and perfect interpretation of the Jewish Torah given by God to Moses. One had to be Jewish and live by the Torah in order to follow Jesus as the ultimate rabbi. The Gospel of Matthew stands very close to this early tradition. The affinity of this tradition with the Qur'anic view of Jesus as a final, exemplary prophet is most evident. The Qur'an does not, however, accept the claim that Jesus is the last and definitive guide for God's people. That honor belongs to Muhammad.

The followers of Stephen, the Deacon, proclaimed Jesus as a universal savior. The proclamation that Jesus was risen to become the

King of a Heavenly kingdom open to all mankind led immediately to Stephen's death (Acts 7) at the hands of the elders of the Sanhedrin, the city council of Jerusalem and chief religious court for Jews in the Roman Empire. The Pharisee Paul took Stephen's place and became the guardian of the pagans who followed Jesus as the savior, the so-called Christians (Acts 11:19ff.). Paul largely created the Christian Church as he untiringly covered the Mediterranean proclaiming the salvation that comes as an act of divine grace apart from the Torah. Inevitably, the followers of Jesus in Jerusalem had to decide if Paul were proclaiming a heresy. This story is played out in the book of Acts, chapters 1–15. The initial decision of James, the presiding elder in Jerusalem (Acts 15), was that both the Christians and the Ebionites, as they were later called, had the right to follow Jesus but that the Christians were dependent upon the authority of the Church in Jerusalem.

The decision of James ignored the key issue. How could one reconcile Paul's claim that the Bible (Torah) had been transcended by an inner, mystical Christian experience open to all races and cultures with the Ebionite claim that the Torah was eternally valid as the sole guide for living according to the will of God? Eventually, the difficult issue was faced and the Ebionites lost. They became a heresy. Pauline Christianity prevailed. Historical events ensured Christian domination of the new faith. The destruction of the Jewish followers during the Roman invasion of Palestine left the Christians as the dominant group. Although a weakened Jewish "christianity" would survive for another 200 years, they were never again a major force in the new movement. The focal point of Christianity shifted to four great patriarchal centers: Jerusalem, Antioch, Alexandria, and Rome. In time, Rome would become the center of Western Christianity and the Bishop of Rome would be declared the Pope, the Holy Father (approximately 1000 C.E.). The Orthodox, or Eastern, Church retains the patriarchy.

Within the new Christian community, a tension developed between the Gnostics and the regular Christians that led to the condemnation of the Gnostics as heretics. This event is critical to our understanding both of the rise of the New Testament canon and the Muslim perception of Christian doctrine. The Gnostic debate was complicated by an important Pauline "side issue": what is the status of the Torah in Christian experience now that it has been superceded by the Gospel?

A Gnostic teacher in Rome named Marcion—a wealthy, retired sea merchant—was the first person to declare a collection of books to be

Christian scripture. Following Paul, Marcion emphasized the mystical experience. He rejected the Old Testament on the grounds that it
was the story of an angry and oppressive god from which Christians
had been liberated by the atoning death of Jesus. Marcion's canon was
the Gospel of Luke, minus the nativity stories, and ten letters that he
considered to have been written by Paul. This initiated the debate
that led after several centuries to a tacit acceptance of the Old
Testament as defined by the Septuagint translation of the Jewish
Bible (150 B.C.E.) and 27 books of the New Testament. At the center
of this controversy with the Gnostics was the question of correct
interpretation of the nature of Christ and of salvation. The Gnostics
were condemned for denying both the humanity of Christ and the
goodness of God's creation.

The Monophysite controversy of the fifth century is another facet
of this christological discussion. The Monophysites, largely from
Egypt, argued "that though Christ was of two natures before the
Incarnation, the divine and the human, he possessed only one nature,
the divine, after his birth" (Cannon, 1960, 27). The orthodox position
enunciated by the Council of Chalcedon stated that "through the
Incarnation Christ was one person with two separate and distinct
natures . . . the divine and the human" (Cannon, 1960, 27). The
Monophysites created a new Christian community that still exists in
the Middle East.

Careful study of the Qur'anic understanding of Christian doctrine
leads to the conclusion that both the Ebionite and the Monophysite
types helped form Muhammad's understanding of Christian teaching
(Andrae, 1960, 87, 100–102). Andrae comments in *Muhammad: The
Man and His Faith* that "it is clear that Muhammad must have been
influenced . . . by the struggle for religious independence that had
given Mani and the Gnostics such a strong position among the peoples of the Orient (106). In addition, the Sufi interpretation of the
Qur'an and its tradition places central emphasis upon "gnosis" or
"mystical knowledge"—a fact explicated most fully by Nasr (1989) in
Knowledge and the Sacred. The Qur'anic understanding of Christianity
tends to offend Christian readers since it places emphasis upon
understandings that Christians relegated to heresy. There can be no
easy blending of Christian and Muslim perspectives. Islam urges
Jews and Christians to abandon their corrupted revelations and submit to the purified message of the Qur'an. The absolute of one tradition is imposed upon another.

The Qur'an

The Qur'an derives solely from revelations received by the prophet Muhammad between 610 C.E. and his death in 632 C.E. The Qur'an was collected and standardized by the caliphs who were his immediate successors. Collection was begun under the first caliph, Abu Baker, and the standard edition was issued by Caliph Uthman ibn Affan in 650 C.E. and deviant texts were destroyed. There is no complicated history of the Muslim canon such as we find in Judaism and Christianity. From this perspective, the Qur'an is radically different from the TANAK and the Christian Bible. A rich patristic debate led to the formation of Christian doctrine and canon through general councils of the Church. Centuries of rabbinic oral teaching and debate led to the Talmud's commentary on the Torah. In Islam, we find the rise of the legal schools that must both interpret the Qur'an and apply it to the life of the Muslim state. Law rather than theology is dominant in Islamic life. This requires that Westerners adjust their concepts of religion. It is the Islamic state rather than the Church or Synagogue that is central for the religious life of the Muslim.

Christians in the West loosely linked the state and the church through the concept of the Holy Roman Empire initiated in 962 by Otto I, the successor of Charlemagne. The Pope crowned the Emperor from 800 until 1562. The French Revolution terminated this alliance in 1806. Under the impact of the Revolution, Christians increasingly separated the obligations of faith and citizenship, as reflected in the term *personal religion* proposed by Rousseau. The Revolution's Declaration of the Rights of Man effectively separated modern Jewish political life from religious life. For the first time since the Jews were expelled from Palestine in 135 C.E., they had the rights of citizenship. This process of secularization has not taken place in Muslim society, where religion and citizenship are theoretically inseparable.

Judaism, Christianity, and Islam agree that their scriptures are holy, the Word of God, but they interpret this claim in very different ways. For Judaism the TANAK is the Word of God revealed in total to Moses in the Hebrew language at Sinai. The Word of God cannot exist in translation lest human intrusions find their way into the text. This further implies that God's act of revelation is instantaneous and perfect but that the process of the human interpretation is an open-ended one. The Muslim claim for the Quran is the same with the exception that the holy language is Arabic rather than Hebrew. Like the TANAK, the Qur'an exists at two levels. Essentially, it is an eternal or archetypal entity in the mind of God. Secondarily, the Qur'an recited by Muhammad is the best possible historical approximation of the heavenly Qur'an. The study and application of the Qur'an through the centuries are a process through which the Muslim comes to understand the Word and Will of God.

For Christians, the true Word of God is Christ. The Bible points to Christ, the Logos. The function of the Bible as a pointer is in no manner disturbed by the act of translation. The Christian Bible is only relatively holy, while the TANAK and the Qur'an are absolutely holy. The Qur'an occupies a place in Muslim life comparable to the place of Christ in the Christian community. The Qur'an, like Christ, is the true Word of God uncontaminated by man. The Muslim doctrine that Muhammad was "unlettered" seeks to protect the Qur'an from such interpretations as would center upon Muhammad as the author. He is merely the pure vehicle used by Heaven. This is similar to the Christian claim that the Virgin Mary was pure and absolutely sinless. She too is the pure vehicle of Heaven. Neither Muhammad nor Mary contaminates the Word of God despite their intimate association with its entry into the historical process.

Muhammad is both the vehicle for the revelation and the best example of how to apply the Qur'an in one's own life. The Sunnah, the customs of the Prophet, is contained in a collection of authenticated testimony, Hadith, to the practice and exemplary behavior of Muhammad. The Sunnah, now contained in the Hadith, is the first commentary upon the Qur'an. Islam, like Judaism, is preeminently a life to be lived according to the plan of God for creation.

The Shariah—the Islamic path defined by the legal scholars—extends the exposition of the life of Muhammad and is regarded as the authoritative guide to the understanding of the Qur'an. Gaetje (1971) observes in *The Quran and Its Exegesis* that in time, "the consensus *(ijma)* of the scholars . . . came to be taken as a practical authority concerning decisions of law and faith, proceeding from a Tradition according to which the Prophet and his community would never agree upon a mistake" (17).

Holy War—Jihad—The Just War

Smith (1993) argues in *What Is Scripture?* that "the meaning of the Qur'an is the history of its meanings—a dynamic, rich, creative, continuing complex; one that is deeply intertwined with the lives of several hundreds of millions of persons over many centuries and many lands" (90). It is from this perspective that we must approach the development of an understanding of the practice of jihad and its relationship to Christian just war theology. There is no central Islamic dictionary from which we may appropriate *the definition*. The practice of jihad must be understood within the context of a multiplicity of Muslim communities through the centuries. The particular application of jihad to contemporary struggles for liberation must be understood in the context of each organization's relationship to the larger Muslim Tradition. In *Unholy War: Terror in the Name of Islam*, John Esposito (2002) stresses that jihad is an integral part of Islam when he writes: "Muslims are enjoined to act, to struggle *(jihad)* to implement their belief, to lead a good life, to defend religion, to contribute to the development of a just Islamic society throughout the world (5). Esposito's point is clear. Jihad is not a theological frill but an integral part of the Muslim life regardless of how jihad may be interpreted in a particular community. The development of the concept of jihad has a rich and varied history, as does the Christian theology of the just war.

The roots of jihad are in the life of the Prophet Muhammad, who waged war in order to establish the first Muslim state in Mecca. It is not the historical achievement of Muhammad that is central for Nasr (1966) in his *Ideals and Realities of Islam* but the universal, or archetypal, characteristics of the Prophet. Muhammad is a model for all to follow. Nasr (1966) writes of Muhammad as "a particular spiritual prototype" of the true life of piety who also

> had a quality of combativeness, of always being actively engaged in combat against all that negated the Truth and disrupted harmony. Externally it meant fighting wars, either military, political or social ones, the war which the Prophet named the "little holy war".... Inwardly this combativeness meant a continuous war against the carnal soul . . . against all that in man tends towards the negation of God and His will, the "great holy war." (73)

Nasr (1966) observes further that the purpose of war from the Muslim perspective is that it tries "to establish equilibrium between all the existing forces that surround man and to overcome all the existing forces that tend to destroy this equilibrium" (73). The goal of jihad is the establishment of harmony either within the psyche (great jihad) or within society (little jihad). War is an acceptable means to achieving a social harmony. It is a medicine for treating social ills.

We tend to have archetypal images of our saints. When we think of Christ, we picture the crucifix—an image deeply rooted in Pearson's (1989) archetypal Martyr soul-plot. We imagine Moses with the two tablets in hand descending the mountain from his discourse with God. He is the Sage, the ultimate Rabbi. Nasr (1966), a Sufi Muslim, suggests that we image the Prophet "as a rider sitting on a steed with the sword of justice and discrimination drawn in his hand and galloping at full speed, yet ready to come to an immediate halt before the mountain of Truth" (1966, 74). Nasr risks activating the Western stereotype of Islam as a warring religion in order to reclaim the truth hidden under the stereotype. It is vital that we contact the archetypal soul-plot that came to expression through Muhammad the Warrior to supplement the images of the Jewish Rabbi and the Christian Martyr. This leads us into the archetypal roots of each tradition.

The Warrior Archetypal Plot and Jihad

The unconscious supplies us with archetypes, that is, soul-plots, typical patterns, or templates for action and understanding. The following description of this archetypal warrior hero plot is based upon Carol Pearson's (1989) Jungian analysis in *The Hero Within* and Joscelyn Godwin's (1981) cultural analysis in *Mystery Religions in the Ancient World.*

The Crusade Model for warriors is well attested in our society from the crusades of the Middle Ages to those of evangelist Billy Graham and other Christian soldiers. The pattern is constant. War must be waged against sinners so that the better world (Kingdom of God) can appear. In variation one of the Warrior plot, sinners are simply killed—burning at the stake being a favorite medieval method. In variation two, sinners are converted into true believers and incorporated into the community. In variation three, one senses the salvivic trends that are moving in the universe and supports them. Jihad can be defined in terms of any of these three stages.

The first approach is presupposed by the Pakistani reformer Maududi (1971) in his *Come Let Us Change This World,* although the rhetoric is shaded to encompass both of the first two stages. He writes:

> We are not opposed to the modern sciences or the technical progress brought about by them. Our rebellion is against that civilization and culture which has been created by the western philosophy of life and its philosophy of morality. . . . We aim at picking out and organizing people who would be ready to fight both backwardness and modernity for

the supremacy of the real Islam of the Quran and the Sunnah. . . . The real thing before us is not a government by Muslims but the government of Islam; of that Islam which embraces the universal principles of honesty and integrity, and a high civic sense. (89, 91)

Taking note of the French Revolution and the Russian Revolution, Maududi calls for the Islamic revolution that is needed to overcome the evil effects of the two prior revolutions (100). Such is the goal of Jamaat-e-Islami in Pakistan.

Esposito (2002) correctly argues that Maududi envisions Jihad primarily as an instrument of social reform. He notes that Maududi argues that Islam needs to transform itself through political action "both against European colonialism and . . . against corrupt, un-Islamic Muslim states" (2002, 54). Nevertheless, Esposito concedes that Maududi approves of a defensive jihad waged by "Islam against colonialism and injustice" (2002, 54). Since many, if not most, Muslims view themselves as the victims of European colonialism, the defensive caveat would allow for a jihad against the "civilization and culture which has been created by the western philosophy of life and its philosophy of morality" (Maududi, 1971, 89). We will see the same possibility of a double reading in the work of Muhammad Qutb, one of Osama bin Laden's professors at King Abdulaziz University in Saudi Arabia (Esposito, 2002, 8). (This is not to suggest that Qutb is responsible for his student's actions.)

In his early work, *Islam: The Misunderstood Religion*, Muhammad Qutb (1964) also explicates jihad in terms of the fight for social justice. He writes, "nothing but evil will result from people's forbearing from the struggle for social justice" (304) as he argues for an equitable distribution of wealth. This position may be somewhat deceptive. Qutb is the brother of Sayyid Qutb, who is "widely acknowledged as the father of militant jihad, a major influence on the worldview of radical movements across the Muslim world, and a venerated martyr of contemporary Islamic revivalism" (Esposito, 2002, 8). It may be that Qutb's work is read differently by Westerners and by those who feel themselves victimized by colonialism and the Western lifestyle. This much, however, is clear. Islamic reform is not new. It was advocated late in the nineteenth century by Jamāl ad-Din al-Afghānī (died 1897), Muhammad 'Abduh (died 1905), and Muhammad Rashīd Ridā (died 1935). Gaetje (1971) notes of these three reformers that "all three viewed the liberation of all Islamic peoples from foreign rule as an essential prerequisite for the revival of Islam" (22). Since this beginning of Islamic reform, the Islamic understanding of jihad has moved from social reform to armed conflict as the Warrior soul-plot has been more tightly linked with the Martyr plot. Soldiers of God fighting in a just cause can expect to reap the rewards of Paradise (Esposito, 2002, 69). From the archetypal point of view, we can see that Saddam Hussein is playing on a partial truth when he claims that suicide bombers are not terrorists, i.e., secular warriors, but martyrs. Of course, it is politically convenient for him to neglect the Warrior plot linkage that this type of martyrdom requires.

The third variation on the Warrior plot is seen in the Sufi interpretation of Nasr (1966). Both the greater and the lesser jihad are in accordance with, in defense of, and for the sake of the Sharī'ah, the divinely revealed Law (1966, 117). All jihad is in support of this cosmic order. War may be required to achieve this goal.

One might ask, "Why don't we just eliminate the Warrior mode of religious existence?" The Warrior soul-plot is deeply rooted in the unconscious. It cannot be eliminated through either education or by force. Nor should we wish to. It is in our capacity as Warrior that we face our fears, assert the true self and live in confidence that the world can be a better place as a result of our positive effort. All members of the Judeo-Christian-Muslim tradition advocate that their members be warriors, social activists. War is a social medicine intended to restore social balance to the body politic. The central question is, "When is war justified and by what means may it be fought legitimately?" Great care must be taken to separate the cause of the war from the actions taken in war. Can terror ever be legitimized as a means even if the cause can be viewed as just? Terror is not a part of the larger Islamic Tradition of jihad or of the Christian just war.

Godwin notes historically that the Warriors' view of the world is dualistic—good and evil, light and dark, angels and demons, heaven and earth, the Greeks and the Barbarians, insiders and outsiders, friends and enemies are self-evident dualities. This dualism may be perceived at every level of the cosmos. In the Warrior's view of the world, the practical values of gaining wealth for self and community tend to attract abstract ideals like justice, truth, and righteousness. Warriors often project their own evil on others, saying things like "My community's war is just," "God is on our side," "Our enemies lie and are villainous but we are righteous persons fighting for 'truth, justice, and the American Way,'" to draw on an allusion from popular culture (e.g., Batman). Warriors tend to associate their enemies with archetypal shadow images, i.e., images of the evils, weaknesses, and unrealized potentials that we refuse to acknowledge in ourselves.

The Warrior's view of the world is also hierarchical. "Our side" is dualistic by rank. One is an officer or a soldier; a knight or a serf; a king or a subject; God or creature. Both Muslim militants and contemporary Christian Fundamentalists share this apocalyptic view that posits "a struggle (jihad) between the forces of God and Satan, good and evil, darkness or ignorance (jahiliyyah) and light" (Esposito, 2002, 53). For Muslims and Christians, the righteous community is the Lord's army in a cosmic battle, an apocalyptic struggle.

The warrior must resign or submit himself or herself to the cause of Justice. Nasr's (1966) suggestion of the warrior image for Muhammad is supported by the very name Islam. According to the Islamic Foundation (England), "'Islam' is an Arabic word. It means the act of resignation to God. The root word is SLM . . . which means peace from which comes the word 'aslama' which means he submitted, he resigned himself. Al-Islam or Islam is the religion which brings peace to mankind when man commits himself to God and submits himself to His will" (Ahmad, 1975, 21). Islam is thus strongly rooted in the Warrior plot where the prime virtue is submission.

The Warrior must learn the virtue of submission in several ways. First, he must place the cause of his country above personal survival; this shifts the focus from his ego to a transcendent idea of God, Cause, or Country. Second, he must submit to hardship in the field. Third, in uniform, he surrenders his individuality to a group identity. Fourth, he must forgo personal judgment and submit to the orders of his superior officers. Maududi (1971) writes apropos of the first and second virtues that the members of Jamaat "are ready to undergo persecution and even imprisonment and tortures and, if it comes to that, are not afraid even of laying down their very lives for the cause" (99). Maududi stresses loyalty to the group and its members as absolute. He warns the prospective member of Jamaat that "ill-feeling against the group, or the harbouring of any grudges, hate, jealousy, or suspicion, or the desire to hurt others, are the worst of crimes, which Allah and His Prophet have condemned. . . ." (101). The bond of the community, however, is not based upon ideology but upon submission to Allah. Members of the Jamaat are not to be blind supporters of the organization. It is the obligation of members to prevent the organization from "swaying from the right path" (103) of Islam lest it become enmeshed in worldly values. The just cause must be supported by right action for Islam to be actualized in the struggle.

The Warrior's primary image of God tends to be that of God the Judge or of God the Avenger. When one must oppose family and friends, it may be difficult to submit to the vocation of killing in the name of justice. The Bhagavad Gita is the story of the great warrior Arjuna, who upon beholding in the ranks of the enemy his "fathers, grandfathers, sons, grandsons" was overcome by grief and despair. He raises a critical question, "Shall we not, who see the evil of destruction, shall we not refrain from the terrible deed?" His god, Krishna, answers with this exhortation:

> Fall not into degrading weakness . . .
> Throw off this ignoble discouragement,
> and arise like a fire that burns all before it . . .
> The wise grieve not for those who live;
> and they grieve not for those who die—for life and death shall pass
>   away . . .
> In death thy glory in heaven, in victory thy glory on earth.
> Arise, therefore, Arjuna, with thy soul ready to fight.
> Prepare for war with peace in thy soul.
> Be in peace in pleasure and pain, in gain and in loss, in victory or in
>   the loss of a battle.
> In this peace there is not sin. (2:3, 48)

The Warrior must learn the virtue of detachment by overcoming his own ambitions and fears. He must act without concern for himself in the heat of battle. He may plan before a battle, but in the field he must rely upon his intuitive sense of how the battle is flowing and change his plans accordingly.

The Warrior can understand life as a war between the forces of healing and those of death and decay. Mankind is an animal with the potential to become a god, but he or she must fight to actualize this potential. Inevitably, this leads one toward peace and community as the most life-fulfilling alternatives to fragmentation and war. When Alexander the Great was questioned by the Brahmins of India as to why he continued to wage war, he replied:

> It is ordained by heavenly Providence that we should be servants of the god's decree . . . Man does not act unless he is impelled by the heavenly Providence. I would willingly desist from making war, but the Lord of my spirit does not suffer me to do so. For if all were of one mind, the cosmos would stand still. (Pseudo-Callisthenes 3,6 cited by Godwin, 1981, 15)

In short Alexander, like many great achievers, understood himself to be called, that is, to have a vocation, by a destiny imprinted upon his soul. Alexander had a transcendental calling to be a warrior. He could not do otherwise and preserve his psychic integrity. The Muslim *mujahidin* (soldiers of God) share this sense of a transcendental calling with Christian soldiers.

From antiquity through the Middle Ages, swords are named and have a genealogy that traces back to ancient heroes or even to the gods. For the ancient and medieval Warrior, the weapon is a transitional object making present the unity of the gods with the warrior himself. Recall that King Arthur receives his sword through a miraculous sign. It was decreed by Heaven that only the true king could pull the sword from the stone. Upon Arthur's death, Excalibur is cast into the lake where it is received by the hand of the Lady of the Lake. This suggests that both Arthur's sword and his destiny arose from Lady Soul (Anima), the inner woman who resides in the unconscious. Nasr (1966) identifies the sword of Muhammad as the sword of discrimination—that psychic quality of cutting through all that is illusory to arrive at the deepest stratum of Truth.

For the Muslim, the key transitional object is the earthly Qur'an and all of its correct interpretation through the ages. The Qur'anic tradition connects one to the Heavenly Qur'an in the mind of God. Submission to God is made possible by means of the Qur'an and the example of Muhammad. The application of Qur'anic principles is the weapon of the Islamic warrior just as the Bible is regarded as the Two-Edged Sword of the Lord Jesus by militant Christians.

The Archetypal Warrior Plot and the Just War

Muslims have the historical example of Muhammad as a warrior and a Caliph, but Christianity did not inherit its commitment to the Warrior plot from Jesus. Certainly, the disciples stood in a tradition of apocalyptic political hope, and they expected Jesus to be the great Warrior King, the Christ, who would appear just prior to the End to lead Israel in battle against her enemies. Victorious, he would establish a final Jewish kingdom that might last a thousand years before the End came. According to the Gospel of Matthew (4:8–10), Jesus rejected Satan's offer to become this king: Jesus said to him, "Away with you, Satan! for it is written, 'Worship the Lord your God, and serve only him'" (Matt. 4:10, NRSV). Jesus chooses to imagine himself as the Servant of God rather than as the Warrior expected by tradition. He rejects the Warrior plot for the Martyr plot. Jesus' followers did not understand this and persisted in the hope that Jesus would be the great warrior, the Messiah (Matt.

26:51–56). When the disciples finally perceived that this was not to be Jesus' role, they fled from the opportunity to embrace the Martyr's plot with Jesus. The disciples were ready to die for the great warrior, the Messiah, but not for a sage or a martyr. Through the early centuries, the Christian had to choose the Martyr plot to the exclusion of the Warrior plot, but slowly this view changed as a theology of the just war developed.

The prototype of the Christian Warrior is the figure of Saint George associated by legend with Lydda in Palestine. There is no historical evidence for the man's existence, but his cult is amply documented. The cult is attested as early as 367 by an inscription in Trachonitis. By the sixth century, churches were dedicated to him throughout the East and the West (Holweck, 1924, 423). His cult came to England in the eighth century (Coulson, 1990, 196). Richard Lionheart placed his crusading army under the protection of St. George; the Teutonic Knights embraced him as their patron saint (Holweck, 1924, 423). The figure of St. George shows us that the later development of the Christian Warrior archetype is strongly influenced by the Christian encounter with the Islamic world. Three orders of Christian soldiers emerged as opponents of the Muslim, protectors of pilgrims, the sick, and Christian civilization: the Knights Templar (1119), the Knights of St. John, or Hospitallers (1070), and the Teutonic Knights (1190).

Andre Jolles (1958) in *Einfache Formen* notes that the legend of St. George arose out of the Diocletian persecution. When this Christian soldier's obligation to the evil emperor proposing the persecution of Christians cannot be reconciled with his responsibility to the Christian faith, George resigns his commission, challenges the emperor's decision, and is martyred. The soldier's vocation clashes with his Christian calling to endure martyrdom in defense of the faith. Legend reflects the practice of the faith. Tomaž Mastnak (2002) in *Crusading Peace: Christendom, the Muslim World, and Western Political Order* notes that "traditionally, the Church had been averse to the shedding of blood . . . [and] participation in warfare was regarded as an evil . . . Even if a Christian stained his hands with blood in a just war, he still sinned" (16).

The legend of St. George evolves with the developing theology of the Church. Jolles (1958) notes that at a later stage in the development of the legend, "the obligation to valor and the obligation to faith coincide'" (48) to form the Soldier-Saint as an archetypal pattern. Mastnak (2002) notes that the term *soldiers of Christ* originally applied to "Christians in general, but from late antiquity onwards the term . . . became increasingly reserved for the monks—in contrast to the 'secular soldiers.'" He quotes Carolingian Abbot Smaragdus speaking in 820 as saying that Christian soldiers "fight against evil so that after death they may gain the reward of eternal life" (22). The Soldier-Saint has appeared. The old dichotomy of Christian and Warrior has collapsed.

Theological developments led to the legitimization of war as a Christian vocation. Mastnak (2002) argues that Odo, abbot of Cluny (926–44), "was one of the first to argue that it was possible to conduct warfare from "proper motives"—and thus to promote a new ethics of war, that is, Christian militarism" (17). By the eleventh century, it could be argued that warfare in service of the Church was legitimate (18). The shedding of blood was acceptable when used to combat the aggression of the Muslim (21) and any who ignored Christ and resisted His Church (43). The legend of St. George again maintained its relevance.

The Christian Soldier became a significant political reality in the First Crusade, proclaimed by Urban II in 1096 for the purpose of rescuing the holy places from the hand of the Muslim. The five crusades, extending from 1096 to 1291, were strategic and spiritual failures. Williston Walker (1959) observes that

> they made no permanent conquest of the Holy Land. It may be doubted whether they greatly retarded the advance of Mohammedanism. Their costs in lives and treasure were enormous. Though initiated in a high spirit of devotion, their conduct was disgraced throughout by quarrels, divided motives, and low standards of personal conduct. (224)

This historical failure did not prevent the Crusades from entering Christian imagination as a glorious war for Christ.

During the twelfth century, the St. George legend came to include the episode of St. George rescuing a king's daughter from a dragon, reminding some of the Perseus myth of the rescue of Andromeda. In this late development of the archetypal pattern, Saint George is no longer the Soldier-Martyr but simply the soldier, the dragon-slayer, and the defender of virtuous young women (Jolles, 1958, 49). St. George was the Defender of the Faith. As the legend was developing in the Christian church along with a theology of the just war, the Arthurian legends were being created in historical and literary works. The Warrior hero pattern is deeply ingrained in both Christian imagination and thought.

Despite the facts documenting military and personal moral failure, the Crusades are remembered as a model of Christian militancy. This conflict between imagination and historical fact is an indication that our image is rooted in an archetypal base. The Christian Knight Crusaders were not evaluated and remembered empirically. They became archetypal figures rooted in the Christian imagination as brave and powerful warriors defending the faith against the infidel, guided by their Christian commitment. On the other hand, the Muslim defenders entered Western imagination as hell-sent bearers of a pagan religion to be imposed by the sword. The Muslim became one of the shadow figures of the Christian world.

The Muslim image of the Crusades is very much the opposite of the Christian image. Any reference to a crusade will call forth a deeply emotional response from a Muslim. Esposito (2002) notes that "the Crusades and European colonialism have had a universal and lasting impact on the Muslim imagination . . . For Muslims, Christianity is the religion of the Crusades and hegemonic ambitions" (74–75). The chilling implication is that the Christian is possibly inseparable in the Muslim mind from the experiences of colonialism and thus a potential enemy of God.

The warrior images of both Christianity and Islamic imagination pose a major barrier to meaningful dialogue. John Renard (1992) comments in *In the Footsteps of Muhammad:*

> Christians, for example, who find it quaint and dangerous that Muslims believe God has prepared rewards in paradise for those who die a martyr's death, might well recall that Christianity too has its tradition of martyrdom. If Jews and Christians take offense at the idea that the God of Islam sanctions certain forms of violence, they would do well to recall not only the just war theory, but the shockingly sanguinary images of God in Deuteronomy and other early sections of the Hebrew scriptures. (19)

Lest images of Deuteronomy seem archaic and irrelevant in the light of the Gospel, one needs to observe that Odo, the abbot of Cluny, argued from the Old Testament that fighting was not precluded by Christian piety since Christians are following in the footsteps of the Patriarchs (Mastnak, 2002, 17). Scripture—of any religion—can be used all too easily as a club, as an easy justification for depriving others of rights, of life, liberty, and the pursuit of happiness.

Conclusion

It is vitally important to recognize that the roots of Christian–Muslim antipathy are to be found in the unconscious. Each side tends to project its images of evil and darkness upon the other. It is only as we are able to withdraw our projections and take responsibility for our own evil that we can hope for meaningful dialogue. We can then explore the historical moments when the Muslim world enriched the Christian world. Where would the West be intellectually, for example, had it not received the works of Aristotle from the Muslim philosophers?

As we approach the Qur'an, we need to be aware of the differences that separate the Jewish, Christian, and Muslim conceptions of scripture. Each tradition has its own unique history of canonical development that cannot fairly be imposed upon another religion. Moses, Jesus, and Muhammad should not be simplistically compared. Each figure is associated with a unique calling. Moses is the Master Teacher; Jesus is the Martyr; and Muhammad is the Warrior-Statesman who perfectly embodies the Universal Man, "the prototype of all creation, the norm of all perfection, the first of all beings" (Nasr, 1966, 88).

Muslims do not have a monopoly upon the theology of the Soldier-Saint. Christians have their own theology of the Just War, and codes for the conduct of Christian soldiers were formulated during the Middle Ages. Muslims and Christians traditionally agree that violence must be controlled even in the just war. The promise of Heaven as a reward for Christian soldiers differs little from the Muslim hope of Paradise for warriors. In the light of historical events in a geographically shrinking world, it is time that we become more aware of our own history and theology as well as better informed about the Muslim tradition. This is no matter of simple Good (Us) challenged by Evil (Them). As we reclaim our projections, we will be empowered to seek understanding and reconciliation.

References

Ahmad, K. (Ed.). (1975). *Islam: Its meaning and message.* London: Islamic Council of Europe.

Andrae, T. (1960). *Muhammad: The man and his faith.* New York: Harper and Row.

Beckwith, R. T. (1990). Formation of the Hebrew Bible. *Mikra: Text, translation, reading and interpretation of the Hebrew Bible in ancient Judaism and early Christianity.* Minneapolis: Fortress.

Cannon, W. R. (1960). *History of Christianity in the middle ages*. Nashville: Abingdon.

Coulson, J. (Ed.). (1990). *The Saints: A concise biographical dictionary*. New York: Hawthorn Books.

Esposito, J. L. (1991). *Islam: The straight path*. New York: Oxford.

Esposito, J. L. (2002). *Unholy war: Terror in the name of Islam*. New York: Oxford.

Fishbane, M. (1990). Use, authority, and interpretation of Mikra at Qumran. *Mikra: Text, translation, reading, and interpretation of the Hebrew Bible in ancient Judaism and early Christianity*. Minneapolis: Fortress.

Gaetje, H. (1971). *The Quran and its exegesis* (A. T. Welsh, Trans. and Ed.). Los Angeles: University of California Press.

Godwin, J. (1981). *Mystery religions in the ancient world*. San Francisco: Harper & Row.

Holweck, F. G. (Ed.). (1924). *A biographical dictionary of the saints*. Saint Louis: B. Herder Book Co.

Jolles, A. (1958). *Einfache formen*. Darmstadt: Wissenschaftliche Buchgesellschaft, 1958.

Josephus, F. (1987). *The wars of the Jews*. In *The works of Josephus, new updated version* (W. Walker, Trans.). Peabody: Hendrickson.

Kasher, R. (1990). The interpretation of scripture in rabbinic literature. *Mikra: Text, translation, reading, and interpretation of the Hebrew Bible in ancient Judaism and early Christianity*. Minneapolis: Fortress.

Mascaro, J. (Trans.). (1978). *The Bhagavad Gita*. New York: Penguin.

Mastnak, T. (2002). *Crusading peace: Christendom, the Muslim world, and Western political order*. Berkeley: University of California Press.

Maududi, A. A. (1971). *Come let us change this world* (K. Siddique, Trans. & Ed.). Karachi: Salama Siddique.

Mulder, J. M. (1990). Introduction. *Mikra: Text, translation, reading, and interpretation of the Hebrew Bible in ancient Judaism and early Christianity*. Minneapolis: Fortress.

Nasr, S. H. (1966). *Ideals and realities of Islam*. Boston: George Allen & Unwin.

Nasr, S. H. (1989). *Knowledge and the sacred*. Albany: SUNY.

Pearson, Carol. (1989). *The hero within: Six archetypes we live by*. New York: HarperSanFrancisco.

Qutb, M. (1964). *Islam: The misunderstood religion*. Kuwait: Darul Bayan Bookshop.

Renard, J. (1992). *In the footsteps of Muhammad: Understanding the Islamic experience*. New York: Paulist Press.

Smith, W. C. (1993). *What is scripture? A comparative approach*. Minneapolis: Fortress.

Stern, M. (1976). Part III: The period of the second temple. *A history of the Jewish people*. Cambridge: Harvard University Press.

Walker, W. (1959). *A history of the Christian church*. New York: Charles Scribner's Sons.

CHAPTER 12

RELIGIOUS METAPHORS CAN KILL

J. Harold Ellens

The Hebrew Bible conveyed an ethical principle to its adherents that was cryptic, direct, and pragmatic. It is simply stated in the Levitical and Deuteronomic Codes. It readily became a rule for life in society and a metaphor for justice in a relatively barbaric world. "An eye for an eye and a tooth for a tooth" (Exod. 21:23–25, RSV), the Bible legislates. We call it the *Lex Talionis*, or the law of the jungle. Much has been written and preached to ameliorate those barbaric tones and their consequences since the ancient regulations were imposed, purportedly by God or on God's authority. Jesus' own words seem the most powerful contradiction of the *Lex Talionis*. He declared, "You have heard that it was said, 'An eye for an eye and a tooth for a tooth.' I say to you, 'If anyone strikes you on the right cheek, turn to him the other also. . . . Love your enemies and do good to those who persecute you so that you may be children of your father who is in heaven'" (Matt. 5:38, 39, 44, 45, RSV).

Few people in the Western world today would speak in favor of running society or personal life by the ancient barbaric code of the law of the jungle. No one reading this book would favor a system consciously devised upon those rubrics. But the problem with metaphors, as Freud and Jung taught us so well, is that they are hatched in the unconscious, accrue their rich and fruitful meaning there, and carry out their function mainly at hidden levels of the psyche, not readily accessible to conscious analysis or discipline. Thus, the ancient cultures of the Eastern Mediterranean adopted that barbaric code, and while Arab societies today claim a Qur'anic grace as their code and the Israelis insist that their society is a democracy, that old barbaric metaphor shapes *and justifies* both the policies of jihad, on the one side, and the exaggerated mayhem of what is now being called "proactive or preemptive defense," on the other: all that in this twenty-first century, in this supposedly civilized Western world.

Freud and Jung were correct in urging that metaphors, reflecting or tuned up to the power of psychological archetypes, function with effects and durability far beyond our wildest imaginations. By reason of wholesome metaphors we create aesthetic and humane civilization, almost as though it were the normal product of daily life. By reason of pathogenic metaphors we continue to recreate destruction, even disaster, in each new generation, as though it were inherited in our genes. Some awful things are inherited genetically, of course. However, much of what continues to defeat the groundswell of civilized decency and aesthetic transcendence, optimistically expected in each new era, is not only such genetically inherited pathologies as borderline syndrome and episodic psychosis. What we inherit culturally in our dominant metaphors persistently defeats the gains in goodness for which we hope. We need not look across the ocean or to international politics to discern this desperate truth.

Exposition

Of course, we human beings do not need exotic explanations of physical or cultural inheritance to account for our violence. We all seem perfectly capable of devising it quite on our own, without metaphoric prodding or genetic pathogenesis. The Palestinians and Israelis have no mortgage on violence; al Qaeda is not unique, but typical, of the universal human pathology; we need only to look within our own psyches or souls.

A Personal Illustration

A few days ago I was driving into my driveway when I suddenly decided to stop for my mail, the mailbox being just to the right of the drive. I slammed on the brakes, threw my vehicle into reverse, and backed up toward my mailbox, nearly putting two cyclists into the hospital in the process—innocent folks out for their afternoon recreation on the fine municipal bike path, in what seemed to them, I am sure, a perfectly safe and peaceful suburb. When I again slammed on my brakes, the fellow right next to my window let out a violent tirade, informing me that I had been viciously irresponsible and incautious.

I am sure his tone was tuned to hysteric levels because of the anxiety he felt about my nearly running down both him and his companion. Mine was too, for the same reason, as well as because of my terror about what physical damage I had nearly done to two human beings, right in my own yard. I opened my window and yelled back at him, giving him as good as I got and bringing my diatribe to a fine rhetorical climax by telling him that this was my driveway, that he used the bike path at the pleasure of the community, meaning mainly me, and that he should shut up and pay more attention to what was going on around him.

The whole thing was scandalous for two purportedly decent old men—and scandalously violent. He seems to have recovered sooner than I did, for the next day there was an envelope taped to my mailbox that read as follows:

> To the motorist I encountered the other day. Pedestrian walkways and bike paths are intended to keep non-motorized traffic out of busy roads—A great idea! These are located in right of ways and require no privilege. In fact, in Michigan, "Driving is a privilege, not a right." You have a great home and property which I have admired many times as I've passed by. However, it is located in a busy section of the city. This calls for extra caution. Cyclists and pedestrians need to be treated as the real traffic they are. When backing up, your range of vision is not as good as when moving and looking forward. Add a cellphone and concern for a mailbox and the risk goes up. PLEASE drive carefully! A couple of seconds are all that are needed to injure someone for life! Or, to avoid an injury. Sorry that I startled you that day!

I wrote him a letter in response and said the following:

> Friend, you are right and I was wrong for running off at the mouth. What ticked me off was what I perceived as your condescending scolding, but in retrospect I can understand your inclination to do so, given the circumstances, though obviously all of us were less cautious than we should have been. In any case, I apologize. I feel terror at what injury I nearly caused, as you note in your missive. The incident confirms what I have long suspected to be a ruling principle in life, namely, that when I feel justified to rise in righteous indignation, the indignation seems to operate automatically, but the righteousness never seems to quite kick in. In any case, thank you for going to the trouble of leaving the note on my mailbox. Perhaps we shall meet sometime for better reasons in a safer environment with opportunity for pleasant fellowship!

I placed this in an envelope with my name and return address. Because he did not sign his letter or indicate his identity, I taped the envelope to my mailbox with this address on it: To the Consummate Cyclist and Gentleman Whom I Nearly Hospitalized. Unfortunately, the next day I found the envelope unopened and ground into the sand, with a discernable heel print on the face of it. Obviously, I miscalculated in my cockiness and elitism. He is not a reader of nineteenth-century novels, and he thought that *consummate*, in this context, was a curse word. I retrieved it from the earth, readdressed it, and put it back on the mailbox with a pastoral prayer that he would come to get it. I would like to see him and sit down over a good martini and redeem my iniquities—and his.

My entire point in relating this hilarious but painful narrative of gross dumbness is that humans, I at least, and most of us I fear, need little provocation for violence of one sort or another. There are things about us that seem to build it in. Even Jesus, despite his nice talk about loving one's enemies, was unacceptably violent in castigating Peter for getting the messianic terminology and vision wrong in what we call the Great Confession (Mark 8:27–33). Jesus was unacceptably violent when he castigated his mother at the wedding at Cana (John 2:3–4), when he cleansed the temple of the money changers (Matt. 21:12–13; Mark 11:15–17), and at consigning the Jewish authorities of his day to a place somewhere below Sodom and Gomorrah in his equivalent of Dante's Inferno (Matt. 11:20–24, 12:38–42; Mark 8:11–12; Luke 11:16, 29–32).

A Sinister Problem

However, what I am concerned about here is something that seems to me to go far beyond that simple, although sinister, human inclination to daily personal violence, characteristic of at least Jesus and me. I am worried about what seems to me to be the societal and institutional violence that has plagued the Western world from its beginnings twenty-five hundred years ago. It is particularly troublesome to consider the role it has played since the rise of Christianity in the first century, of rabbinic Judaism in the third or fourth century, and of Islam in the seventh century. Let me outline the logic of this concern simply and then tease out its details and implications.

Whereas it is true that the early ethical code articulated in the Hebrew Bible is the *Lex Talionis,* it is more importantly true that the later prophets inveighed against this ethic and long before the close of that canon its old barbaric code had been contested and contrasted by what I will call the code of divine and human grace. Micah 7:18–20, for example, declares, "Who is a God like our God? He pardons iniquity, passes over transgression, will not keep his anger forever, delights in steadfast love. He is faithful to us when we are unfaithful to him. He tramples our iniquities under his feet and casts all our sins into the depths of the sea. Moreover, he has guaranteed this to us through our ancestors from the days of old" (author's translation). The Hebrew Bible is full of enjoinders for humans to do likewise.

It requires little argument to demonstrate that it is this Hebrew ethic of grace that Jesus, and thus the New Testament and the early Christian movement, highlighted as the ideal code for the new and distinctive Christian life in the world, both for individuals and institutions. This had been the later Hebrew prophets' way and was to be the Christian Way. However, this ethic did not seem to hold up well in the earliest centuries of the church's life, if we can take seriously the factionalism and heresy trials of early church history. Moreover, this ethic seems to have completely failed as soon as the church was empowered by Constantine as the Queen of the Empire in 313 C.E. Indeed, the conduct of *individual* Christians, Jews, and Muslims seems generally, throughout the last two thousand years, to have been considerably more grace-filled than that of most of the *nations* and other *institutions* of the Western world, which purportedly, in the view of many, were influenced by the rise and presence of Christianity and rabbinic Judaism.

Let us take the example of the Democratic Republic of the United States of America. This nation, which has been influenced in discernable ways by the traditions of Judaism and Christianity, as well as Greek thought, thanks largely to John Locke, has readily and regularly resorted to gross violence to solve its major social and political problems, as well as its relational impasses, throughout its history. The Revolutionary War, if compared with the Canadian experience in disengagement from British Empire, was an unnecessary siege of violence, despite George Washington's Fabian tactics. The Civil War, which killed six hundred thousand American men and disabled, physically and psychologically, three million more, did not discernibly accomplish anything that the abolitionists were not well on the way to accomplishing by 1860.

Even the secession of seven states would have done little of the damage the war did, and by 1900 it would have been clear that the division of the union was so disadvantageous to both sides that a reunion would likely have been achieved. A more wholesome resolution of the issues that produced the Civil War would almost certainly have been achieved by 1900 than was achieved by the horrors of the war and reconstruction. Moreover, as the slightest awareness of history readily suggests, after every major war the society that has victoriously waged it is racked by a sizable increase in domestic social violence for a couple of generations. It is no accident that after having waged the particular butchery of the Civil War, our society went on to channel those pathological energies into the Indian Wars. Not negotiation for land. Rather, theft, encroachment, abuse of treaties, and a policy of extermination of the Americans who happened to inhabit this continent before us.

We have always and we still do resort to gross violence as a nation to solve all of our major problems, despite the fact that this nation was established with what we claimed to be a new kind of spirituality and ethic: equality, liberty, justice, and the commonweal. *Grace* is the one word for that litany of what was supposed to characterize us. What we have proven by our history is the simple fact that we have behaved exactly on the violent model of all the European nations, going all the way back to the violent Christianization of the Roman Empire.

The Inherent Dissonance

What is the inherent dissonance in our system that prevents its clearly articulated idealism from ever grounding, perpetuating, or elaborating itself in a reigning role for grace, love, justice, and decency, for negotiated solutions to major problems in our Western civilization and for statesmanship instead of manipulative politics? The urgency of this question is not decreased by the appropriateness of the U.S. response to the destruction of the World Trade Center Towers on September 11, 2001. What is it that, almost every time we perceive ourselves to be in a temporary crisis, readily, easily, and automatically *justifies* a quick and radical resort to the grossest forms of violence: violence as the exception to the rule of grace, violence always available in any emergency, violence as the exception that has not simply proven the rule, as the old adage says, but has really always functioned *as* the rule?

I want the emphasis in that sentence to fall upon the word *justifies*. Every decent human being will insist that the ethic of divine and human grace is the only worthy thing for human affairs, but we immediately suspend that rule or ethic as soon as we are faced with a really difficult relationship or negotiation in our institutions or nation-states, and often in our personal affairs. We immediately justify the exception—violence!

I believe that this is not just a proclivity for the pragmatic. Most resorts to violence are not the most pragmatic course of action available in any given situation. Barbara Tuchman has brilliantly documented this fact from a survey of Western history, in her fine book, *The March of Folly* (Tuchman, 1984). Moreover, we tend in life and politics to allow things to get to a state in which we cannot think of any solution except violence. We do this precisely because we assume at some subconscious level that if things get bad it is justifiable to resort to violence. Thus, no great care need be taken in advance to prevent that eventuality from arising. Something is going on in our unconscious, as persons, communities, and nations, which leads us so easily to that justification. What is going on down there?

Is it possible that we have, fixed in our individual or collective unconscious, a metaphor that contradicts our conscious commitment to the decency of statesmanship, to the advantages of negotiated conflict resolution, and to the redemptive ethic of grace? Have we forgotten that the Hebrew and Christian prophets fashioned that ethic for us, so that it might stand against the pressures of the barbaric in ourselves and in our communal cultures? I believe that is exactly where the problem lies. My logic is simple. Let my explication of it, therefore, be brief.

Violent Religious Metaphors

Out of the Hebrew form of the *Lex Talionis* came a notion of atonement that corrupted the covenantal theology of grace in the Hebrew Bible. This notion of atonement was a shift away from the equation of a gracious God shepherding and caring for his people and committing himself to a perpetual covenant of grace with them. In that early model the sacrificial system was the presentation to God of the first fruits of flock and field, in grateful response to his covenant of unconditional forgiveness and grace. In that equation God is congenial and good for our health. The relationship between God and humankind is one of pleasant companionship along the pilgrimage of life, albeit in many ways a tragic adventure.

The move away from this grace-equation to the notion of sacrificial atonement was engineered by the Zadokite priests after the decree of Cyrus the Great in 539, releasing the Israelites from Babylonian exile (Boccaccini, 2002). Their system was a shift toward

Christ on the Cross, an early-sixteenth-century
etching by Daniel Hopfer. Library of Congress.

the interpretation of the sacrificial system as a payment for sin. This
was a result of postexilic Judaism trying to come to terms with the
question of how God could possibly be present in history, given the
tragedy of the exile to Babylon. The conclusion, that it could only
make sense on the assumption that Israel had desperately sinned and
God had sent the foreign nations as his servants to punish God's
own rebellious people, led to the supposition that Israel's safety lay
in its ability to mollify God with sacrifices that paid for the iniquity
of God's people, individually and communally. This was a strategy
for balancing the scales of divine justice, or at least resolving God's
wrath and intrapsychic dissonance.

In this model God is a threat and his wrathful judgment can only be turned aside by sacrificial compensation, a very ancient pagan notion exactly opposite to the Hebrew tradition of the covenant of grace. Pauline theology picked up this metaphor and identified it with the crucifixion of Christ as a propitiation for our sins. This atonement theology, elaborated by the early Christian theologians and epitomized in the juridical atonement theory of Anselm, represented God as sufficiently disturbed by the sinfulness of humanity that he had only two options: destroy us or substitute a sacrifice to pay for our sins. He did the latter. He killed Christ.

That has been elaborated in sentimental and well-frosted theological terms, and interpreted so as to make the cross, as substitutionary atonement, appear to be a remarkable act of grace. However, at the unconscious level it is, in fact, a metaphor of the worst kind of violence, infanticide or child sacrifice. The unconscious dynamics of this metaphor have to do with the image or model of God as being so enraged that the only way he can get his head screwed back on right is to kill somebody, us or Christ. In the narrative of the expulsion from the garden of Eden, God cursed his own people (Gen. 3). With the flood of Noah he virtually exterminated them. By the Assyrian and Babylonian exiles he abused them. In the New Testament he crucified a substitute to settle the score (Miles, 1995, 2002), and that is represented in the texts as better behavior on God's part than the earlier Old Testament abusiveness.

That is, the crucifixion of Jesus of Nazareth is an image and a metaphor right at the center of the Master Story of the Western world for the last 2,000 years, which radically contradicts the grace ethic it purports to express and cuts its taproot by the dominant model of solving ultimate problems through resort to the worst kind of violence. With that kind of metaphor at our center, and associated with the essential behavior of God, how could we possibly hold, in the deep structure of our own unconscious motivations, any other notion of ultimate solutions to ultimate questions or crises than violence— human solutions that are equivalent to God's kind of violence?

The God in Our Master Story

My father was without exception and by a wide margin the very best man I ever knew. He was the epitome of grace, patience, and self-control. I would like myself a lot better if I were more like him. He would not have spoken sharply to the cyclist but would have acknowledged the humanness of the situation, and the affair would have ended in friendship and decency. I easily project upon God the image and metaphor that my father has become in my conscious and unconscious mind, and so to me God is the epitome of grace, patience, and decency. There is much in the Bible to illumine and certify this. I could never know or believe in any other kind of God. Any other kind is a monster, given the needs of the likes of us, caught as we are in our human predicament, not designed or selected by us. I need the God of Micah 7:18–20. But that is not the God of the Western world at the institutional level. Then who is the God at that level?

Is it possible that, beyond the mayhem that lousy chemistry wreaks upon us through psychologically sick human beings, and beyond the mayhem of our pettiness and fear that life's inadvertencies, such as running over cyclists, bring to the fore, there is at the core of our collective selves a divine monster, who, when he gets to feeling a little crazy about something like our human frailty, goes out looking for somebody to murder? Are we stuck with a monster god in our inaccessible psyches, who plays out his devilish game under the flag of our expediencies? Somebody ought to find out.

The American tragedy of September 11, 2001, is not just economic or political. It is not just the insupportable psychospiritual anguish about the death of 5,000 people at the hands of terrorists, together with the immense grief and loss of the survivors and the families of the dead. All that is sufficiently overwhelming by itself. However, the real depth of the tragedy lies in the fact that an entire community of human beings, pseudo-Islamic Fundamentalists, perpetrated this immense disaster upon another community of innocent humans, and did it under the banner of a religious metaphor: jihad. The tragedy of that terrorism is severe enough at the physical and material level to gain global attention and concern. However, the real tragedy of violence lies in the fact that it is a state of the soul or psyche, conditioned and twisted by specific religious archetypes. Those terrorists apparently really believed that their action was an execution of the will and intention of God and for it they would have "exceedingly great reward."

The noted Roman Catholic scholar René Girard addressed at length, as well as in depth, the question of the metaphors and archetypes of violence in the Master Stories of the great religions. He analyzed the manner in which they shape human culture (Girard, 1987. Cf. also Williams, 1996). It is his contention that murder of a key symbolic figure or group has been a crucial element in establishing and maintaining sociocultural stability since the beginning of the human experiment.

Girard employed the ancient Greek term so important to Aristotle, *mimesis*, as the construct by which to explicate his theory. He claims that the natural human process of modeling on key historic figures or past generations produces competition regarding who in the community is truest to the ancient or historic model or tradition being remembered and celebrated. From this competition, judgments are made regarding who is good and who is bad. This mimetic and competitive process eventually becomes institutionalized in the structures of dogmas, orthodoxies, codes of social control, and rituals. Those who do not achieve well or conform are progressively valued negatively. Those who exceed the performance level of the masses may pose a threat and need to be leveled to the mean or may be negatively valued as well. As these perceptions harden, the process eventually arrives at the point at which the underperformer, the nonconformist, the threatening superachiever, or the heretic must be eliminated. Societal justification of the murder of this singled-out person or group inevitably follows.

There are a number of implications one might draw from or build upon Girard's model. Let us briefly explore a few of these. The process of societal justification, mentioned above, may take the form of remembering the eliminated figure as victim of his own evil, thus as a symbol of the purification of the society, or as the heroic agent who has given his life for the society's redemption. The decision between the two is a deep-structure psychodynamic decision shaped by the unconscious archetypes prevailing in the society and the Master Story metaphors that dominate the community. Which of those two roles is the one adopted in any given case depends upon which metaphor the society most needs at the time and the degree of ambiguity within the society regarding the character and quality of the one sacrificed.

Girard believed that human civilization is the product of this violent action designed to control the inevitable violence of the rivalry inherent to mimetic process. Thus, in the early chapters of Genesis, Cain's murder of Abel focuses and unleashes the energy for the construction of cities, industry, arts, crafts, and ordered, enriched human society. Only those who take the victim's side report this as evil. Girard contends that from the outset the mimetic process of chaotic rivalry required a reduction of dissonance. In the Genesis narrative this dissonance is radically reduced with one definitive act focused upon Abel, the counterforce of progress. He is murdered.

Ithamar Gruenwald (2003), in his work on ritual theory in cultural development, suggests that it is not insignificant that Abel is a nomadic shepherd and Cain an agrarian cultivator of fixed spaces who moves thence to urban life. Gruenwald notes that this dissonance between the idealization of the nomadic shepherd and the pastoral-agrarian persists throughout the Hebrew Bible and can be seen clearly in the New Testament, as well. Eventually the biblical metaphor settles down as a picture of chronic tension between the pastoral-agrarian images and the urban vision. The scriptures narrate the story from the side of the victim and depict the ideal people as the remnant that harks back to the ancient nomadic model of the shepherd, those close to the earth and heavily dependent upon God moment by moment, despite the fact that the world has long since permanently passed them by in its progress from the garden (Gen. 3) to the idealized city (Rev. 22).

Progressively the dissonance indicated in the story of Cain and Abel developed into a tension and lethal rivalry between the urban and pastoral-agrarian Israelites. This persistent dissonance played an important part in much of the history of Israel recorded in the Bible, including the conflict between the urbanized exiles returning from captivity, and "the people of the land," in the narratives about the release from Babylon. Thus, among many other things, this set of scriptural metaphors and their intrinsic tensions may have contributed significantly to the disappearance of the royal line of David during the fifth century B.C.E.

Three Pillars of Violence

Girard saw three crucial elements in the mimetic process of employing violence to reduce dissonance in a society and to maintain order and peace in the face of the natural tendency to dissonance, chaos, and disorder. The first is the codification of control structures or prohibitions, second, the creation of rituals for enacting both the event of redemptive violence and the patterns of required conformity within the society, and third, the killing of the scapegoat. Regarding the second element, Weaver has this to say,

> These rituals—games, dramas, animal sacrifices—provide approved outlets for expression of mimetic rivalry within a culture, and thus limit the actual violence perpetrated. While prohibitions and ritual appear as opposites—prohibition versus acting out—their function is the same. They both limit mimetic violence and contribute to the maintenance of order. But eventually a mimetic crisis develops, when prohibitions and rituals can no longer control rivalry and maintain order. At this point, the third pillar of culture and religion comes into play, the killing of a scapegoat. (quoted in Girard, 1987, 103)

Weaver continues this line of thought by describing the dynamics of the subsequent process. Tensions in the community continue to grow and eventually resurge. During this developmental social process a search begins to find someone to blame for the conflict or crisis. One can imagine that at first this quest is unconscious, then subconscious, and finally conscious. When the scapegoat is identified, properly blamed, and exterminated, the crisis subsides because a rationale has been established for it, so its reasons can be managed and its apparent resolution or cure has been accomplished. The violence has redeemed the society and its fruits are peace. The community experiences the logic of this transaction in such a manner and to such a degree that ritual repetitions of the event of murdering the scapegoat are celebrated. The community's decorum is maintained by reenactment of the formative event through sacred rituals, and by substitution of new scapegoats, thus ensuring a continuation of the miraculous peace.

Anyone familiar with anthropological research or with ancient mythology will realize, of course, that the scapegoat story is even more universal in the cultures of history than is the narrative of the lost continent of Atlantis. Weaver (2001) summarizes the point concisely.

> The founding events of societies—the murders on which they are founded—are portrayed in myths, which contain enough historical data to locate the origins in history. At the same time, the function of the myth is to disguise the founding murder so that it does not appear as murder. The story of origins is always told from the perspective of the majority, ruling order, which enables the majority to hide the innocence of the scapegoat victim and to affix blame to it for society's problems. Removing the scapegoat then takes on the appearance of a necessary and noble deed that is done in order to preserve the society. Killing the scapegoat becomes not an act of murder but an act of salvation. Life appears to come from death. Exposing the innocence of the victim would reveal the deed as murder, and thus undercut its efficacy as a saving event. Thus the function of ritual and of religion is to limit the violence to a single victim or single group of victims while simultaneously disguising the fact that it is a ritual murder and providing transcendent validation of the process. (47–48)

Psychodynamics of Violence

It seems clear that under Girard's model lies a good deal of the conflict theory of Jung and Freud, as well as the fulfillment theory of Adler (Freud, 1997. Cf. also Gay, 1988, 1993). Freud seems to have been substantially dependent upon the brief but brilliant work of a

Sigmund Freud reading Moses' manuscript, 1938. Library of Congress.

Russian psychoanalyst, Sabina Spielrein, a former student and mistress of Jung. Spielrein wrote a definitive paper in 1911 that spelled out the contours of the foundations for theories of violence as resolution of intrapsychic dissonance. It was published as "Die Destruktion als Ursache des Werdens" in the *Jahrbuch fur psychoanalytische und psychopathologische Forschungen* (Spielrein, 1912). In this publication she speculated on the dynamic processes of destructive impulses contained in sexual drives, with the claim that here lie the essence and wellspring of the entire process that leads to the social necessity of violence as resolution of mimetic dissonance in society.

Jungian theory suggests that individuation, maturation, and wholeness in personality development require reduction of intrapsychic conflict or dissonance. Such dissonance is inherent and inevitable to the processes of birth and coping. Its reduction depends upon externalizing, acting out, the internal conflict, really or symbolically. The polarities within us, such as those between our anima and animus, must be synthesized. If they are not adequately synthesized or are resolved in a pathological direction or manner, the dialectical process becomes destructive. In Jungian terms the atonement, or the killing of the scapegoat, is a dialectical synthesis of these polarities, for example, between justice and mercy, between animus and anima, at the deep-structure level. Conflict and violence are at the core of Jung's framework (Jung, 1997; cf. also Fierz 1991; Homans 1979; Jung 1938, 1957; Hogenson 1983; Palmer 1997; Rollins 1983).

Adler, in his fulfillment theory, illumines Jung's model by pointing out that this "constructive violence," or scapegoating, is meant to end destructive violence in society by transforming violence itself into an act of grace for the community (cf. Miles, 2002). Adler contends that the act of symbolic violence is designed to disarm the very ideologies that create the dissonance and conflict in the first place. For these theorists, the absence of conflict and of its violent externalization or aggressive ritual sublimation, sterilizes a person, leaving that person and society in an unresolved and potentially chaos-inducing state.

Weaver acknowledges the nature of this violent scapegoat dynamic in human existence and argues with Gustav Aulen and J. Christiaan Beker that the violent metaphor at the center of the Master Story of Western tradition, namely, God's crucifixion of his son, is designed as an act of grace to disarm the powers of the violent evil inherent to human persons and society (Aulen 1969; Beker 1980, 1982; cf. also Wink 1984, 1986, 1992). However that may seem in idealistic models of theology or psychoanalysis, the case is that the disarming has failed. Moreover, the entire construct that violence quells violence is, on the face of it, absurd, whether theologized or psychoanalyzed. The violence that is supposed to afford a resolution of the mimetic competition and its consequent social dissonance provides a *temporary* release of the destructive human energies at best.

Even a superficial look at the sweep of history, to say nothing of a profound study of it, informs one immediately of the fact that violence breeds violence and does not quell it. The most common and most universally agreed-upon reality of history is the fact that quelling violence and social or intrapsychic dissonance by a violent or physically aggressive action that victimizes a person or a people as scapegoat merely breeds a festering and irrepressible counter force and ferment. This eventually manifests itself in another revolution. This is true and obvious whether the conflict is adolescent individuation and disengagement from parents, or civil war, or international strife.

Jihad means "struggle against evil." Humane Muslims have long interpreted this to mean the human personal struggle against the counterproductive and self-defeating forces that lie within our own inner selves. However, Muhammad himself, in the process of establishing his hegemony in Arabia, at the outset called for jihad as a military struggle in which anyone who died in the heroic cause could be assured of the reward of immediate translation to heaven. This metaphor created an authoritative model identified with the prophet himself. There can be no doubt that it is this metaphor, which has been raised to the level of an unconscious archetype in Muslim culture, that drives the al Qaeda terrorists in their passion to destroy the secularized Western world.

This behavior, which struck down the World Trade Center Towers, is little different in nature, motive, spirit, and method from the Israeli extermination of the Canaanites in the biblical narrative in the Book of Joshua. Nor does it differ significantly, in any of these categories, from the Christian Crusades of the High Middle Ages. All three of these great religions of the world have at their core a religious metaphor grown into a psychological archetype that legitimates violence in the grossest imaginable forms, justifying it on the grounds of divine order and behavior.

Conclusion

Undoubtedly, it would be difficult to persuade the general human community, much less the perpetrators of the specific gross tragedies of human history, that their motives are unconscious and their drives are moved and shaped by a divine metaphor that works like a monster deity at unaware levels of their psyches. Most of us are certain of what we are doing and confident that we know why we are doing it. Of course, this is almost never so. It is never true to the degree of clarity or transparency that we constantly and universally believe and claim.

Psychoanalytic theories have taught us a crucial thing about our role in what John F. Kennedy called "this tragic adventure" of human existence. They have given us the clue to the sources and forces at play in our psyches and societies that make violence inevitable. What their model fails to do is to provide a mechanism for exorcising the monster deity from the center of our souls or selves, a thing that is forever unlikely as long as the function of that monster is constantly reinforced by the cultural metaphors of radical violence at the center of our Master Stories.

Until we are ready to analyze those Master Stories and eradicate from them their violent core metaphors, it is impossible for us to develop at the unconscious level, where this action is, warrantable nonviolent alternatives for our strategies in conflict resolution.

Warrantable alternatives are required that carry more and better authority than we now get automatically from the destructive metaphors of violent divine behavior inhabiting the dark caves of our individual and collective unconscious. We will never be able to accede to that better authority until we can substitute constructive metaphors for violent ones and exchange manipulative power struggles for true democracy. We cannot gain ground here until we are ready for the risks of authentic mutual acceptance of each other's needs and claims. That requires taking the time to hear and negotiate those needs and claims in good faith and, thus, to give up the notion that narcissism and justice are preeminent over grace and mercy.

This will not happen until we eliminate from our framework of thought the unconscious perception that atonement is a phenomenon necessary for psychosocial equanimity and we transcend the notion that life is a quid pro quo contest. These destructive structures cannot be eradicated as long as the unconscious god in our psyches is a violent monster who cannot achieve intrapsychic stasis without killing someone, even "his beloved son."

Note

This chapter first appeared in C. Stout (Ed.), (2002), *The Psychology of Terrorism*, Westport: Praeger, and is republished here with permission.

References

Aulen, G. (1969). *Christus victor: An historical study of the three main types of the idea of atonement* (A. G. Herbert, Trans.). New York: Macmillan.

Beker, J. C. (1980). *Paul the Apostle: The triumph of God in life and thought.* Philadelphia: Fortress.

Beker, J. C. (1982). *Paul's apocalyptic gospel: The coming triumph of God.* Philadelphia: Fortress.

Bettelheim, B. (1984). *Freud and man's soul.* New York: Random House-Vintage.

Boccaccini, G. (2002). *Roots of rabbinic Judaism: An intellectual history, from Ezekiel to Daniel.* Grand Rapids: Eerdmans.

Cox, D. (1959). *Jung and St. Paul.* New York: Association Press.

Fierz, H. K. (1991). *Jungian Psychiatry.* Einsiedeln: Daimon Verlag.

Freud, S. (1997). *Selected writings.* New York: BOMC.

Gay, P. (1984). *The bourgeois experience: Victoria to Freud: Vol 1. Education of the senses.* New York: Norton.

Gay, P. (1986). *The bourgeois experience: Victoria to Freud: Vol. 2. The tender passion.* New York: Norton.

Gay, P. (1988). *Freud: A life for our time*. New York and London: Norton.

Gay, P. (1993). *The bourgeois experience: Victoria to Freud: Vol. 3. The cultivation of hatred*. New York: Norton.

Gay, V. P. (1983). *Reading Freud: Psychology, neurosis, and religion*. Chicago: Scholars Press.

Girard, R. (1987). *Things hidden since the foundation of the world* (S. Bann & M. Metter, Trans.). Stanford: Stanford University Press.

Gruenwald, I. (2003). *Rituals and ritual theory in ancient Israel*. Leiden: Brill.

Guirdham, A. (1962). *Christ and Freud*. New York: Collier.

Hogenson, G. B. (1983). *Jung's struggle with Freud*. Notre Dame: Notre Dame.

Homans, P. (1979). *Jung in context: Modernity and the making of psychology*. Chicago: University of Chicago Press.

Jung, C. G. (1938/1963). *Psychology and religion*. New Haven: Yale.

Jung, C. G. (1957). *The undiscovered self* (R.F.C. Hull, Trans.). Boston: Little, Brown.

Jung, C. G. (1997). *Selected writings*. New York: BOMC.

Kung, H. (1979). *Freud and the problem of God*. New Haven: Yale.

Miles, J. (1995). *God: A biography*. New York: Knopf.

Miles, J. (2001). *Christ: A crisis in the life of God*. New York: Knopf.

Palmer, M. (1997). *Freud and Jung on religion*. New York and London: Routledge.

Rollins, W. G. (1983). *Jung and the Bible*. Atlanta: John Knox.

Scharfenberg, J. (1988). *Sigmund Freud and his critique of religion*. Philadelphia: Fortress.

Schlusser, G. H. (1986). *From Jung to Jesus: Myth and consciousness in the New Testament*. Atlanta: John Knox.

Spielrein, S. (1912). Die Destruktion als Ursache des Werdens. *Jahrbuch fur psychoanalytische und psychopathologische Forschungen, 4*, 465–503.

Stout, C. (Ed.). (2002). *The psychology of terrorism* (Vols. 1–4). Westport: Praeger.

Tuchman, B. (1984). *The march of folly*. New York: Knopf.

Weaver, J. D. (2001). *The non-violent atonement*. Grand Rapids: Eerdmans.

Williams, J. G. (Ed.) (1996). *The Girard reader*. New York: Crossroad.

Wilmer, H. A. (1994). *Understandable Jung: The personal side of Jungian psychology*. Wilmette: Chiron Publications.

Wink, W. (1984). *The powers: Vol. 1. Naming the powers: The language of power in the New Testament*. Philadelphia: Fortress.

Wink, W. (1986). *The powers: Vol. 2. Unmasking the powers: The invisible forces that determine human existence*. Philadelphia: Fortress.

Wink, W. (1992). *The powers: Vol. 3. Engaging the powers: Discernment and resistance in a world of domination*. Minneapolis: Fortress.

Afterword

Chris E. Stout

Series Editor
Contemporary Psychology

Religion and politics. Lightning rods and powder kegs. Such are the thoughts and images that may be conjured up reviewing this dynamic collection of works. Few topics can stir more opinion, bring more varied viewpoints, stimulate more debate and contention, or spark more potentially volatile reactions than discussions of religion as a motivator for murder, terrorism, and even war. Dr. Ellens has successfully assembled some of the best and the brightest contemporary scholars to expound on this most controversial, yet classically delicate, relationship.

So it is fitting that this set of volumes launches the new Praeger Series in Contemporary Psychology. In this series of books, experts from various disciplines will peer through the lens of psychology to examine human behavior as this new millennium dawns. Including modern behaviors rooted back through history, the topics will include positive subjects like creativity and resilience, as well as examinations of humanity's current psychological ills, with abuse, suicide, murder, and terrorism among those. At all times, the goal of the series remains constant—to offer innovative ideas, provocative considerations, and useful beginnings to better understand human behavior.

Developing a collection of the size, substance, and quality shown in *The Destructive Power of Religion* is no easy task. Indeed, I first met Dr. Ellens when he contributed to my earlier, similar four-volume set,

The Psychology of Terrorism (Westport: Praeger, 2002). The goal was to organize well-researched content and weave it into a fabric appealing to readers of differing backgrounds and interests. Certainly, this goal was achieved in Dr. Ellens' volumes.

While no editor of such a work wishes for homogenization of the content, it becomes a fine balance between maintaining thematic consistency among chapters with a healthy tension between differing perspectives. Therein again, this collection succeeds.

The first time I had the honor and the pleasure of meeting Dr. Ellens, he struck me as a virtual Roman candle of intellectual enthusiasm. Therefore, it comes as no surprise that he has been successful in gathering some of the greatest thinkers on the topic from around the world, including a Pulitzer Prize–winning author.

There is potential for these volumes to unleash a Niagara of discussion and debate.

Ideally, there is potential for these volumes to spark understanding that will trigger solutions to the problem of destructive powers unleashed in the name of religion.

This is to Dr. Ellens' credit, and it is to us readers' marked benefit.

Index

ABOUT THE SERIES

As this new millennium dawns, humankind has evolved—some would argue has devolved—exhibiting new and old behaviors that fascinate, infuriate, delight, or fully perplex those of us seeking answers to the question, "Why?" In this series, experts from various disciplines peer through the lens of psychology telling us answers they see for questions of human behavior. Their topics may range from humanity's psychological ills—addictions, abuse, suicide, murder, and terrorism among them—to works focused on positive subjects including intelligence, creativity, athleticism, and resilience. Regardless of the topic, the goal of this series remains constant—to offer innovative ideas, provocative considerations, and useful beginnings to better understand human behavior.

Chris E. Stout
Series Editor

About the Series Editor and Advisory Board

CHRIS E. STOUT, Psy.D., MBA, holds a joint governmental and academic appointment in Northwestern University Medical School and serves as Illinois' first chief of psychological services. He served as an NGO special representative to the United Nations, was appointed by the U.S. Department of Commerce as a Baldridge examiner, and served as an adviser to the White House for both political parties. He was appointed to the World Economic Forum's Global Leaders of Tomorrow. He has published and presented more than 300 papers and 29 books. His works have been translated into six languages.

BRUCE E. BONECUTTER, Ph.D., is director of behavioral services at the Elgin Community Mental Health Center, the Illinois Department of Human Services state hospital, serving adults in greater Chicago. He is also a clinical assistant professor of psychology at the University of Illinois at Chicago. A clinical psychologist specializing in health, consulting, and forensic psychology, Bonecutter is also a longtime member of the American Psychological Association Taskforce on Children and the Family.

JOSEPH A. FLAHERTY, M.D., is chief of psychiatry at the University of Illinois Hospital, a professor of psychiatry at the University of Illinois College of Medicine, and a professor of community health science at the University of Illinois College of Public Health. He is a founding member of the Society for the Study of Culture and Psychiatry. Dr. Flaherty has been a consultant to the World Health Organization, to the National Institutes of Mental Health, and also to the Falk Institute in Jerusalem.

MICHAEL HOROWITZ, Ph.D., is president and professor of clinical psychology at the Chicago School of Professional Psychology, one of the nation's leading not-for-profit graduate schools of psychology. Earlier, he served as dean and professor of the Arizona School of Professional Psychology. A clinical psychologist practicing independently since 1987, his work has focused on psychoanalysis, intensive individual therapy, and couples therapy. He has provided disaster mental health services to the American Red Cross. Dr. Horowitz's special interests include the study of fatherhood.

SHELDON I. MILLER, M.D., is a professor of psychiatry at Northwestern University and director of the Stone Institute of Psychiatry at Northwestern Memorial Hospital. He is also director of the American Board of Psychiatry and Neurology, director of the American Board of Emergency Medicine, and director of the Accreditation Council for Graduate Medical Education. Dr. Miller is also an examiner for the American Board of Psychiatry and Neurology. He is founding editor of the *American Journal of Addictions* and founding chairman of the American Psychiatric Association's Committee on Alcoholism.

DENNIS P. MORRISON, Ph.D., is chief executive officer at the Center for Behavioral Health in Indiana, the first behavioral health company ever to win the JCAHO Codman Award for excellence in the use of outcomes management to achieve health care quality improvement. He is president of the board of directors for the Community Healthcare Foundation in Bloomington and has been a member of the board of directors for the American College of Sports Psychology. He has served as a consultant to agencies including the Ohio Department of Mental Health, Tennessee Association of Mental Health Organizations, Oklahoma Psychological Association, the North Carolina Council of Community Mental Health Centers, and the National Center for Health Promotion in Michigan.

WILLIAM H. REID, M.D., MPH, is a clinical and forensic psychiatrist and consultant to attorneys and courts throughout the United States. He is clinical professor of psychiatry at the University of Texas Health Science Center. Dr. Miller is also an adjunct professor of psychiatry at Texas A&M College of Medicine and Texas Tech

University School of Medicine, as well as a clinical faculty member at the Austin Psychiatry Residency Program. He is chairman of the Scientific Advisory Board and medical adviser to the Texas Depressive & Manic-Depressive Association, as well as an examiner for the American Board of Psychiatry and Neurology. He has served as president of the American Academy of Psychiatry and the Law, as chairman of the Research Section for an International Conference on the Psychiatric Aspects of Terrorism, and as medical director for the Texas Department of Mental Health and Mental Retardation.

About the Editor
and Advisers

J. HAROLD ELLENS is a Research Scholar at the University of Michigan, Department of Near Eastern Studies. He is a retired Presbyterian theologian and ordained minister, a retired U.S. Army Colonel, and a retired professor of philosophy, theology, and psychology. He has authored, coauthored, and/or edited 86 books and 165 professional journal articles. He served 15 years as Executive Director of the Christian Association for Psychological Studies and as founding editor and Editor-in-Chief of the *Journal of Psychology and Christianity*. He holds a Ph.D. from Wayne State University in the Psychology of Human Communication, a Ph.D.(Cand.) from the University of Michigan in biblical and Near Eastern studies, and master's degrees from Calvin Theological Seminary, Princeton Theological Seminary, and the University of Michigan. He was born in Michigan, grew up in a Dutch-German immigrant community, and determined at age seven to enter the Christian ministry as a means to help his people with the great amount of suffering he perceived all around him. His life's work has focused on the interface of psychology and religion. He is the founder and director of the New American Lyceum.

LeROY H. ADEN is Professor Emeritus of Pastoral Theology at the Lutheran Theological Seminary in Philadelphia, Pennsylvania. He taught full-time at the seminary from 1967 to 1994 and part-time from 1994 to 2001. He served as Visiting Lecturer at Princeton

Theological Seminary, Princeton, New Jersey on a regular basis. In 2002 he coauthored *Preaching God's Compassion: Comforting Those Who Suffer* with Robert G. Hughes. Previously, he edited four books in a Psychology and Christianity series with J. Harold Ellens and David G. Benner. He served on the Board of Directors of the Christian Association for Psychological Studies for six years.

ALFRED J. EPPENS was born and raised in Michigan. He attended Western Michigan University, studying history under Ernst A. Breisach, and receiving a B.A. (Summa cum Laude) and an M.A. He continued his studies at the University of Michigan, where he was awarded a J.D. in 1981. He is an Adjunct Professor at Oakland University and at Oakland Community College, as well as an active church musician and director. He is a director and officer of the Michigan Center for Early Christian Studies, as well as a founding member of the New American Lyceum.

EDMUND S. MELTZER was born in Brooklyn, New York. He attended the University of Chicago, where he received his B.A. in Near Eastern Languages and Civilizations. He pursued graduate studies at the University of Toronto, earning his M.A. and Ph.D. in Near Eastern Studies. He worked in Egypt as a member of the Akhenaten Temple Project/East Karnak Excavation and as a Fellow of the American Research Center. Returning to the United States, he taught at the University of North Carolina–Chapel Hill and at the Claremont Graduate School (now University), where he served as Associate Chair of the Department of Religion. Meltzer taught at Northeast Normal University in Changchun from 1990 to 1996. He has been teaching German and Spanish in the Wisconsin public school system and English as a Second Language in summer programs of the University of Wisconsin–Stevens Point. He has lectured extensively and published numerous articles and reviews in scholarly journals. He has contributed to and edited a number of books and has presented at many national and international conferences.

JACK MILES is the author of the 1995 Pulitzer Prize winner *God: A Biography*. After publishing *Christ: A Crisis in the Life of God* in 2001, Miles was named a MacArthur Fellow in 2002. Now Senior Adviser to the President at J. Paul Getty Trust, he earned a Ph.D. in Near Eastern languages from Harvard University in 1971 and has been a Regents Lecturer at the University of California, Director of the Humanities Center at Claremont Graduate University, and Visiting

Professor of Humanities at the California Institute of Technology. He has authored articles that have appeared in numerous national publications, including the *Atlantic Monthly*, the *New York Times*, the *Boston Globe*, the *Washington Post*, and the *Los Angeles Times*, where he served for 10 years as Literary Editor and as a member of the newspaper's editorial board.

WAYNE G. ROLLINS is Professor Emeritus of Biblical Studies at Assumption College, Worcester, Massachusetts, and Adjunct Professor of Scripture at Hartford Seminary, Hartford, Connecticut. His writings include *The Gospels: Portraits of Christ* (1964), *Jung and the Bible* (1983), and *Soul and Psyche: The Bible in Psychological Perspective* (1999). He received his Ph.D. in New Testament Studies from Yale University and is the founder and former chairman (1990–2000) of the Society of Biblical Literature Section on Psychology and Biblical Studies.

GRANT R. SHAFER was educated at Wayne State University, Harvard University, and the University of Michigan, where he received his doctorate in Early Christianity. A summary of his dissertation, "St. Stephen and the Samaritans," was published in the proceedings of the 1996 meeting of the *Societe d'Etudes Samaritaines*. He has taught at Washtenaw Community College, Siena Heights University, and Eastern Michigan University. He is presently a Visiting Scholar at the University of Michigan.

About the Contributors

LeROY H. ADEN is Professor Emeritus of Pastoral Theology at the Lutheran Theological Seminary in Philadelphia, Pennsylvania. He taught full-time at the seminary from 1967 to 1994 and part-time from 1994 to 2001. He served as Visiting Lecturer at Princeton Theological Seminary, Princeton, New Jersey, on a regular basis. In 2002 he coauthored *Preaching God's Compassion: Comforting Those Who Suffer* with Robert G. Hughes. Previously, he edited four books in a Psychology and Christianity series with J. Harold Ellens and David G. Benner. He served on the Board of Directors of the Christian Association for Psychological Studies for six years.

PAUL N. ANDERSON is Professor of Biblical and Quaker Studies and Chair of the Department of Religious Studies at George Fox University, where he has served since 1989 except for a year as a visiting professor at Yale Divinity School (1998–99). He is author of *The Christology of the Fourth Gospel: Its Unity and Disunity in the Light of John 6* and *Navigating the Living Waters of the Gospel of John: On Wading with Children and Swimming with Elephants*. In addition, he has written many essays on biblical and Quaker themes and is editor of *Quaker Religious Thought*. He serves on the steering committee of the Psychology and Biblical Studies Section of the Society of Biblical Literature and teaches the New Testament Interpretation course in the Psy.D. program of George Fox University. His Ph.D. in the New Testament is from Glasgow University (1989), his M.Div. is from the

Earlham School of Religion (1981), and his B.A. in psychology and B.A. in Christian ministries are from Malone College (1978).

DONALD CAPPS, Psychologist of Religion, is William Hart Felmeth Professor of Pastoral Theology at Princeton Theological Seminary. In 1989 he was awarded an honorary doctorate from the University of Uppsala, Sweden, in recognition of the importance of his publications. He served as president of the Society for the Scientific Study of Religion from 1990 to 1992. Among his many significant books are *Men, Religion, and Melancholia: James, Otto, Jung, Erikson and Freud; The Freudians on Religion: A Reader; Social Phobia: Alleviating Anxiety in an Age of Self-Promotion;* and *Jesus: A Psychological Biography.* He also authored *The Child's Song: The Religious Abuse of Children.*

RAFAEL CHODOS has been a practicing business litigation attorney in the Los Angeles area for nearly 25 years. He holds a B.A. in philosophy from UC–Berkeley (1964). He earned his way through college teaching Hebrew, Latin, and Greek, intending to become a rabbi. But after graduating from Berkeley he entered the then-fledgling computer software field, where he worked for 15 years. He founded his own software company, which developed expert systems and sold them to most of the Fortune 500 companies. He then returned to law school and received his J.D. from Boston University in 1977. He is the author of several articles on legal topics as well as topics relating to computers, software design, operations research, and artificial intelligence. He has authored two books: *The Jewish Attitude Toward Justice and Law* (1984) and *The Law of Fiduciary Duties* (2000).

JOHN J. COLLINS is Holmes Professor of Old Testament Criticism and Interpretation at Yale University. He previously taught at the University of Chicago and at Notre Dame. He received his Ph.D. from Harvard (1972). His more recent books include a commentary on *The Book of Daniel* (1993), *The Scepter and the Star: The Messiahs of the Dead Sea Scrolls* (1995), *Jewish Wisdom in the Hellenistic Age* (1997), *Apocalypticism in the Dead Sea Scrolls* (1997), *Seers, Sibyls, and Sages* (1997), *The Apocalyptic Imagination* (revised ed., 1998), and *Between Athens and Jerusalem: Jewish Identity in the Hellenistic Diaspora* (revised ed., 2000). He has served as editor of the *Journal of Biblical Literature*, as president of the Catholic Biblical Association (1997), and as president of the Society of Biblical Literature (2002).

CHARLES T. DAVIS III studied at Emory University with Dr. Norman Perrin, graduating with the B.D. and Ph.D. degrees after special study at the University of Heidelberg. Although specializing in New Testament Studies, he has also published articles and book reviews in the fields of American religion, computers and the humanities, philosophy, and Buddhist studies. He is the author of the book *Speaking of Jesus* and currently serves as Professor of Philosophy and Religion at Appalachian State University, where he teaches biblical literature, Islam, and seminars on symbols and healing.

SIMON JOHN DE VRIES, an ordained minister in the Presbyterian Church, was born in Denver. He served in the U.S. Marines during World War II as a First Lieutenant, pastored three churches, and received his Th.D. from Union Theological Seminary in New York in Old Testament Studies before beginning seminary teaching in 1962. He is the author of numerous scholarly articles and reviews in the field of Old Testament exegesis and theology in addition to nine books, the latest of which is *Shining White Knight, A Spiritual Memoir.*

J. HAROLD ELLENS is a Research Scholar at the University of Michigan, Department of Near Eastern Studies. He is a retired Presbyterian theologian and ordained minister, a retired U.S. Army Colonel, and a retired professor of philosophy, theology, and psychology. He has authored, coauthored, and/or edited 86 books and 165 professional journal articles. He served 15 years as Executive Director of the Christian Association for Psychological Studies and as founding editor and Editor-in-Chief of the *Journal of Psychology and Christianity.* He holds a Ph.D. from Wayne State University in the Psychology of Human Communication, a Ph.D.(Cand.) from the University of Michigan in biblical and Near Eastern studies, and master's degrees from Calvin Theological Seminary, Princeton Theological Seminary, and the University of Michigan. His publications include *God's Grace and Human Health* and *Psychotheology: Key Issues,* as well as chapters in *Moral Obligation and the Military, Baker Encyclopedia of Psychology, Abingdon Dictionary of Pastoral Care, Jesus as Son of Man, The Literary Character: A Progression of Images,* and *God's Word for Our World* (2 vols.).

MARK ADAM ELLIOTT holds M.Div. and Th.M. degrees from the University of Toronto and a Ph.D. in New Testament from the University of Aberdeen, U.K. His area of concentration is Christian origins in Judaism. His first major publication was *Survivors of Israel:*

A Reconsideration of the Theology of Pre-Christian Judaism (2000). He has served as pastor in both the United Church of Canada and Baptist Convention of Ontario and Quebec, and taught biblical studies in two Ontario universities. Presently, he is executive director of the *Institute for Restorationist and Revisionist Studies* (www.irrstudies.org) and carries out research at the University of Toronto.

ALFRED J. EPPENS was born and raised in Michigan. He attended Western Michigan University, studying history under Ernst A. Breisach, and receiving a B.A. (Summa cum Laude) and an M.A. He continued his studies at the University of Michigan, where he was awarded a J.D. in 1981. He is an Adjunct Professor at Oakland University and at Oakland Community College, as well as an active church musician and director. He is a director and officer of the Michigan Center for Early Christian Studies, as well as a founding member of the New American Lyceum.

JACK T. HANFORD is a Professor Emeritus of Biomedical Ethics at Ferris State University in Michigan. He is a member of the American Philosophical Association, the American Academy of Religion, the Christian Association for Psychological Studies, and the Association of Moral Education. He is also an associate of the Hastings Center, the foremost center for biomedical ethics, the American Society of Bioethics and Humanities, the Center for Bioethics and Human Dignity, and the Kennedy Institute of Ethics, as well as several other societies. He has published many professional articles, including those in *Religious Education*, the *Journal for the Scientific Study of Religion*, the *Journal of Psychology and Christianity*, and the *Journal of Pastoral Psychology, Ethics, and Medicine*. His highest degree is a Th.D.

RONALD B. JOHNSON has worked as a clinical psychologist in private practice for 30 years. His academic background includes a B.S. at the University of Wisconsin, M.Div. at Denver Seminary, and M.A. and Ph.D. in psychology from the University of Iowa. He is currently working on a Post-Doctorate in Neuropsychology. He holds licenses in several states and in Canada. His interests are in therapy with men and children, the psychology of men, psychological evaluations, and forensic psychology. He writes in the areas of "friendly diagnosis," which includes personality type, intelligences, gender differences, personal development, and theological-psychological integration.

D. ANDREW KILLE received his Ph.D. from the Graduate Theological Union in Berkeley in Psychological Biblical Criticism.

He is the author of *Psychological Biblical Criticism: Genesis 3 as a Test Case* (Fortress Press, 2001). A former pastor, Dr. Kille teaches psychology and spirituality in the San Francisco Bay area and is principal consultant for Revdak Consulting. He has served as cochair of the Psychology and Biblical Studies Section of the Society of Biblical Literature and on the steering committee of the Person, Culture, and Religion Group of the American Academy of Religion.

CASSANDRA M. KLYMAN is Assistant Clinical Professor at Wayne State University College of Medicine, where she teaches Ethics, and the Psychology of Women to residents in psychiatry and supervises their clinical cases. Klyman is also a lecturer at the Michigan Psychoanalytic Institute and chairperson of the Michigan Psychoanalytic Society's Committee on Psychoanalysis in Medicine. She is a Life-Fellow of the American Medical Association, the American Psychiatric Association, and the College of Forensic Examiners. She is also Past-President of the Michigan Psychiatric Society. She has published papers nationally and internationally in peer-reviewed journals. Most of her time is spent in the private practice of psychoanalysis and psychoanalytically informed psychotherapy. She earned her M.D. at Wayne State University.

EDSON T. LEWIS is an ordained minister (emeritus) of the Christian Reformed Church. During 47 years of active ministry, he served a suburban New York City congregation for 8 years, an inner-city parish in Hoboken, New Jersey, for 12 years, and the campus of the Ohio State University, Columbus, Ohio, for 17 years. He is a graduate of Calvin Theological Seminary (B.D.), New York Theological Seminary (STM), and Trinity Lutheran Seminary (D.Min). During the 1990s, he played a key role in the revitalization of the church's higher education ministries in the United States and Canada. His participation in antipoverty and peacemaking ministries has been extensive.

ZENON LOTUFO JR. is a Presbyterian minister (Independent Presbyterian Church of Brazil), a philosopher, and a psychotherapist, specializing in Transactional Analysis. He has lectured for undergraduate and graduate courses at universities in São Paulo, Brazil. He coordinates the course of specialization in Pastoral Psychology of the Christian Association of Psychologists and Psychiatrists of Brazil. He is the author of the books *Relações Humanas* (Human Relations) and *Disfunções no Comportamento Organizacional* (Dysfunctions in

Organizational Behavior), and coauthor of *O Potencial Humano* (Human Potential). He has also authored numerous journal articles.

CHARLES MABEE is Full Professor and Director of the Masters of Divinity Program at the Ecumenical Theological Seminary in Detroit, Michigan. He is also a Visiting Lecturer and United Ministries in Higher Education Ecumenical Campus Minister at Oakland University, where he founded two subsidiary institutions, the Institute for the Third Millennium and the Detroit Parliament for World Religions. He is a founding member of the Colloquium on Violence and Religion, chairman of the American Biblical Hermeneutics Section of the Society of Biblical Literature/American Academy of Religion, southeast region, and has been Chair of the Department of Religious Studies at Marshall University in West Virginia. Early in his career, he was a Research Associate for the Institute for Antiquity and Christianity at Claremont Graduate University.

J. CÁSSIO MARTINS is a Presbyterian minister (Presbyterian Church of Brazil) and a clinical psychologist. As a minister, he held pastorates in São Paulo and Rio de Janeiro. As a psychologist, he runs his own clinic in São Paulo. He holds a Master of Theology degree from Union Theological Seminary, Richmond, Virginia. He is one of the coordinators of the course of specialization in Pastoral Psychology of the Christian Association of Psychologists and Psychiatrists of Brazil. He has taught psychology at the Methodist University in São Paulo, as well as courses and seminars to pastors and psychologists throughout Brazil, leading the creation of and exercising the Office of Pastoral Support of his denomination until July 2002. He has written numerous articles on psychology and theology.

MARTIN E. MARTY is the Fairfax M. Cone Distinguished Professor Emeritus at the University of Chicago Divinity School, where he taught for 35 years and where the Martin Marty center has since been founded to promote "public religion" endeavors. An ordained minister in the Evangelical Lutheran Church of America, he is well known in the popular media and has been called the nation's "most influential interpretor of religion." He is the author of 50 books, including *The One and the Many: America's Search for a Common God*, as well as a 3-volume work entitled *Modern American Religion*. He has written more than 4,300 articles, essays, reviews and papers. Among his many honors and awards are the National Humanities Medal, the National Book Award, the Medal of the American

Academy of Arts and Sciences, and the Distinguished Service Medal of the Association of Theological Schools. He has served as president of the American Academy of Religion, the American Society of Church History and the American Catholic Historical Association. Marty has received 67 honorary doctorates.

CHERYL McGUIRE is a member of the Colloquium on Violence and Religion, and her work was presented at Purdue University during the colloquium in 2002. She is a graduate of the University of Michigan master's program in Ancient Civilizations and Biblical Studies and is now involved with postgraduate work at the University of Detroit.

EDMUND S. MELTZER was born in Brooklyn, New York, and attended Erasmus Hall High School. He developed a passion for the ancient world, especially Egypt, and attended the University of Chicago, where he received his B.A. in Near Eastern Languages and Civilizations. He pursued graduate studies at the University of Toronto, earning his M.A. and Ph.D. in Near Eastern Studies and working in Egypt as a member of the Akhenaten Temple Project/East Karnak Excavation. He also worked as a Fellow of the American Research Center in Egypt. After returning to the United States, he taught at the University of North Carolina–Chapel Hill and at the Claremont Graduate School (now University), where he served as Associate Chair of the Department of Religion. In 1990, Meltzer and his family traveled to China, where he taught at Northeast Normal University in Changchun for six years. Subsequently he has been teaching German and Spanish in the Wisconsin public school system and English as a Second Language in the summer programs of the University of Wisconsin–Stevens Point. He has lectured extensively and published numerous articles and reviews in scholarly journals. He has contributed to and edited a number of books and has presented at many national and international conferences.

JACK MILES is the author of the 1996 Pulitzer Prize winner, *God: A Biography*. After publishing *Christ: A Crisis in the Life of God* in 2001, Miles was named a MacArthur Fellow in 2002. Now Senior Adviser to the President at J. Paul Getty Trust, he earned a Ph.D. in Near Eastern languages from Harvard University in 1971 and has been a Regents Lecturer at the University of California, Director of the Humanities Center at Claremont Graduate University, and Visiting Professor of Humanities at the California Institute of Technology. He has authored articles that have appeared in numerous national publications, including the *Atlantic Monthly*, the *New York Times*, the *Boston Globe*, the *Washington Post*, and the *Los Angeles Times*, where he served for 10 years as Literary Editor and as a member of the newspaper's editorial board.

MICHAEL WILLETT NEWHEART is Associate Professor of New Testament Language and Literature at Howard University School of Divinity, where he has taught since 1991. He holds a Ph.D. from Southern Baptist Theological Seminary and is the author of *Wisdom Christology in the Fourth Gospel; Word and Soul: A Psychological, Literary, and Cultural Reading of the Fourth Gospel*, and numerous articles on the psychological and literary interpretation of the New Testament.

DIRK H. ODENDAAL is South African and was born in what is now called the Province of the Eastern Cape. He spent much of his youth in the Transkei in the town of Umtata, where his parents were teachers at a seminary. He trained as a minister at the Stellenbosch Seminary for the Dutch Reformed Church and was ordained in 1983 in the Dutch Reformed Church in Southern Africa. He transferred to East London in 1988 to minister to members of the United Reformed Church in Southern Africa in one of the huge suburbs for Xhosa-speaking people. He received his doctorate (D.Litt.) in 1992 at the University of Port Elizabeth in Semitic Languages. At present, he is enrolled in a Master's Degree course in Counseling Psychology at Rhodes University.

RICARDO J. QUINONES is Professor Emeritus of Comparative Literature at Claremont McKenna College. He is author of *Renaissance Discovery of Time* (1972), *Mapping Literary Modernism* (1985), *The Changes of Cain: Violence and the Lost Brother in Cain and Abel Literature* (1991), and several volumes on Dante, including *Foundation Sacrifice in Dante's Commedia* (1996). He is also Founding Director of the Gould Center for the Humanities.

ILONA N. RASHKOW is Professor of Judaic Studies, Women's Studies, and Comparative Literature at the State University of New York, Stony Brook. She has also been the visiting chair in Judaic Studies at the University of Alabama. Among her publications are *Upon the Dark Places: Sexism and Anti-Semitism in English Renaissance Bible Translation* (1990), *The Phallacy of Genesis* (1993), and *Taboo or Not Taboo?: Human Sexuality and the Hebrew Bible* (2000). Her areas of interest include psychoanalytic literary theory as applied to the Hebrew Bible and, more generally, as applied to Judaic studies, religious studies, feminist literary criticism, and women's studies.

WAYNE G. ROLLINS is Professor Emeritus of Biblical Studies at Assumption College, Worcester, Massachusetts, and Adjunct Professor of Scripture at Hartford Seminary, Hartford, Connecticut. His writings include *The Gospels: Portraits of Christ* (1964), *Jung and the Bible* (1983), and *Soul and Psyche: The Bible in Psychological Perspective* (1999). He received his Ph.D. in New Testament Studies from Yale University and is the founder and former chairman (1990–2000) of the Society of Biblical Literature Section on Psychology and Biblical Studies.

GRANT R. SHAFER was educated at Wayne State University, Harvard University, and the University of Michigan, where he received his doctorate in Early Christianity. A summary of his dissertation, "St. Stephen and the Samaritans," was published in the proceedings of the 1996 meeting of the *Societe d'Etudes Samaritaines*. He has taught at Washtenaw Community College, Siena Heights University, and Eastern Michigan University. He is presently a Visiting Scholar at the University of Michigan.

DONALD E. SLOAT, is licensed as a psychologist in Arizona, California, and Michigan. His training includes a B.A from Bethel College (Indiana), an M.A. from Michigan State University, and a Ph.D. from the University of Southern Mississippi. Since 1963, he has devoted his professional life to helping damaged people find healing for their pain. He has worked most often with people who have been trauma victims, including those with post-traumatic stress disorder (PTSD) and other effects of physical, emotional, verbal, sexual, and spiritual abuse. He has worked with Detroit's Youth for Christ, with outpatient drug-treatment programs, a community health center, psychiatric hospitals, and in his current private practice. He authored two books detailing spiritual abuse, *The Dangers of Growing Up in a Christian Home* and *Growing Up Holy and Wholly*. In addition, he has presented workshops on spiritual abuse and shame at national conferences. His professional affiliations include the American Psychological Association, American Association of Christian Counselors, Christian Association for Psychological Studies, and the International Society for the Study of Dissociation. He has served on the advisory board of the National Association for Christian Recovery. His private practice is in Michigan.

MACK C. STIRLING was born in 1952 in St. George, Utah. He was a Mormon missionary in Norway from 1971 to 1973 and graduated from Brigham Young University studies in chemistry in 1975. He received the M.D. degree from Johns Hopkins University in 1979 and thereafter underwent specialty training at the University of Michigan, where he was Assistant Professor of Thoracic Surgery from 1987 to 1990. Since 1990, he has been Director of Cardiothoracic Surgery at Munson Medical Center in Traverse City, Michigan.

ARCHBISHOP DESMOND TUTU is best known for his contribution to the cause of racial justice in South Africa, a contribution for which he was recognized with the Nobel Peace Prize in 1984. Archbishop Tutu has been an ordained priest since 1961. Among his many accomplishments are being named the first black General Secretary of the South African Council of Churches and serving as archbishop of Cape Town. Once a high school teacher in South Africa, he has also taught theology in college and holds honorary degrees from universities including Harvard, Oxford, Columbia, and Kent State. In addition to the Nobel Peace Prize, he has been awarded the Order for Meritorious Service presented by President Nelson Mandela, the Archbishop of Canterbury's Award for outstanding service to the Anglican community, the Family of Man Gold Medal Award, and the Martin Luther King Jr. Non-Violent Peace Award. The many publications Archbishop Tutu has authored, coauthored, or made contributions to include *No Future without Forgiveness* (2000), *Crying in the Wilderness* (1986), and *Rainbow People of God: The Making of a Peaceful Revolution* (1996).

JOHAN S. VOS is Associate Professor of New Testament, Faculty of Theology, Vrije Universiteit te Amsterdam, The Netherlands. He was born in Gouda, The Netherlands. He studied theology at the University of Utrecht, the University of Tübingen, and Union Theological Seminary in New York. He received his Th.D. from the University of Utrecht in 1973 and was Assistant Professor of New Testament Studies at the University of Leiden in 1974 and 1975. From 1975 to 1981, he worked as a social therapist at a psychiatric clinic for delinquents in Nijmegen. He has been Associate Professor at Vrije Universiteit since 1981 and has published many articles on New Testament subjects. He recently authored *Die Kunst der Argumentation bei Paulus* (The Art of Reasoning in the Letters of Paul), WUNT 149, 2002.

WALTER WINK is Professor of Biblical Interpretation at Auburn Theological Seminary in New York City. Previously, he was a parish minister and taught at Union Theological Seminary in New York City. In 1989 and 1990, he was a Peace Fellow at the United States Institute of Peace. His most recent book is *The Human Being: The Enigma of the Son of the Man* (2001). He is author of a trilogy, *The Powers: Naming the Powers: The Language of Power in the New Testament* (1984), *Unmasking the Powers: The Invisible Forces That Determine Human Existence* (1986), and *Engaging the Powers: Discernment and Resistance in a World of Domination* (1992). *Engaging the Powers* received three Religious Book of the Year awards for 1993, from Pax Christi, the Academy of Parish Clergy, and the Midwestern Independent Publishers Association. His other works include *Jesus and Nonviolence* (2003), *The Powers That Be* (1998), and *When the Powers Fall: Reconciliation in the Healing of Nations* (1998). He has published more than 250 journal articles.